BIG TIME FUNDRAISING
FOR TODAY'S SCHOOLS

*This book is dedicated to all those people who believe in
the public schools and who tirelessly give their time and resources to
ensure that all children receive a quality education and realize their full potential.*

STANLEY LEVENSON

BIG TIME FUNDRAISING
FOR TODAY'S SCHOOLS

Foreword by Wendy D. Puriefoy

CORWIN PRESS
A SAGE Publications Company
Thousand Oaks, CA 91320

Copyright © 2007 by Corwin Press

For information:

Corwin Press
A Sage Publications Company
2455 Teller Road
Thousand Oaks, California 91320
www.corwinpress.com

Sage Publications Ltd.
1 Oliver's Yard
55 City Road
London EC1Y 1SP
United Kingdom

Sage Publications India Pvt. Ltd.
B-42, Panchsheel Enclave
Post Box 4109
New Delhi 110 017 India

Printed in the United States of America

Library of Congress Cataloging-in-Publication Data

Levenson, Stanley.
Big-time fundraising for today's schools/Stanley Levenson.
        p. cm.
Includes bibliographical references.
ISBN: 1-4129-3915-1 or 978-1-4129-3915-7 (cloth)—1-4129-3916-X or 978-1-4129-3916-4 (paper)
    1. Educational fund raising-United States. 2. Proposal writing for grants-United States.
3. Education-United States-Finance. I. Title.
LC243.L488 2007
378.1'06—dc22   2006021817

This book is printed on acid-free paper.

06   07   08   09   10   10 9 8 7 6 5 4 3 2 1

Acquisitions Editor:	Elizabeth Brenkus
Editorial Assistant:	Desirée Enayati
Production Editor:	Beth A. Bernstein
Copy Editor:	Cate Huisman
Typesetter:	C&M Digitals (P) Ltd.
Proofreader:	Colleen Brennan
Indexer:	Sylvia Coates
Cover Designer:	Michael Dubowe
Graphic Designer:	Lisa Riley

Contents

Book Cartoons

On page 4

On page 11

On page 15

On page 21

On page 25

On page 58

Foreword

PUBLIC EDUCATION IS EVERYONE'S RESPONSIBILITY

Public education is the single most important public institution in a democratic society. It is our ultimate department of defense against poverty, ignorance, hatred, and intolerance. It is the vehicle by which we transmit democratic and civic values to future generations, and it is the means by which we produce an educated citizenry capable of civic leadership, personal virtue, public deliberation, and economic and social vitality.

The institution of public education is deeply woven into the fabric of American life. Today, with more than 48 million children attending America's public schools, we can justifiably take pride in the scope of and access to public education that exists in this nation. But scope and access are only half the story. Today, public and governmental responsibilities in education and the strong connection that Americans have with their public schools are being put to a serious test. The battle in education is for equity and for the right of every child to a quality education, and this is a battle we must win.

Every generation of Americans has had to wrestle with the challenge of educating its youth. This generation is no exception, and, fortunately, we now know what it takes for all children to learn. We know it takes qualified teachers, capable school leaders, supportive learning environments, adequate resources, a rigorous curriculum, high expectations linked to standards, fair diagnostic assessments, and nonacademic supports that help students build strong minds and healthy bodies. But one vital ingredient has been missing in this formula for education excellence, and that ingredient is public responsibility.

This is where the talents, experience, and passion of Stan Levenson are making an important difference for public schools. As Stan points out, private fundraising for public schools has gone big time. School fundraising from nonpublic sources has grown by leaps and bounds in the last few decades, from schools seeking hundreds of dollars for individual classroom projects to schools seeking millions of dollars for long-delayed construction and to meet instructional needs that clearly are not being met. This book makes a clear and compelling case for the role that big-time fundraising will play in improving all American schools. The book is a concise primer for classroom teachers, parents, and administrators in their pursuit of outside funding for their schools.

Many school districts have created school foundations to raise and manage donations from outside contributors, including individuals, businesses, fundraising events, and grants from governmental and philanthropic agencies. There are a great variety of shapes and sizes of school fundraising staff and organized school foundations. They can range from a part-time staff member who writes grants to entrepreneurial parent groups that raise money through car washes and golf tournaments to multimillion-dollar campaigns that allure wealthy patrons and partner with big businesses.

Learning about and adopting the techniques of big-time fundraising helps schools to move away from nickel-and-dime fundraising activities, like bake sales and candy sales, into the world of big bucks that colleges and universities have long enjoyed as a boost to their ability to become world-class learning institutions. When it comes to big-time fundraising, Stan's book is the most specific and most comprehensive book ever written on the subject for the public schools. It includes actual methods and techniques for securing monies from individual donors as well as from corporations, foundations, and a wide array of governmental agencies.

The book is worth its asking price for its extensive bibliography and Web addresses alone, which will save readers hundreds of hours of mind-numbing online research. In addition, the examples of winning grant applications and proposals will help save readers from the frustration of starting from scratch or from the head-slapping realization that they have spent important time reinventing the wheel. Stan describes in great detail the previously unrevealed shortcuts of school fundraising. These well-kept secrets used by wealthy and advantaged school districts are laid out in the open for everyone to use to help improve public education for all children.

Stan Levenson is uniquely qualified to map the terrain of school fundraising. For nearly four decades, he has served as a dedicated classroom teacher and school administrator. He is a successful fundraiser and a respected author. His work has appeared in esteemed professional publications such as the *School Administrator,* the *American School Board Journal,* and *Principal Leadership.* His previous book, *How to Get Grants and Gifts for the Public Schools,* has proven to be an indispensable training manual for school fundraisers.

Stan is a pragmatist. Schools need more money, and he is here to help show them how to get it. He helps fundraisers understand the entire spectrum of the fundraising process: Donor research, appeal-letter and proposal writing, goal development, program evaluation, effective stewardship, and budgeting are just a few of the topics he ably examines.

Throughout this process, he is guided by a strong moral compass. At no time does he overpromise results. Money does not grow on trees, and schools will not raise significant sums of money unless they are organized, clear about their needs, honest in their dealings, accountable to donors for results, and endlessly thankful to their patrons.

Like many informed and engaged citizens, Stan is working with schools to identify private sources of support to help address today's unmet needs. At the same time, he is working to increase public understanding of the need to make public education our number-one public priority, so that the important instructional needs of schools are met by public tax dollars.

But, as much as schools need money, they need friends in local communities, in state houses, and in the White House. Stan knows that effective stewardship in public education requires citizens to vote not only with their checkbooks but also in the ballot box. As citizens, we take responsibility for our public schools when we vote for the candidates and provide the public funding that support and advance education equity. As elected officials, we take responsibility when we keep the promises we made while campaigning and when we fight for the resources our public schools need. As school administrators and teachers, we take responsibility when we put into place appropriate teaching and learning practices so that *all* children can learn to high standards. As community leaders, we take responsibility when we provide long-term money, support innovation, give new ideas time to take root, and give educators time to work out the kinks and make a genuine difference. We are all responsible.

We as a nation cannot afford to stand by and allow our public schools become wastelands of mediocrity, ill equipped to meet the needs of our society or educate the future citizens of our democracy. We must not allow millions of children to grow up unaware of their rights and responsibilities as citizens and unprepared to support themselves and their families, with little or no stake in society's welfare. We must not accept achievement gaps, tolerate inequitable funding systems, make do with deteriorating buildings and outdated textbooks, and defend failing schools and substandard teaching.

Stan Levenson provides both insightful analysis and proven tools and strategies to help schools think creatively about making new, more powerful allies and friendships when it comes to harnessing private financial resources. Had this book been published 25 years ago, the current landscape of public education would be different as a result. His book adds greatly to our understanding of the need for public schools to be proactive in seeking outside funds for support.

Ensuring that every child in America has a quality public education takes time, takes money, and, most of all, requires acceptance of our personal and collective responsibility. Schools ignore this imperative to engage the public at their own peril. Stan adds to our understanding of public school fundraising, of the profound financial needs of public schools, and of the political pressures that we must resolve so that we can reclaim, revitalize, and reestablish public education as the powerful engine of democratic principles and progress it is meant to be. His book begs us as a nation to rethink our public commitment to public education. At the same time, Stan helps communities harvest the ripe fruit of personal and collective generosity. His book, which is extremely constructive and just plain valuable, helps communities to leave no stone unturned in the search for funds that will help improve student learning. In shifting our sights to the new world of big-time fundraising, Stan has made a groundbreaking, noteworthy, and lasting contribution to the field of public school improvement and reform.

—Wendy D. Puriefoy

Wendy D. Puriefoy is president of Public Education Network (PEN), a national organization of local education funds and individuals working to improve public schools and build citizen support for quality public education in low-income communities across the nation.

Preface

The public schools in America are in financial trouble, and teachers and administrators are feeling the pinch. The cost of providing a world-class education has gone well beyond what is provided by taxpayer dollars. In many districts, worthwhile programs such as those for music, art, physical education, foreign languages, and team sports have been curtailed or eliminated. Some neighborhood schools have been shut down. Teachers, administrators, and staff have lost their jobs. School boards are overwhelmed trying to pay for teacher and staff salaries, fringe benefits, materials, equipment, and technology, as well as for maintenance of buildings and grounds.

There are many people all over this country who want to experience the joy and elation of giving gifts to the schools, and many want to become personally involved. These people don't want just to give their money away; they want to invest in worthy causes that change people's lives. There are few causes more worthy and more life altering than public schools. Our task as fundraisers is to help people understand that their gifts can change the lives of children for generations to come. Showing how to ask for such gifts is a major purpose of this book. Colleges, universities, and private schools have been doing it for years. Now it's time for the public schools to learn how to solicit large grants and gifts as never before.

This book, written for teachers, principals, superintendents, school board members, parents, school foundation members, volunteers, and others, is an outgrowth of my original book, *How to Get Grants and Gifts for the Public Schools*, published in 2002. But it goes way beyond the original book and zeros in on practical, down-to-earth ideas and suggestions that will make your job easier as you pursue grants and gifts from corporations, foundations, the government, and individual donors. My insights into big-time fundraising at private schools, colleges, and universities, combined with my 35 years of experience working in the public schools, provided a strong basis and impetus for the approach to fundraising presented in this book.

Of particular note are a host of suggestions on how to ask for big gifts from individuals. This is key to big-time fundraising, because more than 80 percent of all grants and gifts to colleges, universities, and private schools come from individual donors. The same should hold true for the public schools!

The techniques that I have outlined in this book will enable you to pursue grants and gifts from corporations, foundations, the government, and individual donors. This is serious and demanding work, but the payoff can be enormous. Once you learn how to do it, you are well on your way to helping all children reach their fullest potential, and your budget shortfalls will turn into budget windfalls!

The book is organized into 14 chapters. Chapter 1 presents an overview of the needs of the schools and the opportunities that are out there. Chapter 2 explains what big-time fundraising is, and it describes the need for school districts to establish development offices as well as to delineate roles and responsibilities in a big-time fundraising effort. Chapter 3 concentrates on public school foundations and public education funds, describes how to establish a foundation in your school or school district, and shows the impact of such foundations around the country. Chapter 4 covers individual giving and the effect it can have on a big-time fundraising effort in the public schools. It includes a multistep approach to securing a major gift and other specific ideas on how to ask for gifts. Chapter 5 describes the differences among annual campaigns, capital campaigns, and planned giving. Also included is a description of different approaches used in raising monies in an annual campaign, such as direct mail solicitation; use of telephone, radio, and television; Internet fundraising; and special events. A matrix is provided that shows the size and number of gifts needed to achieve a campaign goal in a capital campaign, and noncash gift ideas are described for a planned giving program, including bequests, charitable gift annuities, appreciated marketable securities, real estate, life insurance, and others.

Chapter 6 will help you learn how to apply for corporate and foundation grants and describes the gains that K–12 schools have made in pursuing these funding opportunities. Chapter 7 provides an 11-step strategy for winning corporate and foundation funding and includes a list of 101 foundations and corporations interested in giving to K–12 schools. Chapter 8 teaches you how to write a minigrant and includes a blank minigrant program application. Chapter 9 teaches you how to go from the minigrant to writing a major grant application, opening doors to big federal and state dollars. This chapter provides detailed information and suggestions on how to write the sections on needs assessment, goals and objectives, and activities; these sections are included in all major grant proposals. Chapter 10 teaches you how to prepare the evaluation component of a government grant application, including both internal and external evaluations. Chapter 11 shows you how to prepare the application budget; break down each component, including direct and indirect costs; and write the budget narrative and the dissemination plan. It also includes 14 helpful hints to improve your chances of getting funded.

Chapter 12 covers what happens after you receive a grant as well as how to be a good steward of all grants and gifts received. It also covers what happens when monies run out and the options that are open to you then. Chapter 13 provides actual examples of two winning minigrants and a winning government grant that will enable you to familiarize yourself with appropriate formats and writing styles and to gauge the amount of work required. Chapter 14 provides a conclusion and summarizes the entire book. An extensive bibliography lists books, articles, grantwriting resources, periodicals, software, directories, and guides. Also included are 6 special Web sites and 28 additional Web sites that will save you much time and effort in your pursuit of grants and gifts. The resources include a comprehensive list of available grant opportunities for K–12 schools, sample ads for key positions, a sample cover letter to accompany a foundation grant request, and a glossary of terms.

With this collection of tools, a supportive school community, and a lot of work, you should be able to find the funding your schools need and your students deserve. Good luck along the way.

Acknowledgments

I would never have been able to complete this book without the help of many friends and colleagues as well as the help of teachers, parents, and administrators who have participated in my workshops and classes around the country. Thanks to Elizabeth "Lizzie" Brenkus, acquisitions editor at Corwin Press, who not only convinced me to write for Corwin Press, but also worked with me on a continuing basis to see the manuscript through to publication. Also, thanks to Desirée Enayati, editorial assistant at Corwin Press, who answered all my questions and concerns and provided needed direction related to marketing. I also want to thank Beth A. Bernstein, production editor, for her able assistance, as well as Cate Huisman, copy editor, who assisted in making the manuscript clear and concise. I am indebted to my daughter, Carla Levenson, a great writer in her own right, for all of the editorial and computer work on the manuscript. A big thank-you goes to my son, Mark Levenson, for his insightful organizational and marketing suggestions. Also, I am grateful to Dave Carpenter, one of the great cartoonists in America, for his perceptive and hilarious cartoons. Finally, to my wife, Kay Pantelis, a wonderful public school teacher, I owe a debt of gratitude for her insistence that I make the manuscript as practical and readable as possible. To all, I couldn't have done it without you!

Corwin Press gratefully acknowledges the contributions of the following reviewers:

Richard L. Austin
Professor Emeritus
University of Nebraska, Lincoln
Lincoln, NE

Mary Ann Burke
Grants Coordinator
Oakland Unified School District
Oakland, CA

Carol Cash
Principal
Hanover High School
Mechanicsville, PA

John W. Davis
Principal
Juan Cabrillo Elementary School
Malibu, CA

About the Author

Dr. Stan Levenson is a nationally known author, speaker, and fundraising consultant to the public schools. He has more than 35 years experience in public education as a classroom teacher; principal; grantwriter; coordinator of special projects; university professor; director of corporate, foundation, and government grants; and fundraising consultant. Levenson has raised more than $50 million in grants and gifts for the public schools, and the people he has trained have raised more than $100 million. The Public Education Network has referred to him to as "a fundraising guru." His book, *How to Get Grants and Gifts for the Public Schools,* received worldwide attention. Levenson has written on fundraising for major publications, including the *American School Board Journal, Principal Leadership,* the *School Administrator, Leadership for Student Activities,* and others. He provides consultant services to school districts around the country, is invited to speak at national conferences and workshops, and is interviewed and quoted in newspapers, magazines, and Web sites across America. He resides in San Diego, California, and can be contacted via Web site at www.grantsandgiftsforschools.com.

1

From Needs to Opportunities

The public schools in America are having financial difficulties, and everyone knows it. The cost of providing a world-class education for students has gone well beyond what is available from taxpayer dollars. Budgets are strained paying for teacher salaries and fringe benefits; purchasing materials, books, and equipment; remodeling and maintaining buildings and grounds; keeping up with the latest innovations in school technology; and meeting state and federal testing mandates. The public schools are also being impacted by declining enrollments brought on by homeschooling, school vouchers, charter schools, attendance of more children in private and religious schools, failing tax overrides, and cuts in local, state, and federal funding. Worthwhile programs such as those for music, art, physical education, and foreign languages have been curtailed or eliminated. Sports and other extracurricular activities have also taken a hit, and neighborhood schools have been shut down. Most disturbing is that in many areas of the country, the ax is falling on core academic programs, and the trend is likely to continue.

THERE'S GOOD NEWS ON THE HORIZON

There are millions of people in America who are strong supporters of the public schools. While some don't always agree with everything going on in the schools, they nevertheless want to see the schools succeed. They view the public schools as being truly representative of our democratic ideals and values as a nation. They see the public schools as a civic treasure that has taken almost 200 years to achieve. Most of these men and women are graduates of the public schools. They are our doctors, dentists, lawyers, professors, and teachers. They are our mothers, fathers, grandmothers, and grandfathers. They are our blue-collar workers, our police, our firefighters, and our postal workers. They are our homemakers, scientists, engineers, pilots, mathematicians, musicians, artists, actors, and realtors. They are our writers, editors, secretaries, business owners, corporate and foundation executives, program officers, government workers, congressional representatives, senators, retirees, and philanthropists. These products of the public schools represent all ages, ethnic groups, colors, and religions. They represent everything that's right with our schools and everything that's right with America.

For years, colleges and universities—especially public institutions—have struggled under similar budgetary constraints. But they have found a way to keep class sizes down, hire and retain high-quality staff, add buildings and grounds, and expand important academic and nonacademic programs. How do they do it? By organizing highly sophisticated development offices, hiring experienced fundraisers, and raising billions of dollars. These entities see the development office as a profit center that goes after big grants and gifts to augment building programs, sports programs, academic programs, creative and performing arts programs, and other vital programs that make for world-class institutions. In essence, they have become big-time fundraisers.

While bake sales, candy sales, carnivals, and car washes create a sense of community for a school or district, these labor-intensive, time-consuming fundraising activities—used so effectively for more than 100 years—can no longer carry the burden for our financially strapped schools. If the schools are to compete for needed dollars, superintendents and their staffs, principals, teachers, parents, school board members, school foundation members, volunteers, and others must aggressively apply the fundraising strategies used so effectively by these other organizations. The public schools must turn their attention to more lucrative ways of raising extra money. They must become big-time fundraisers!

CORPORATIONS, FOUNDATIONS, AND INDIVIDUAL DONORS ARE INTERESTED

Corporations, foundations, and individual donors are becoming more and more interested in helping the public schools. The Foundation Center in New York City reported that in 2004, K–12 schools (including private schools) received more grant monies for education from corporations and foundations than colleges and universities. People like the late Walter Annenberg, Bill and Melinda Gates, Eli Broad, and others have poured millions of dollars into the public schools because they believe in the schools and because they have some of their own ideas on how to improve public education. The schools are beginning to listen.

THE FEDERAL GOVERNMENT IS INVOLVED

The federal government continues to give significant dollars to the schools in competitive and noncompetitive grants. More than $40 billion was provided to public schools in 2004 by the U.S. Department of Education, the Department of Health and Human Services, the Department of Agriculture, the Department of Energy, the Department of the Interior, and the Department of Defense. Go to the Web sites of these organizations to find out more about government grant opportunities. Also, go online to your state department of education's Web site for information about funding opportunities in your state.

CONTRIBUTIONS TO WORTHY CAUSES ACROSS AMERICA HAVE INCREASED

According to the American Association of Fundraising Counsel, more than $248 billion was contributed to worthy causes across America in 2004 (see Figure 1.1). Of this amount, approximately $34 billion (13.6 percent) went to education, which was second only to religion in grants and gifts received. Most interesting is the fact that more than 80 percent ($197 billion) of all contributions, including bequests, come from individual donors, and more than $40 billion comes from corporations and foundations (see Figure 1.2). What does all this mean to public schools trying to bring in outside monies? It means that the schools need to learn how to pursue individual donors as never before. It also means that going after grants and gifts from corporations and foundations should also be a part of your overall fundraising strategy.

Figure 1.1　2004 Contributions: $248.52 Billion by Type of Recipient

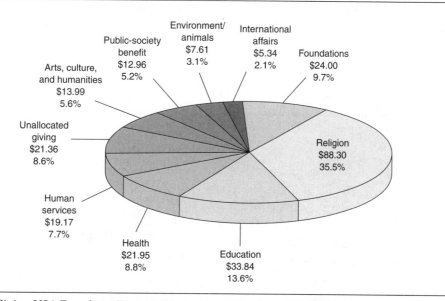

SOURCE: Giving USA Foundation™, AAFRC *Trust for Philanthropy/Giving USA 2005.*

Figure 1.2　2004 Contributions: $248.52 Billion by Source of Contributions

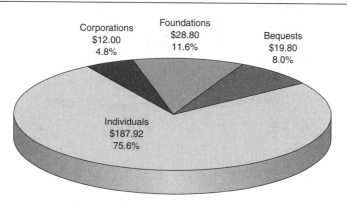

SOURCE: Giving USA Foundation™, AAFRC Trust for Philanthropy/*Giving USA 2005.*

THE TRANSFER OF WEALTH IN AMERICA WILL HELP

When it comes to studying and understanding wealth in America, I have been excited about the research and writings of Paul Schervish and John Havens of the Center on Wealth and Philanthropy at Boston College. The materials coming out of their offices on the transfer of wealth in the United States have been truly mind-boggling. For example, Schervish reported in 2002 that within 50 years, $40.6 trillion will be inherited by many people living today, including mothers, fathers, children, grandchildren, friends, and relatives of past and present public school students. Schervish emphasizes that his figures are low estimates, basing them on a meager two percent growth rate. He indicates that with a growth rate of three percent, $73 trillion will transfer, and with a growth rate of four percent, $136 trillion will transfer. The people inheriting this wealth will be looking for causes to contribute to. Why not the public schools?

Schervish points out in his writing that an increasing number of wealth holders, at ever-younger ages, are no longer focusing exclusively on accumulating more money. They are recognizing that they have reached a certain financial level and now have enough for themselves and their families to achieve their desired standard

of living for generations to come. These new wealth holders are beginning to look at wealth as a tool to achieve higher purposes. They want to give to worthy causes like the public schools, but they also want to have a say in how the money is spent. Consider, for example, Bill and Melinda Gates. These billionaires, through their own foundation, have given more than a billion dollars to the public schools or to non-profit organizations working with the public schools in areas that they are primarily interested in. These areas are mainly redefining the American high school and creating small high schools that offer the new 3R's—rigorous instruction, a relevant curriculum, and meaningful, supportive relationships. If urban high schools want to buy into this approach and apply for funds, it appears that they have a chance of getting funded. If they don't agree philosophically with the vision of the Bill and Melinda Gates Foundation, they probably won't get funded.

Many new wealth holders are forming foundations and thinking very seriously about giving to the public schools. It is important to understand that there might be some strings attached to their giving. The way they look at it, it's their money, and they want a say in how the money is going to be spent. I wouldn't hesitate to accept their monies and allow them the opportunity to feel the joy of giving to a noble cause, provided that their interests mesh with my school's or district's needs.

The public schools are at the threshold of one of the biggest booms in the history of philanthropy, and we need to crank up our fundraising systems now. Many men and women who will be inheriting millions of dollars in cash, equities, real estate, and insurance are products of the public schools. They want to help the schools as never before. We need to learn how to involve these people in our schools and learn how to ask for big gifts. The time for action is now!

2

What Is Big-Time Fundraising?

Big-time fundraising concentrates on the needs of the students as the driving force in obtaining large and small grants and gifts from a variety of funding sources, including corporations, foundations, the government, and individual donors. Schools and school districts involved in a big-time fundraising effort understand that there are many avenues to obtaining big grants and gifts. They know that corporate, foundation, and government grant applications are important. They recognize that letter writing and phone solicitation are important, as is soliciting grants and gifts on the Internet. They are aware that special-events fundraising can be very rewarding. But most of all, they understand that soliciting grants and gifts from individual donors is the most lucrative avenue to obtaining big grants and gifts.

ESTABLISHING A DEVELOPMENT OFFICE

At this time of tight education budgets, budget shortfalls, and a desire to improve public education for all students in America, superintendents of schools, with the approval and support of their school boards, should establish development offices in their school districts and become personally involved in the overall fundraising effort just as college and university presidents do. Experienced, qualified staff should be employed, and volunteers should be recruited and trained as needed. With reasonable expectations, the development office will be one of the few profit centers in the district. Based upon my experience and the experience of others, it should take a development office two to three years or less to become a profit center. Is it worth the investment? You bet it is!

Any school district or school foundation that wants to get involved in a big-time fundraising effort usually has a number of paid, full-time staff or paid consultants or both. In large urban districts, full-time staff might include a director of development;

specialists in individual giving, in alumni relations, and in corporate, foundation, and government grants; and full-time grantwriters. Secretarial staff and facilities would be made available. In smaller school districts, where employees wear many hats, staff might include one full-time person or a part-time person and a number of volunteers. As more grants and gifts come in, additional staff would be employed.

Full-Time Staff

A good way to find full-time, qualified staff for your development office is by placing an announcement in the *Chronicle of Philanthropy*. (See the bibliography for contact information for this and other publications.) Reading the *Chronicle* will also assist you in identifying consultants and consultant companies. Going to the *Chronicle's* Web site is also recommended to familiarize yourself with the enormousness of the fundraising field. Be selective in choosing staff to assist in organizing your development office and in obtaining grants and gifts. There are many good candidates out there looking for new employment opportunities, including people now working in the private schools, colleges, and universities. Many of these men and women have a great deal of experience and expertise, have big-time track records, and are ready, willing, and able to assume leadership positions in public school development offices all across America. Take a look at these people. They are out there for the asking!

To help you get started with recruitment efforts, I have provided job descriptions in Resource B for the positions of director of development; director of individual giving; coordinator of corporate, foundation, and government grants; and grantwriter. For examples of additional job descriptions, look at the *Chronicle of Philanthropy's* Web site under Careers.

As far as titles and salaries are concerned, development office staff should be given salaries and fringe benefits comparable to those of others in the district having similar titles and responsibilities.

Consultants

Consultants are independent contractors who are responsible for their own benefits, office space, and secretarial space, unless other arrangements are made. They normally sign a contract with the district to complete a specific task by a specific date for a specific fee. Consultants can be of great help when starting a big-time fundraising effort. They can augment existing staff, provide staff development, and contribute their time and expertise to the total fundraising effort. When a district works with consultants in this manner, district staff have an opportunity to be trained appropriately and to meet immediate needs for accomplishing specific tasks, and the district is not obligated to long-term contracts and fringe benefits.

A good way to find qualified consultants is to go to the Web sites of the *Chronicle of Philanthropy* and the *NonProfit Times*. When considering consultants for your cause, take a look at their recent track records. Ask about their experience at the elementary and secondary school levels. Check their references to find out if they are able to work cooperatively with teachers, principals, parents, volunteers, and others. Finally, inquire about their fee schedules. Most consultants will charge you a daily rate and multiply that rate by the number of days they estimate it will take them to complete a project or the number of days you want them to work in the district.

Specifications for Hiring Full-Time Staff and Consultants

A qualified full-time staff member or a fundraising consultant should

- Have fundraising experience at the K–12 level.
- Know how to obtain corporate, foundation, and government grants as well as grants and gifts from individuals.
- Know how to do prospect research and respond to Requests for Proposals (RFPs).
- Know how to match up school district needs with corporate, foundation, and government interests and funding levels.
- Understand the importance of getting to know many of the wealthy people in the community who give to good causes, and know ways of soliciting monies from these individuals.
- Know how to conduct and manage annual and capital campaigns.
- Understand what planned giving is and how to implement a planned giving program.
- Know how to work cooperatively with district-level administrators, principals, evaluators, teachers, parents, and community leaders.
- Relate well to program officers and chief executive officers of funding agencies and understand the nurturing process that takes place before a grant is awarded.
- Be articulate and knowledgeable about education issues and needs from prekindergarten through Grade 12.
- Set a good example for the grantwriting team by being a successful grantwriter, being well organized and articulate, making good use of technology, and meeting all deadlines.
- Have established a successful track record of assisting schools and school districts in obtaining funding on a continuing basis and being called upon to teach others how to do it.
- After a realistic period of time (two to three years or sooner), assist in bringing in a substantial number of grants and gifts so that the development office becomes a profit center for the school or district.

Note that the above specifications can be used as a hiring matrix for full-time staff and consultants.

Be Wary of Consultants Who Propose to Work for No Up-Front Fees

Some consultants will propose to work for you for no fee up front, instead asking for a percentage of the money they bring in. These consultants are usually just getting started and are attempting to get their feet in the door. To get a contract, they will make this kind of proposal. This arrangement is not recommended, even though it sounds enticing. For example, if the consultant was working on 15 percent of gross for a winning grant that comes in at $1 million, are you prepared to justify to your community and your school board paying the consultant $150,000 for one grant? Also, which category of the budget would this fee come out of, and would it be legal to do this in your state? My suggestion would be to employ qualified consultants as needed, and pay them for their time and effort.

It should be mentioned that some school districts encourage consultants to write themselves into grant applications as program directors, project developers, trainers, and evaluators. In doing so, the consultant (contractor) brings a unique perspective and expertise to the project's development and remains vested in the project, helping to ensure project funding and development success.

A DOZEN BIG-TIME FUNDRAISING STRATEGIES AND TECHNIQUES THAT WIN EVERY TIME

To yield maximum results in implementing a big-time fundraising effort, utilize the following strategies and techniques:

1. Form a local education foundation on a districtwide or individual school basis, if you haven't already done so. The foundation should be a nonprofit 501(c)(3) organization that is tax-exempt. Invite prominent members of the community to be members of the foundation board. Local education foundations broaden the school constituency, keep the community informed, and facilitate the acquisition of grants and gifts. (See Chapter 3 for more information on forming a local education foundation.)

2. Devote the necessary resources to make your fundraising effort successful.

3. Employ full-time, qualified staff as needed, or start by hiring part-time consultants and volunteers.

4. Identify influential community leaders, including your town's mayor, local congressional representatives, corporate sponsors, business leaders, wealthy people, alumni, friends, parents, and grandparents. Nurture these people and make them part of the total fundraising effort.

5. Become familiar with fundraising publications, including the *Chronicle of Philanthropy*, the *NonProfit Times*, and *Planned Giving Today*.

6. Access the Web site of the Foundation Center in New York City, and become familiar with its services.

7. Attend or host training classes and workshops on fundraising, including soliciting gifts from individuals; writing grants; and seeking corporate, foundation, and government grants.

8. Learn how to write a case statement that details your district's needs and priorities. Use the case statement as a basis for obtaining grants and gifts.

9. Alert the local media about your fundraising efforts. They can reach a broad audience faster and more efficiently than you can.

10. Get together with other school foundations and other school districts in your state and area to share ideas, speakers, and information.

11. When writing a grant proposal, attempt to collaborate with colleges and universities in your area. Funding agencies look at this approach very favorably.

12. Encourage the superintendent of schools and other key staff to become involved in the fundraising effort just as the presidents of colleges and universities do.

ROLES AND RESPONSIBILITIES IN A BIG-TIME FUNDRAISING EFFORT

Many people are involved in a big-time fundraising effort. Below you will find a description of the roles and responsibilities of each of these people, including superintendents, principals, classroom teachers, subject matter specialists, coaches, parents, volunteers, and people with money.

The Role of Superintendents

The superintendent of schools, with the blessings of the board of education, is the overall leader in a big-time fundraising effort. This responsibility includes, but is not limited to, the establishment of a districtwide development office, including the employment of competent, experienced development office staff.

Working with the development office staff, the local education foundation, central office staff, principals, teachers, parents, volunteers, consultants, and the board of education, the superintendent can bring power, prestige, and creativity to the overall needs and vision of the school district.

Recently, I visited two foundations in the San Francisco Bay Area with a Southern California superintendent of schools. In both instances, the executive directors of the foundations indicated that this was the first time that they had ever met with a superintendent of schools on their turf. They were both very pleased that the superintendent took some valuable time and felt it was important to make a personal visit to the foundation to discuss the district's needs and vision. Needless to say, both foundations funded the school district in a major way, and the superintendent discovered that if the CEO of a school district meets the CEO of a foundation or corporation, good things start to happen.

The superintendent of schools should learn how to ask for gifts from wealthy individuals and others within the school constituency. Once training takes place, the superintendent will be ready to be a part of a solicitation team. This approach, used so effectively by college and university presidents, will reap major rewards. If the superintendent of schools takes the time and makes the effort to meet with potential donors on a personal basis, good things will also start to happen, and monies will start pouring in. Remember, if you don't ask, you won't get!

The Role of School Board Members

Individual school board members are key players in the overall big-time fundraising effort for the school district. Most board members I know have many friends and contacts in the community and elsewhere, including key people in the business world. I recommend that board members utilize these great contacts for the overall good of the school district by soliciting gifts from some of their friends and colleagues. If the opportunity is there, and school board members are able to make gifts themselves, why not? Board members in the nonprofit world, as well as at private schools, colleges, and universities, are contributing regularly to the good causes they represent. Why not in the public schools?

School board members should be strong supporters and advocates of a big-time fundraising effort in their school district. They should approve of the establishment of a development office and should expect the office to be a profit center in two to three years or sooner. School board members should also understand that more than 80 percent of all grants and gifts to good causes come from individual donors. Therefore, they should encourage and support the superintendent and the development office staff to personally go after big grants and gifts from individuals. School board members should assist in identifying and soliciting others in the community who have the ability to and interest in contributing to the schools. By setting a good example of contributing to the schools themselves, school board members will create a lot of excitement and interest in donating to the schools.

The Role of Principals

Principals are key players in the overall big-time fundraising effort. They can make or break a program by their attitude and their involvement. I look at principals in almost the same way as I look at superintendents. Principals are the leaders of their schools just as superintendents are the leaders of their school districts. The more involved a principal gets in the individual giving program, the more money will flow in. Therefore, I see principals making personal visits, along with the superintendent, to wealthy constituents and others in the attendance area of the school. I also recommend that principals be part of the visitation team that meets with program officers and CEOs of corporations and foundations interested in funding a specific school.

The Role of Classroom Teachers, Specialists, Coaches, and Band Directors

Classroom teachers, specialists, coaches, and band directors are at the heart of a big-time fundraising effort. These are the people on the firing line each and every day. They make the community proud of their involvement and commitment to kids. School band directors, choral directors, coaches in all sports as well as for academic decathlons, classroom teachers, and teachers of creative and performing arts are key players in each school and school district. These people represent all the good that is going on in the schools. If individuals are going to give big money to the schools, they probably know one or more of these people through their kids or grandkids, have been influenced by their good work, and want to help out in any way they can. We need these people in our big-time fundraising programs.

The Role of Parents and Volunteers

Parents and volunteers are very important team members in the total big-time fundraising effort. If you involve them on your team, you will reap major rewards in time and money. Most parents want to help the schools that their children attend. Many of them are tired of nickel-and-dime fundraising efforts and want to learn how the big boys and girls do it. Additionally, many parents and volunteers have very good contacts in the school community and know who the wealthy people are. Having these contacts, they should be invited to make personal visits to prospects along with other members of the solicitation team. They should also be encouraged to make their own contributions as well.

The Role of People With Money

Wealthy people, especially those who are graduates of the public schools or have taught in the public schools, should take an active role in both giving to the schools and in helping to solicit grants and gifts from their friends and family. A number of these people have already felt the joy of giving to other causes in their communities. They would welcome an invitation to give back to the schools by contributing their time and money. Many of these people with money have children and grandchildren in the schools and would be receptive to giving a large gift in their behalf. Invite these people into the schools and involve them in your cause. Ask them to assume leadership positions—such as chairman of the board, secretary, or treasurer—in your school or district foundation. If they contribute large sums of money, consider naming a facility in their honor. It's being done everywhere else. Why not the public schools?

An Example From New York City

Fundraising is already beginning to change in some schools and school districts around the country. For example, Joel I. Klein, New York City schools chancellor, appointed Caroline Kennedy (daughter of John F. Kennedy) to the position of chief executive of the Office of Strategic Partnerships that oversees the development and management of strategic partnerships between the New York City public schools and the private sector. In her new role, Ms. Kennedy (who earns $1 per year) is working cooperatively with key staff to identify educational needs throughout the school system and then to secure and target private-sector resources for reform efforts. Ms. Kennedy brought more than $150 million in grants and gifts to the New York City schools in a short period of time, with more to come. Is there a person in your community who has very good contacts, who doesn't need or want a salary, and who would be honored to be asked to serve the children, parents, teachers, principals, superintendent, and board of the public schools? If there is, go after this person with gusto!

SOME IMPORTANT ISSUES

There are a number of issues that you should be aware of as you begin thinking about implementing a big-time fundraising effort in your school or school district. These issues include the following:

- Many taxpayers believe that it is the school district's responsibility, as well as the responsibility of the state and federal governments, to provide the monies needed for the public schools. They don't believe that the public schools should be put in a position to have to raise significant amounts of monies from outside sources, especially to restore core academic programs and to pay for teacher and staff salaries lost to budget cutbacks.

- The success of school fundraising tends to be directly proportionate to household income in a school's attendance area. Therefore, high-income areas are able to raise significantly more monies than low-income areas.

- Affluent parents in the richer schools and school districts are better able to keep programs alive than parents in poorer schools and school districts, thus worsening the divide between the rich and the poor and not providing equal educational opportunities for all kids.

- School foundations in rich schools and school districts are able to raise significantly more money than school foundations in poorer schools and school districts. People are calling for a leveling of the playing field.

- Some policy experts and school officials say that private financing for public schools carries real risks, including loss of government funding for schools and donors playing a disproportionate role in shaping school policy. This, they say, is enabling to legislators and taxpayers who might shrug off their responsibility to support public education.

- Many teachers are spending their own monies to pay for books, materials, and equipment in the classroom and are also feeling pressured to write grants to meet basic needs.

- Individual school foundations, local education foundations, and districtwide foundations are being formed in many schools and school districts around the country without proper coordination and cooperation with the total school community. In some instances, there are multiple foundations in one school. In others, there are multiple foundations within the school district. This has resulted in duplication of effort, problems with one program being favored over another, friction among foundations, and a waste of human resources. Learning how major colleges and universities handle this issue is important to avoid misunderstandings and disputes.

- In some schools and school districts, local education foundations are in an adversarial position with the superintendent of schools, the teachers, and the school board. This is not in the best interest of the schools and the kids. It's important that positive lines of communication remain open at all times and that foundations make every effort to work cooperatively with districts, with the ultimate objective being the improvement of public education for all children.

Issues Are Legitimate

The issues being raised are legitimate and should be addressed by the total school community. At this time, there are large infusions of monies going to poor, urban schools and school districts. The federal government is aware of the negative impact that poverty has on learning, and through Title I of the Elementary and Secondary Education Act of 1965 and other programs, it has provided significant amounts of federal dollars to schools in an effort to improve and equalize learning opportunities. Corporations, foundations, and individual donors are becoming aware of these issues as well, and they are beginning to address them through their own giving programs. Alumni associations at various high schools around the country are contributing to scholarship programs and endowments for poor high school students to attend colleges and universities.

A number of school and district foundations are developing strategies to equalize funding throughout the district so that the poorer schools won't be at a disadvantage in soliciting grants and gifts from the community. This includes putting all gifts into one pot and distributing the monies equally. It also includes minigrants for teachers based upon the submission of grant applications. After all is said and done, every advocate for public education in the United States should insist that the schools receive their fair share of tax dollars and not be put in a position to have to raise significant amounts of outside dollars to meet basic needs. It is the duty of every legislator in the country and every taxpayer to make this a reality.

The public schools are in their infancy when it comes to big-time fundraising. Some schools and school districts are continuing to study their options. Others are just getting started. A number are making some serious progress. One thing is for certain: Big-time fundraising at the K–12 level is here to stay!

3

Public School Foundations

Foundations are relatively new phenomena in the public schools. Howie Schaffer, public outreach director for the Public Education Network (PEN) in Washington, DC, estimates that there are more than 5,000 foundations in the approximately 16,000 school districts across the United States. These foundations come in many shapes and sizes and are as unique as the schools they serve. Some are not very active and raise small amounts of money, while others are large and sophisticated and raise in the millions. Any foundation that brings in less than $10,000 per year does not have to file an IRS Form 990, which is the information form that charities and foundations file with the Internal Revenue Service. Because of this, it is very difficult to track actual numbers of foundations at individual school sites. My estimate, taking into account all foundations regardless of size, is that there are more than 10,000 public school foundations in the United States.

The San Francisco Education Foundation, founded in 1979, is recognized as being one of the first public school foundations in the United States. PEN is also considered one of the pioneers in this fast growing movement, having received a grant from the Ford Foundation in 1982 to assist in the establishment of approximately 50 local education funds (LEFs). PEN's network of LEFs operates in 34 states, the District of Columbia, and Puerto Rico, serving 11.5 million students in more than 1,600 school districts. LEFs are community-based advocacy organizations focused on serving poor and disadvantaged students and engaging local citizens in public education reform. Though independent of their local school districts, LEFs work closely with public school administrators, teachers, and school boards as well as with parents, community leaders, businesses, and students. LEFs are located in communities with populations ranging from less than 10,000 to almost 10 million. They operate with annual budgets of under $100,000 to budgets of more than $20 million.

Most public school foundations are nonprofit 501(c)(3) tax-exempt organizations raising monies for the schools. The foundations give members of communities around public schools an opportunity to contribute their time and monies to the schools and show that they really value public education. Foundations come in various shapes and sizes and are not based upon one model. For example, some foundations represent just one school, while others represent an entire school district. In some schools and school districts, there are multiple foundations representing differing goals, objectives, and community support.

HOW ARE PUBLIC SCHOOL FOUNDATIONS ORGANIZED?

There are four broad categories of public school foundations around the country. These are the following:

- Foundations that are organized at an individual school to foster excellence by supporting innovative classroom practices and by supplementing, augmenting, and complementing the curriculum by providing for programs and activities not otherwise available, such as music, art, and physical education. Many of these school foundations also provide minigrants for teachers.

- Foundations that are independent, community-based organizations that see themselves as advocates for public education, school improvement, and school reform. These foundations look to broaden the constituency and keep the community informed about the strengths, challenges, and needs of the schools. Example of these types of foundations would be local education funds sponsored by PEN.

- Foundations that are organized on a districtwide basis as an arm of the school district just as at colleges, universities, and private schools. This type of school foundation coordinates and facilitates the district's total fundraising effort through a development office with full-time staff and financial support of the school district.

- A combination of any of the above.

Public school foundations around the country have been established by local efforts of groups such as parents, civic groups, chambers of commerce, alumni, booster clubs, and friends of the schools. Additionally, school boards and school districts have provided the impetus for the establishment of a large number of districtwide foundations.

Many public school foundations are becoming serious about their roles as big-time fundraisers and advocates for the public schools. These foundations want to learn how the private schools, colleges, universities, and nonprofit organizations raise billions of dollars each year. They want to roll up their sleeves and compete for needed dollars in these times of budget shortfalls and diminishing financial resources.

Ten Basic Steps to Starting a Public School Foundation

When you start a public school foundation, it is critical that you do it correctly. Make certain to consult with an attorney or a technical assistance agency whose staff has experience in this area.

According to the California Consortium of Education Foundations, there are 10 basic steps that should be followed when starting a local education foundation:

1. Establish a core leadership group.

2. Define your reason for being.

3. Share your plans with school and community leaders.

4. File for tax-exempt status.

5. Develop bylaws.

6. Recruit a board that reflects your community.

7. Establish committees and draft policies.

8. Develop a priority project list and an allocations process.

9. Create a fundraising plan and outline, identifying your unique resources.

10. Celebrate your success and evaluate your progress.

Things to Consider When Starting a Public School Foundation

PEN provides leadership and direction to school districts around the country wanting to start foundations. They have the following suggestions, adapted by the Oklahoma Foundation for Excellence:

- Research existing local education funds. Pay particular attention to those with school districts of similar size and demographics. You can start by reviewing our list of members as well as other sources such as education foundations.
- Call or e-mail the Public Education Network national office for additional materials or resources. PEN member services team will provide advice and guidance on starting a Local Education Fund. (202) 628–7460 or www.public education.org
- Become familiar with your state's provisions regarding nonprofit organizations. Contact your state association of the National Center for Nonprofit Associations.
- Assess interest of the community, school board, and school district administration in starting a local education fund.
- Identify community residents who are committed to the LEF concept and ask them to join a steering committee to establish the organization. Include civic and business leaders, parents, school district leaders, teachers, minority representatives, and attorneys and accountants who are familiar with 501(c)(3) nonprofit organizations. Having a representative of the local newspaper on the committee is also very helpful.
- Invite enthusiastic veteran board members and administrators from existing LEFs to talk with the steering committee about their experiences in starting an LEF. You can find nearby LEFs in our directory.
- Convene the steering committee to review materials, plan the organization, determine its general mission and goals, and identify the prospective board of trustees.
- Draft preliminary articles of incorporation and bylaws.

- File a request for incorporation as a nonprofit organization with the proper state agency.
- File federal form SS-4 to obtain an employer identification number from the federal government. This should be obtained early in the process, since it will be needed for many next steps.
- Select a nominating committee from the steering committee members to nominate the board of directors. Consider a board of 11 to 21 members. Be sure to thoroughly spell out the expected duties of board members when asking prospects to join the board.
- Hold an organizational meeting of the steering committee to elect the board of directors and officers. Ratify the mission and approve the bylaws and initial budget. Appoint someone to record the minutes from this organizational meeting.
- File federal form 1023 with the IRS to apply for 501(c)(3) status within 15 months of incorporating: The form requires a three-year operating budget and a board of directors. You will receive a temporary exemption (advance ruling) from the IRS. After the advance-ruling period, the IRS will request additional information to grant a permanent exemption status. You must maintain these papers in a permanent file.
- Establish financial records, including controls over donor records and financial reporting standards to the board and community. Ask your accountant to set up a chart of accounts, the general ledger and journals, and draft a set of financial statements. Set up a receipt system to comply with IRS contribution reporting requirements for 501(c)(3) organizations. Determine if an outside firm or an internal audit committee will do your audit. If possible, use an outside auditor.
- Complete additional filings with the tax commission in your state and a Form 990 with the IRS at the end of the fiscal year in lieu of an income tax form.
- Determine responsibilities and assign work to board members and committees. Develop procedures for staff reporting to the board of trustees. BoardSource is a good starting place to learn about nonprofit governance. (www.boardsource.org)
- Begin detailed planning for program development and fundraising.
- Inform the community of your LEF's existence, goals, and needs.
- Begin a fundraising campaign and programs.
- Apply for membership in Public Education Network.

WHAT'S HAPPENING AROUND THE COUNTRY?

A number of public school foundations around the country are becoming big-time fundraisers. Some have employed consultants to help them get organized and train staff. Others have hired full-time executive directors, grantwriters, and specialists to solicit grants and gifts from individual donors, including alumni and friends. Many foundations have their own Web sites and solicit grants and gifts via the Internet. Some foundations are training and using a bevy of volunteers to help in obtaining grants and gifts from individual donors and to assist with capital campaigns, bequests, and endowments.

Public school foundations in America are beginning to enjoy the benefits of private philanthropy as never before. Described below is the work of 12 foundations that are making a difference around the country. They represent just a small sampling of what is happening. Much more needs to get done!

TWELVE PUBLIC SCHOOL FOUNDATIONS
THAT ARE MAKING A DIFFERENCE

1. Wake Education Partnership in Raleigh, North Carolina, has an annual budget of $1.5 million. In their fundraising campaigns, they engage hundreds of volunteers and more than 5,000 donors, including corporations, parents, teachers, and others.

2. Franklin-McKinley Education Foundation, located in a primarily low-income area of San Jose, California, raised more than $1.2 million through corporate and foundation giving.

3. P.S. 87 in Manhattan, influenced by Jean C. Joachim, teacher and author of *Beyond the Bake Sale,* has been raising $200,000 a year for more than 10 years.

4. The Portland Schools Foundation in Portland, Oregon, has raised more than $360 million for the Portland schools over the past 10 years. During one span of time, the foundation raised $10 million in six weeks. The foundation also was responsible in helping to attract a $10 million gift from the Bill & Melinda Gates Foundation.

5. The Achieve Minneapolis Foundation, which has a full-service development office, has been raising more than $4 million a year for the past five years.

6. The Coronado Schools Foundation in Coronado, California, has been raising more than $100,000 per year for the public schools through its dinner auction.

7. The Rancho Bernardo High School Foundation in the Poway Unified School District in California has raised more than $700,000 for construction of a new music hall on campus.

8. The Alumni Association of P.S. 6 in New York City has raised $750,000 for a new library on campus by tapping into its prominent alumni base.

9. The Moreland School District's all-volunteer foundation in the San Jose and Cupertino, California, areas has raised nearly $300,000 in two years and has restored staff positions that were going to be cut.

10. The Lincoln Public Schools Foundation in Lincoln, Nebraska, has raised more than $13 million since 1989. Most of the monies go to financing minigrants for teachers through an innovative "Fund a Need" program. The foundation has also gotten into estate planning, including individual bequests. See their Web site.

11. The Education Fund in Miami, Florida, with a staff of more than 15 along with an additional 30 AmeriCorps volunteers, is raising more than $3 million a year for the Miami–Dade County Public Schools. They have also made inroads into corporate and foundation giving programs, and local businesses have contributed more than 5,000 laptops to the schools.

12. San Diego High School Foundation in San Diego, California, has an endowment of more than $350,000 primarily because of dedicated alumni. Most parents are not able to contribute financially to the school, and the alumni, because of their love, dedication, and fond memories, have stepped to the plate and provided needed funds.

As public school foundations become successful in their acquisition of funds from outside sources such as corporations, foundations, and individual donors, it is important to set up district procedures for the proper acceptance of foundation checks. This entails procedures for loading budgets, processing expenditures, and meeting the fiscal and program reporting requirements of funding agencies. Also, service fees that cover the cost of using a foundation as a fiscal agent or for fiscal management of school district initiatives should be agreed upon through memorandums of understanding or other such agreements.

4

How to Get Big Gifts From Individual Donors

There are thousands of people all over this country who want to experience the joy and elation of giving big gifts to the schools, and many want to become personally involved in your cause. These people don't want to give their money away, but they do want to invest in worthy causes that change people's lives. There are few causes more worthy and more life altering than the public schools. Our task as fundraisers is to help people understand that their gifts can change the lives of children for generations to come. Learning how to ask for such gifts will reap major rewards. The colleges, universities, and private schools have been doing it for years. Now it's time for the public schools to learn how to do it.

WHY HAVEN'T WE GONE AFTER BIG GIFTS?

Solicitation of big gifts from individual donors is practically nonexistent in the public schools. There are many reasons for this, but suffice it to say that teachers and administrators have been reluctant as a group to ask constituents for major gifts of cash, materials, equipment, buildings, and grounds. Maybe it is because the public schools are tax supported that they are inhibited from asking. However, so are the University of California, the State University of New York, the University of Michigan, the University of Iowa, and other state-supported institutions.

These entities have been raising billions of dollars each year, while the public schools have been idly standing by. I believe the major reason the public schools have not been soliciting major gifts from potential donors is that superintendents of schools, principals, classroom teachers, school board members, and parents are inexperienced in asking for such gifts and have been reluctant to ask. This must change if the public schools are to compete for needed dollars.

When I teach a class or speak to groups around the country, I always ask how many participants attended private or religious schools. There usually are a number of people in the audience who raise their hands. Then I ask if they ever hear from these schools and if they have ever been asked for money. Their response: "All the time." I then ask whether the audience members receive calls or mailers from their alma maters and if those colleges and universities regularly ask for contributions. Again: "All the time." Finally, I ask if they ever heard from the public schools they attended. Silence. Why not the public schools?

Many potential donors are graduates of the public schools, live or work in our communities, own businesses in our communities, and have children or grand-children attending our schools. These people want the public schools to succeed and at the same time want to experience the joy of giving to the schools in their time of need. This reminds me of a story: A pig and a cow were talking in a barnyard one day. The pig said, "I don't get it! I give away bacon, pork chops, baby back ribs, and pig's feet, and nobody ever recognizes me for this. I never receive any credit for my worthy contributions. In fact, I give away my life, and you, Ms. Cow, just give away milk, butter, and cheese but seem to get all the honors, rewards, and appreciation. There's something wrong here, and I don't know what it is." To that Ms. Cow replied, "Hmm, maybe it's because I give while I'm still alive." There's an element of truth to this story as more and more people are choosing to experience the joy of giving before they pass on.

Decisions on giving to the schools (and other good causes) usually come from the gut. The person or family making the gift feels a sense of commitment, joy, excitement, friendship, and love. They see themselves changing students' lives and contributing to making a major impact on the education of children in the schools for many years to come.

Recently, I established an endowment for a college scholarship and met the first recipient of my gift. It was pure joy and excitement! I have made a friend for life! Each year, while I am alive, I will be making new friends and looking forward to meeting and corresponding with the next scholarship recipient. What an opportunity to make a difference in a person's life! And best of all, the life is mine!

DEFINING BIG GIFTS

From my perspective, a big gift from an individual or family would be a gift of $25,000 or more. However, you can designate any amount you wish. Big gifts are usually solicited for endowment purposes, scholarships, buildings, grounds, equipment, and any other program or facility that needs a large infusion of money. These gifts are asked for infrequently, and the giver can spread their delivery over three to five years. If you are looking for big gifts, you'll get them by "friendraising" with potential donors and meeting with them in person. Solicitation on a person-to-person basis is the most effective way to raise serious dollars.

There is an old adage that says, "People contribute money to people with causes and not just to causes." This is not to say that donors are not interested in causes, because they are, but it is the dynamics of a face-to-face meeting with someone who is a friend that helps snare the gift.

For those new to fundraising, you will discover that it is easier to get people to give than it is to ask for the gift. Learning how to ask for the gift is key to big-time fundraising. Always remember, if you don't ask, you won't get!

HOW TO SNARE BIG GIFTS FROM INDIVIDUAL PROSPECTS

There are many ways to solicit big grants and gifts from individual donors in your school community. The most desirable, but most difficult, is to approach people on an individual basis. Because of the personal nature of this strategy and its importance to you and your cause, ask for a "visit" with a potential donor, rather than using the more formal term "appointment." Make the visit only after going through a comprehensive training program taught by someone who has been on the firing line before and has learned how to snare big grants and gifts.

Arranging a visit to secure the gift is one of the toughest things that you will accomplish. It is much easier to set up a visit with a prospect if the person arranging the visit is a close friend or relative or is a leader in the school district such as a principal, the superintendent of schools, or a school board member. Once you set up the visit, you are well on your way to securing the gift. Below is a step-by-step approach on how to do it based upon my own work in the field as well as the work of others mentioned in the bibliography.

THE STEPS TO SECURING A MAJOR GIFT

Utilizing a group process technique, prepare a *case statement* of two to five pages in length that is clear, concise, and compelling. The case statement should indicate what you need the money for and highlight the staff's competence and ability to deliver. It is imperative that you include in the case statement the precise reason for your appeal, what you will achieve if your objectives are met, and the students and staff who will benefit. The case statement should be reproduced on good-quality 8½ x 11 inch paper, or made into an attractive multicolored brochure, depending on your budget. In either case, the content is more important than the format used for the statement. Prepare multiple copies of the statement for handout purposes, and train the staff and volunteers on how to use the materials to achieve maximum results.

Recruit volunteers in your community to work on the fundraising committee. Include, among others, prominent citizens who are well known and well thought of. Invite these people to an orientation meeting held by some of the key people in the school district, such as the superintendent, principals, board members, teachers, community leaders, and others. Use a PowerPoint presentation or other powerful audiovisual means to communicate your message and highlight your cause. Answer all questions and concerns in a forthright and efficient manner. Ask participants to make a commitment of time and money before the meeting is concluded.

Make certain that the volunteers contribute their gifts first, before they approach prospective donors. This will help by providing them with "boasting rights" and will demonstrate to prospective donors that the cause is so worthy that the volunteers have already made contributions.

Utilize the services of a good fundraising consultant if at all possible, unless you have someone on staff that can train volunteers. Have this person provide a comprehensive training program that involves role-playing and videotaping (if possible). Use prepared scripts and prepared situations such as "overcoming objections," "asking for the gift," and "deciding how much to ask for." Training programs are included in some of resource materials listed in the bibliography. The training program should be mandatory for all members of the fundraising committee.

Develop a list of prospective donors in cooperation with the fundraising committee. Decide as a group how much you plan to ask each person to give. The committee should identify the names of wealthy parents, grandparents, teachers (including retired teachers), administrators, staff, friends, alumni (elementary, middle school, and high school), business people, politicians, retirees, and others that reside in the school community. Try to match up the list of prospective donors with people on the fundraising committee who might know the prospects as friends, relatives, or acquaintances. Ask these committee members to make the contact with these people once the committee members have gone through the training program.

Two people should approach a potential donor as a team. The team might include a principal and a volunteer, the superintendent and a volunteer, a board member and the superintendent, a teacher and a volunteer, or other groups of two. However, in a situation where a major contributor has already made a gift to your cause and is interested in soliciting a friend to make another major gift, it is suggested that you encourage him or her to solicit the friend on an individual basis. This approach seems to work with major donors all across America.

Visits to prospective donors should take place in a quiet, peaceful atmosphere not disturbed by telephone calls, interruptions, and extraneous conversation and noise. My first choice would be at the home or office of the potential donor. A second choice would be in a meeting room at the school or district office. I do not recommend luncheon or dinner meetings or meetings held in public places such as on the golf course or on the tennis court. Meetings at these locations have a tendency to get away from the business at hand. The major consideration is the comfort level of the prospect to be in an environment to discuss a gift. Remember, when you arrange a visit to meet with a prospective donor, you are actually going on a *business call* to ask for the order.

Visits with prospects should be arranged for no more than 30 to 45 minutes. If additional time is needed, let the prospect decide to extend the meeting.

If you do not know the individuals you are assigned to visit with, you must do prospect research before the visit takes place. You should discover, if possible, their educational and business backgrounds, their financial backgrounds, their family backgrounds, the organizations to which they belong, their social affiliations, and their interests and hobbies. Find out where they received their degrees and whether they sit on any important corporate or nonprofit boards. You should also determine if any member of their family attended or is attending your district schools, if the potential donor is involved in any school activities or functions, and if the family has given monies to the schools in the past. If you do comprehensive prospect research concerning each potential donor, your chance of receiving gifts increases substantially, because you will be able to connect with the prospect in human terms.

When visiting with a potential donor, make sure you break the ice by talking about areas of mutual interest that you have discovered in your prospect research. For example, if you are a tennis player and the potential donor is a tennis player, you might say something like, "I understand that you are a tennis player. How often do you play?" If you are or your dad is a graduate of Harvard University and you discover that the potential donor is a graduate of Harvard, you might say, "I graduated from Harvard," or "My dad graduated from Harvard," and then add, "What was your major?"

During the first visit, no solicitation of money usually takes place. It is a time to be a good listener. By being a good listener, you will discover the prospect's needs and greatest joys. You will also discover the prospect's concerns. The first visit is also the time to establish rapport with your prospect, to show your energy, commitment, and enthusiasm for your cause. It is during the second or third visit that you ask for the money.

On this visit, explain why you are visiting with the potential donor. This is a time to impress this person and discuss your cause. You might mention the outstanding staff that you have and any additional staff that you intend to put into place. Talk about the benefits and advantages of having this new and innovative program (or some other cause) and about how beneficial the program will be to the prospective donor. Be sure to provide the prospect with a copy of the case statement. When presenting your case, listen aggressively and pay close attention to the potential donor. Watch for signs of approval or disapproval. Watch for body language that might be indicative of the comfort level of the prospect.

Treat objections as questions the potential donors have rather than as attacks on your program or credibility. (If they really had no intention of giving you a gift in the first place, they would not be meeting with you at all.) Handle objections as they come up, and never let an objection lead to an argument. Always hear an objection out and respond with solutions. One approach is to convert the objection into an answerable question. You might say, "I realize that you are concerned about the district's reading program. Would you be interested in participating on the district's reading committee?" Finding common ground with the prospect is another way of turning negatives into positives. "I realize that our reading program can improve. This is why we are seeking your help." Make sure to identify honest objections and respond with facts. Do not make excuses, and respond candidly. You might say, "I realize our reading scores went down this year in fifth grade, but did you know that our overall scores are still considerably higher than those of most school districts in the area?" Another option is to empathize: "I am delighted that you brought this matter up. I, too, do not like the fact that our scores went down."

When making the "big ask," always request a little more than you expect to receive, and then remain silent. It is critical to know how much to ask for, and this is decided after doing extensive prospect research. Once research is complete, and you are meeting with the prospect, you might say, "We're hoping that you will consider an investment in our reading program by making a contribution of $50,000." Pause and let the request sink in and observe the prospect's behavior.

Not asking for a large enough gift could lead to receiving a smaller gift than anticipated or not receiving a gift at all. People with money usually do not get upset if you ask them for more than they are considering. In fact, they might feel honored that you think they are more wealthy than they really are and surprise you with a gift that is larger than you expected.

Do not accept a gift if you feel the gift is too small. It is better to make another appointment to further explore opportunities for giving a gift. You might say, "Let us leave the materials so you can study them, and then we'll get together again in two weeks to answer any questions that you might have."

If you receive a gift pledge from a prospect that you are happy with, express your appreciation enthusiastically, and ask the person to complete and sign a pledge card. A sample pledge card is provided in Figure 4.1. There are also software programs available that include computerized pledge cards; these are listed in the bibliography at the end of this book.

Continue to cultivate those prospects that did not make a gift the first time they were approached, and continue to seek out new prospects. Keep careful records for all prospects. For those that did not contribute, analyze why they did not make a pledge based upon your conversation with them, and go back again in three to six months. Maintain records for those people who did contribute to your cause also, so that when you return and ask for an additional gift in the future, you will know to ask for a larger gift then the one previously received.

Acknowledge all those people who contributed to your fundraising campaign by sending them personal thank-you notes. The volunteers can help you with this task. Also, do not forget to recognize the volunteers themselves by thanking them publicly at a luncheon or dinner celebration. For major gift givers, you might want to hold a black-tie reception at which the superintendent can personally thank them. By doing all of these things, you are helping to ensure that all previous participants will continue to support your programs into the future.

Be good stewards of all monies, gifts, and bequests received by having them invested with an investment banker or certified financial planner. A competent certified real estate management company should manage gifts of real estate. It is essential that all management companies and individuals that assist the school district or public school foundation be reliable and conservative in their investment approaches. The foundation board or the school board should monitor the investment program for all grants and gifts on a continuing basis.

Soliciting big grants and gifts from individual donors is serious and demanding work, but the payoff can be enormous. Learning how to ask for such gifts is key in a big-time fundraising effort. Once this takes place, you are well on your way to helping all children reach their fullest potential.

Figure 4.1   A Sample Pledge Card

XYZ School District
100 Ferryboat Lane
Anywhere, USA
Computer Laboratory Fund Campaign

No. _____

Name _____   Date _____

Address _____

Telephone _____   E-mail _____

In consideration of the gifts of others and the obligations to be incurred based upon pledges received from the under-signed and others, I/we promise to pay the XYZ School District, Computer Laboratory Fund Campaign, the sum of

_____dollars $_____

X _____
    Signature   Date

Please remind me _____Annually _____ Semi-Annually _____ Quarterly

For _____years ending _____Month _____ Day _____ Year

- -

No. _____ Category/Division _____ Volunteer _____

Evaluation _____ Pledge _____ Project _____

Remarks _____

_____

_____

_____

_____

_____

5

Annual Campaigns, Capital Campaigns, and Planned Giving

Annual campaigns are ongoing yearly appeals that provide support for the schools. Gifts in annual campaigns tend to be smaller than gifts in capital campaigns, which have loftier goals. New donors are solicited each year in an annual campaign, and previous donors are courted to increase their contributions from the previous year. Spouses do not have to be consulted when approaching donors in an annual campaign, as they do for capital campaigns and planned giving, and monies are usually given out of donors' incomes, rather than from their savings or investments. Individual staff members, parents, administrators, or volunteers can solicit these gifts, and while personal visits would be desirable, they are not mandatory. Cash is the most prevalent gift given in an annual campaign.

ANNUAL CAMPAIGNS

Some of the fundraising approaches used in annual campaigns are direct mail solicitation; telephone, radio, and television solicitation; Internet fundraising; and special events fundraising. Below is a sampling of each approach. For a more complete overview, see the books listed in the bibliography.

Direct Mail Solicitation

This is a very practical way to reach many small gift prospects within your school community without having to recruit and train a big work force. Once a good letter is drafted, a small group of volunteers could handle this type of solicitation.

An effective fundraising letter makes an appeal from one person (or family) to another. It gives the person (or family) an opportunity to support a worthy cause while meeting their personal need to help the schools. It also invites the person (or family) to make a specific gift that will have a positive impact on the schools and explains the benefits derived from making the gift. In his book, *Write Successful Fundraising Letters,* Mal Warwick talks about six qualities that are shared by the most productive fundraising letters. These are clarity, cohesiveness, authenticity, ease of response, appropriateness, and engaging copy. See the bibliography for more resources for direct mail campaigns.

Telephone, Radio, and Television Solicitation

These can be worthwhile if proper preparation and training take place and if the community is informed of your intentions, including dates and times to expect a solicitation call or dates and times that you will be conducting your telethon or radio solicitation.

Telephone solicitation has been around for years. We have all heard from the colleges and universities we attended, haven't we? This kind of solicitation takes a lot of training and practice with scripts prepared ahead of time. It is important for solicitors to learn how to overcome objections as well as how to respond to being put off. There are a number of consultants and consultant companies that specialize in this type of solicitation, including companies that will do the solicitation for you for a price.

Some local radio and television stations, as a public service, are donating airtime to schools and school districts around the country. In some instances, television and radio personalities are assisting in the fundraising effort. Ask for some of this airtime to fundraise, and request some volunteer assistance. There's money out there if you put in the time and effort.

Fundraising on the Internet

Raising monies on the Internet is becoming more and more popular. With more than 100 million people connected worldwide, the potential of raising serious dollars is enormous.

One of the finest Internet fundraising sites in the country for public schools is DonorsChoose. (Contact information for this organization and others mentioned in this chapter is given in the bibliography.) The theme for the DonorsChoose Web site is, "Every teacher a grantwriter, every citizen a philanthropist." The site was originally thought of and developed by a new teacher in the New York City schools who wanted to assist other teachers with finding outside funding sources for projects and materials that the teachers were paying for themselves or just going without. Teachers are encouraged to submit minigrant proposals to the site, listing their needs and desires, and philanthropists from around the country fund the projects using their credit cards. Once projects are funded, teachers are informed, given the name and address of the donor, and provided with a disposable camera with which to take pictures. The students are encouraged to write thank-you notes that are sent to the donor along with photos of the project in action. The donor gets immediate feedback on how the gift is being spent.

I am proud to say that I funded a project through the DonorsChoose Website to purchase a bookbinding machine for a fifth-grade class in the New York City schools. The machine is being used for student-authored books. Once the project was funded, the classroom teacher sent me a thank-you note and photos of the machine in action with her kids. The children also sent me individual thank-you notes. Needless to say, this gift has brought me much joy and satisfaction, because I met an immediate need with my philanthropy, and I got to see the program in action through the photos that were forwarded to me.

Web sites such as DonorsChoose are popping up all over the country. Thus far, DonorsChoose has raised more than $6 million, and there are now branches of DonorsChoose in San Francisco, Chicago, and North Carolina, with additional sites planned for other parts of the country. Why not have a similar Web site designed for your school or school district, or utilize your present Web site for this purpose? You can also contract with a company like Kintera to do Internet fundraising for you.

Special Events Fundraising

A number of schools and school districts around the country are raising big bucks sponsoring special events like golf tournaments, tennis tournaments, 5K and 10K runs and walks, dinner-dances, and silent auctions. In San Diego County, where I live, schools like Coronado High School and Torrey Pines High School raise between $100,000 and $200,000 in one evening at their annual dinner-dances that include silent auctions. Of course, it should be mentioned that these schools are located in some of our most affluent areas!

CAPITAL CAMPAIGNS

Capital campaigns have loftier goals than annual campaigns, and because of this, gift amounts are set far higher than gift amounts for annual campaigns. Capital campaigns are very new to the public schools, and some school districts are beginning to recognize this tremendous potential resource for external fundraising. Time frames in capital campaigns generally extend over several years, such as a three-year campaign (or a five-year campaign) to build a new creative and performing arts center. Prospects are asked to pledge a certain amount of money over a specific time period, such as three to five years.

Capital campaigns are exciting in a school community, because the goals are tangible and the results are highly visible. These campaigns are usually organized for endowment purposes as well as for purchasing buildings and equipment. People who make major gifts to a capital campaign receive great joy over their lifetimes.

Capital campaigns require a great deal of time and energy and are not easy to conduct. Collaborative efforts between all parties in the fundraising community are essential for maximum success. In smaller school districts, where staffing is limited, reliance on community volunteers is key to striking it rich.

I have found that identifying someone in the community to make a *lead gift* before the capital campaign officially begins is a good way to get started. One way to obtain a lead gift is to provide the opportunity for the donor to have a facility on campus named in his or her family's honor, such as "The Alice Jones Performing Arts Center." This is done all the time in the private schools, colleges, and universities. Why not the public schools?

Once the lead gift is made, funding opportunities for naming other portions of the performing arts center should be made available. Donors can also receive public recognition for funding the main lobby, the stage, the lighting, dressing rooms, the seats, and other things. The opportunity for recognition and service is the reason that capital campaigns have such great appeal to prospective donors and the reason many donors become motivated to make major contributions.

Named Gifts and Naming Rights

Named gifts have been around for a long time on private school campuses, colleges and universities, and nonprofit facilities like YMCAs, YWCAs, and Boys and Girls Clubs. The public schools should take a close look at this fundraising opportunity and realize that the schools are a wonderful place for a family to leave a lasting legacy by having a school building, a ball field, or a seat in a little theatre named after them. At this time, a number of schools and school districts are exploring ways of giving commercial vendors opportunities for naming rights. If you move in this direction, it is recommended that the naming rights be awarded for a specific period of time (5 to 10 years, more or less) after which new negotiations should take place or the contract should be rescinded.

Number and Size of Gifts
Needed to Achieve a Campaign Goal

Over the years, fundraising professionals at the college, university, and private school levels have been following industry standards related to the number and size of gifts needed to achieve a campaign goal. It is interesting to discover that a few major gift givers will contribute more than 80 percent of the funds needed to meet your campaign goal, while all the others together contribute the remaining 20 percent. This is sometimes referred to as the *80/20 rule*. Tables 5.1, 5.2, and 5.3 show some examples of capital campaign goals and the number and size of the gifts you will need to achieve your desired outcome. Of course, these are provided as a guide only and are subject to change based upon the wishes, desires, and generosity of the school community.

Table 5.1   Campaign Goal: $50,000

Gift Range	Number of Gifts Needed	Subtotal	Cumulative Subtotal
$5,000	1	$5,000	$5,000
$2,500	2	$10,000	$15,000
$1,500	4	$6,000	$21,000
$1,000	7	$7,000	$28,000
$750	6	$4,500	$32,500
$500	10	$5,000	$37,500
$499 or less	15	$12,500	$50,000
Totals	45	$50,000	$50,000

Table 5.2   Campaign Goal: $100,000

Gift Range	Number of Gifts Needed	Subtotal	Cumulative Subtotal
$10,000	1	$10,000	$10,000
$7,000	1	$7,500	$17,500
$5,000	4	$20,000	$37,500
$3,500	6	$21,000	$58,500
$2,500	8	$20,000	$78,500
$1,500	10	$15,000	$93,500
$1,499 (or less)	15	$7,000	$100,000
Totals	45	$100,000	$100,000

Table 5.3   Campaign Goal: $1,000,000

Gift Range	Number of Gifts Needed	Subtotal	Cumulative Subtotal
$100,000	1	$100,000	$100,000
$75,000	1	$75,000	$175,000
$50,000	2	$100,000	$275,000
$35,000	3	$105,000	$380,000
$25,000	4	$100,000	$480,000
$20,000	6	$120,000	$600,000
$15,000	8	$120,000	$720,000
$10,000	10	$100,000	$820,000
$5,000	12	$60,000	$880,000
$2,500 or less	80	$120,000	$1,000,000
Totals	127	$1,000,000	$1,000,000

NOTES: The above are examples only. Note the pyramid effect. A small number of donors, if approached effectively, can carry the major burden of a capital campaign.

PLANNED GIVING

Planned giving refers to the process of making a charitable gift of cash or noncash assets to one or more nonprofit organizations, including the public schools. Charitable gifts are a tangible way for donors to contribute to the schools. The gift, when made, usually requires consideration and planning in light of the donor's overall estate plan and tax situation. Legal documents should be completed in cooperation with the donor's financial advisors and should be made part of the overall estate plan of the donor.

Like capital campaigns, planned giving is very new to the public schools. It can be time-consuming and complicated at times, but the payoff can be enormous. If possible, it is important that competent, qualified staff be employed for this purpose, and that volunteers be trained to assist in the solicitation process. In small school districts, where administrators wear many hats, volunteers can be trained to work in the planned giving area.

There are many tax advantages to giving noncash assets, including appreciated assets. While gifts of cash are always welcome, gifts of stock, bonds, shares in mutual funds, a home or farm property, vacant land, vacation or rental property, commercial or income property, life insurance, and other noncash gifts can be made to the schools. Because of the size and potential impact of such gifts on an estate, a donor should be advised to consult with his or her professional advisors before completing the process. Additionally, the school district should consult with its legal advisors concerning implementation of a planned giving program and develop policies to receive and administer such gifts.

As part of an overall estate plan, a donor may choose to make a gift over time; that is, a donor can plan for a gift to be made after the donor no longer needs the asset. The gifts may earn donors charitable tax deductions at the time they set up the gifts, while increasing their income levels during their lifetimes and lowering their estate taxes.

There are tax advantages when giving cash and noncash assets to a nonprofit organization such as a public school foundation. Giving noncash assets may be attractive to supporters of the schools in that they are donating to a good cause, and there are favorable tax implications for this kind of gift. Examples of appreciated assets are

1. Stocks

2. Bonds

3. Shares in mutual funds

4. A home or farm property

5. Vacant land

6. Vacation or rental property

7. Commercial property

8. Other assets held in a form other than cash

Property that has increased in value and has been owned on a long-term basis generally brings the most in tax savings for the donor. People also find that giving property leaves their cash available for other purposes. Most long-term appreciated property is deductible for its full fair market value when the gift is made to a charitable organization or a school. In addition, capital gains tax is not due on property that is donated rather than sold. Under current law, gifts of appreciated property worth up to 30 percent of the donor's adjusted gross income may be deducted in the year of the gift, and excess deductions may be carried over for as many as five years if deductions are itemized. There are many ways to make gifts of appreciated and marketable securities and real property to the schools that provide significant tax advantages for the donor. Of course, gifts of cash are always welcome.

The next section discusses noncash gifts and presents an explanation of gifts of cash that could be given to schools outright or bequeathed upon the death of the donor. In either case, a tax attorney or other certified accountant should be consulted before any transfer of ownership is made.

POSSIBLE NONCASH GIFT IDEAS FOR THE PUBLIC SCHOOLS

Appreciated Marketable Securities

One of the most attractive methods givers can use to realize their charitable intentions toward the schools is giving appreciated marketable securities. A gift of listed stocks, bonds, or other publicly traded securities entitles the giver to a charitable income tax deduction equal to the full fair market value of the securities on the date of the gift, provided that the giver owned the securities for at least one year. In addition, the donor does not incur capital gains tax on the sale of such securities when they are transferred to the schools.

Entire Interest in Real Estate

An outright gift of unencumbered real estate may enable the giver to make a significant gift to the schools without incurring capital gains tax on the sale of the appreciated asset. The gift will entitle the giver to a charitable income tax deduction equal to the fair market value of the interest in the property on the date of the transfer, provided that the giver owned the property for more than one year.

Charitable Remainder Trusts

A charitable remainder trust is a tax-saving alternative for donors who want to make a gift to a school, district, or school or district foundation. Gifts can be made in cash, highly appreciated stock, real estate, or a closely held business interest. In exchange for a charitable gift of this type, the school district pays income to the donors (e.g., husband and wife) for a fixed period of time or for life, while also generating tax benefits for the donors. The minimum payout rate is 5 percent of the value of the trust, and the maximum rate can go as high as 50 percent. To generate this payout, the organization receiving the gift sells the assets and reinvests the proceeds in an income-producing asset. Upon the death of the donor(s), the remaining balance in the trust is distributed to the organization receiving the gift.

Charitable Gift Annuities

A charitable gift annuity is a contract between a donor and a school, district, or school or district foundation based upon a charitable gift typically funded with cash or from the sale of real estate, securities, or other assets. The organization receiving the annuity pays the donor an amount of money, called an *annuity*, each year based on the value of the gift. The annuity can be set up to continue for the life of the donor as well as for the life of the donor's spouse or designee. The rate paid out is based upon the donor's age and the age of the spouse or designee. The older you are, the higher the rate. The American Council on Gift Annuities recommends rates that are followed by most nonprofit organizations.

Tangible Personal Property

A person might wish to consider making a gift of personal property such as art objects, books, and other collectibles to the schools. If the schools can use and are expected to use the gift of such property toward the furtherance of their educational mission, and if the giver has owned the property for more than one year, the giver will be eligible for a charitable income tax deduction equal to the fair market value of the property. The giver will not owe capital gains tax on any appreciation of the property—as he or she would if the property were sold—and will receive a tax credit for the fair market value of the property.

Life Insurance

If a person owns a life insurance policy and no longer requires its protection, he or she may wish to consider transferring ownership of the policy to the schools, or to name the schools as a beneficiary to receive all or a portion of the policy proceeds. Another possibility is to purchase a new policy and transfer ownership to the schools. Each gift will generate a charitable income tax deduction roughly equal to the cash surrender value of the policy on the date of the gift. A person might also want to use the cash value of policies that have outlived their original purposes to immediately give a gift to the schools.

Social Security Checks

There are many people all across America whose retirement lifestyle does not require the income they receive from social security. Donating these benefits to a worthy cause like the public schools would not only give donors great satisfaction, but would also reduce their overall tax bill. Potential donors can sign paperwork authorizing their banks to automatically send part or all of the proceeds of their social security checks to your school or school district. Make certain that potential donors consult with their tax advisors before going ahead with this plan.

Bequests

A bequest is a very popular way to make a deferred gift. Here are eight generally accepted ways for potential donors to make a bequest to the schools:

1. **Specific bequest.** This is a gift of a specific item to a specific beneficiary. An example is, "I give my 2006 Mercedes Benz to EYZ School." If that specific property has been disposed of before death, the bequest fails and no claim can be made to any other property. (In other words, XYZ School cannot claim some other property.)

2. **General bequest.** This is usually a gift of a stated sum of money. It will not fail, even if there is not sufficient cash to meet the bequest. An example is, "I give $50,000 to XYZ High School." If there is only $2,500 cash in the estate, other assets must be sold to meet the bequest.

3. **Contingent bequest.** This is a bequest made on the condition that a certain event must occur before distribution to the beneficiary. An example is, "I give $100,000 to XYZ School provided that Mr. Jones remains the principal for the next five years." A contingent bequest is specific in nature and fails if the condition is not met.

4. **Residuary bequest.** This is a gift of all the "rest, residue, and remainder" of the donor's estate after all other bequests, debts, and taxes have been paid. For example, a school or school district can be named in a person's estate to receive a residuary bequest.

5. **Unrestricted bequest.** This is a gift made to a school or school district that can be used for general purposes, at the discretion of the school board. A gift like this—without conditions attached—is frequently the most useful, as it allows

the school or school district to determine the wisest and most pressing need for the funds at the time of receipt.

6. **Restricted bequest.** This type of gift allows the donor to specify how the funds are to be used. An example is, "The gift is to be used to build a new creative and performing arts center for XYZ High School." Potential givers of restricted gifts to individual schools and school districts should be encouraged to discuss their plans and ideas with the building principal, the superintendent of schools, and anyone else who needs to know.

7. **Honorary or memorial bequest.** This is a gift given in honor or in memory of someone. An example is, "The gift in the amount of $1 million is given in honor of my dear mother, Mabel Moneybags, to the XYZ School District."

8. **Endowed bequest.** This bequest allows donors to restrict the principal of their gift, requiring the school district to hold the funds permanently and use only the investment income the funds generate. Creating an endowment in this manner means that your gift can continue into perpetuity.

Outright Gifts of Cash

For some people, an outright gift of cash is the most comfortable gift to give. It would also be very much appreciated by the schools, in that cash is easy to administer and can be used for multiple purposes. Many philanthropists give cash gifts to worthy causes and are more comfortable in giving in this manner. Sometimes people have a specific cause within the schools to which they want to contribute, and they will designate that their cash gifts be used for this purpose. This is referred to as a *restrictive gift*. Others will give cash and not place any restrictions on how the money is spent. This is considered an *unrestrictive gift*. Needless to say, unrestrictive gifts offer more flexibility than restrictive gifts. However, any gifts of cash are always appreciated.

A CLOSING CAVEAT

All information pertaining to tax benefits listed above is subject to change. Federal and state tax laws change on a continuing basis. When working with potential donors, encourage them to talk with their accountants or tax attorneys concerning any of the above. Accompany them, if they so desire, to discuss their objectives and the opportunities available to them. Also, involve the attorneys for the school district as well. For additional information on planned giving, see the publications listed in the bibliography.

6

Applying for Corporate and Foundation Grants

Just a few short years ago, most public schools in America were applying only for government grants. Now, many schools and school districts are going after corporate and foundation funding with vigor and gusto. In fact, in 2004, corporations and foundations gave more grant dollars to K–12 schools (including private schools) than were given to colleges and universities. This is the first time that this phenomenon has occurred, and schools and school districts around the country should be congratulated for going after these monies as never before.

For those of you who are new to corporate and foundation funding or want to improve your chances of getting more money, let it be known that corporations and foundations are committed to supporting public education at all grade levels. Pursue grants and gifts from those corporations and foundations located in your city, state, or region first, before requesting funds from out of state, unless you are responding to a Request for Proposal (RFP), or have some special contacts.

CORPORATE GIVING

Corporations provide support to nonprofit organizations, including the schools, through their own private foundations, direct-giving programs, or both. It is estimated by the Giving USA Foundation that corporate foundations gave more than $12 billion to worthy causes in 2004. These separate legal entities maintain close ties with their parent organizations, and their giving philosophies usually mirror company priorities and interests. Corporations are interested in forming partnerships with the public schools and in contributing dollars and equipment to them. They are also involved in providing technical assistance, including in-kind assistance such as staffing for particular projects or providing speakers for classes and career days. Corporations typically contribute in those communities where their employees live and work; therefore it is not recommended that you apply for these grants out of your area unless your are responding to an RFP.

Corporate foundations are required to follow the laws and regulations governing private foundations, including filing an annual form 990-PF with the Internal Revenue Service. The 990-PF provides a complete grants list, the names of the foundation's trustees and officers, and other relevant information. Having access to 990-PFs will assist you in determining the giving trends of a particular foundation as well as the size of the grants made and other vital data. Fortunately, 990-PFs are public records, and you can access these documents through the GrantSmart Web site and other search engines, including those of the cooperating libraries of the Foundation Center and of the offices of state attorneys general, where tax returns for foundations are kept on file. The Foundation Center's Web site also has additional information on accessing 990-PF forms. (See the bibliography for information on how to access all these sites.)

In addition to giving through corporate foundations, corporations give through direct-giving programs. These giving programs are not separately incorporated, and for the purposes of these gifts, the IRS does not require the corporation to adhere to private foundation laws or regulations, including the requirement to file form 990-PF. Corporations are allowed to deduct up to 10 percent of their pretax income from their taxable income if they use this money for charitable purposes. Check out the corporations in your community, and become familiar with their giving priorities.

FOUNDATION GIVING

In 2004, foundations (including community foundations; see more about them below) gave twice as much money to public schools as corporations gave in the same year. Foundations are required by federal tax law to give away an average of at least five percent of their assets to charity over a three-year period. As foundation assets and businesses continue to grow, and as individuals and families begin to inherit enormous amounts of wealth and establish their own foundations, the opportunities look bright for the public schools to tap into this vast resource. Why not? Private schools, colleges, universities, and nonprofit organizations have been reaping the rewards for years!

Independent Foundations

Independent (private) foundations contributed more than $28 billion to worthy causes in 2004. These foundations are nongovernmental, usually have a principal fund or endowment, are managed by a board of trustees and directors, and give cash and gifts to nonprofit organizations, including the schools. In recent years, America's 1,000 leading private foundations have given more than $5 billion annually to colleges, universities, nonprofit organizations, and the schools. They typically support charitable, educational, religious, and other causes that serve the public good.

Independent foundations are interested in funding excellence in the public schools. They typically have not been interested in compensatory education or remedial types of programs, although some foundations are beginning to support these efforts. Independent foundations are concerned with bringing about change in a positive manner or in enhancing and supplementing existing programs. Some foundations support math, science, and the environment, while others are interested in music, art, and dance. Other foundations give preference to computer technology and literacy, while still others are interested in health education, parent education, and staff development. Some independent foundations support the acquisition of capital equipment such as computers, printers, scanners, and video and sound equipment; however, they support these purchases only insofar as the equipment is directly related to a clear vision for its use and an overall program plan. In other words, they normally do not fund the purchase of hardware only. When applying for a foundation grant, try to match your needs with the foundation's interests. Usually, it is easier to get a foundation grant from a local foundation, or a foundation within your state or region, than from a national foundation.

Community Foundations

There are more than 600 community foundations across the United States, and their assets together total more than $39 billion. These foundations gave away more than $3 billion in 2004 to good causes, including K–12 schools. Individuals, businesses, and organizations in a specific community or region financially support community foundations. Within certain parameters, anyone can be a donor to a community foundation. Donors can give cash or assets, including stocks, bonds, real estate, insurance, or other assets to a community foundation. These gifts can usually be made within the lifetime of the donors or through their estates, with the donors receiving maximum tax benefits.

There are community foundations located in every state in the United States. Grants from these foundations help to support charitable groups and programs working to improve the quality of life within a specific community or region. Over the past several years, I have observed community foundations become more interested in giving to the public schools. Competitive minigrant programs for teachers are being funded by a number of community foundations around the country, as are programs that improve teaching and learning in the foundations' communities. Community foundations are sprouting up all over the country. They are a good source of funding for teachers, schools, and school districts. Take the time to locate the community foundations in your area of the country, and begin to dialogue with them.

OBTAINING CORPORATE AND FOUNDATION FUNDING IS EASIER THAN YOU THINK

Corporations and foundations give to the public schools through three processes:

1. **Requests for proposals (RFPs).** These are usually announced on the corporations' or foundations' Web sites, on other Web sites, or in newsletters, newspapers, or other publications. By announcing an RFP, the funding agency is pinpointing and

targeting its specific areas of interest and indicating how much money to apply for. One advantage of responding to an RFP is that knowing what the funding agency is interested in and how much money to apply for makes your job easy if your needs match the funding agency's interests. Some disadvantages of responding to an RFP are that your focus will be narrowed down to what the funding agency's interests are and that you will have more competition in obtaining the grant.

2. Direct contact. Corporations and foundations also give to the public schools when the schools make direct contact with them. It should be mentioned that, at times, these funding agencies initiate the contacts themselves and invite schools or districts to partner with them. This usually takes place in large urban school districts across the country and not in smaller districts.

3. Corporate-school partnerships. There are many corporate-school partnerships operating around the country. In a number of instances, corporations or businesses make the initial contact with the school or school district to establish the partnership. In other situations, the school or district initiates the contact. Many corporations encourage staff to work in schools as tutors, speakers, consultants, and helpers. Corporations also provide materials, equipment, staff, and outright gifts of cash to the schools. If you do not have any corporate-school partnerships going on in your school or school district at this time, you might want to make some contacts with local businesses and corporations through your chamber of commerce, Rotary club, and other organizations in your community. Again, it is important for the school board to establish policies and procedures for setting up corporate-school partnerships and for the acceptance of grants, gifts, and services.

The Foundation Center

One of the great resources for corporate and foundation funding and information is the Foundation Center. Established in 1956, the Foundation Center's mission is to strengthen the nonprofit sector by advancing knowledge about U.S. philanthropy. To achieve the mission, the Foundation Center collects, organizes, and communicates information on U.S. philanthropy. It also conducts and facilitates research on trends in the field, provides education and training on the grantseeking process, and ensures public access to information and services through its outstanding Web site and other print and electronic publications. The Foundation Center is headquartered in New York City and has field offices located in Atlanta, Cleveland, San Francisco, and Washington, DC. Additionally, there are cooperating collections of the Foundation Center located in all 50 states and in Puerto Rico and Washington, DC. The cooperating collections are funding information centers in libraries, community foundations, and other nonprofit resource centers that provide a core collection of Foundation Center publications and a variety of supplementary materials and services in areas useful to grantseekers. Use of these collections is free.

The Foundation Center reports that there are more than 66,000 corporate, independent, and community foundations in the United States, with the number growing weekly. The total assets of these foundations are more than $476 billion. Go to the Foundation Center Web site and access the site map for a wealth of information that will be of use to you as you pursue corporate and foundation grants and gifts.

Reasons for Applying for Corporate and Foundation Funding at This Time

There are three good reasons for applying for corporate and foundation funding at this time:

1. Corporations and foundations are interested in providing grants to schools, and many teachers and administrators have not yet discovered this funding opportunity. If you know how to obtain corporate and foundation funding, you will be at an advantage over other people who are not yet aware of this funding source. Therefore competition will not be as keen for corporate and foundation grants as it will be for other grants that are more well known, such as federal grants. This, of course, will not be going on forever, so take advantage of it now and reap the rewards. A word of caution should be mentioned. Just because a corporation or foundation indicates in its literature that it funds education doesn't necessarily mean that it funds K–12 education. Make sure that you read the eligibility guidelines very carefully before you apply for funding.

2. Most corporate and foundation funding agencies require an application of just 2-10 pages or a 1-page letter of application. This is reason enough to apply for corporate and foundation funding. Teachers and administrators are very busy people. So are program officers and other staff at the funding agencies. When application requirements are short and to the point, everybody wins.

3. Most corporations and foundations fund more than once a year. This is a delight! Some of these agencies fund 4 times a year, and others fund every time the board meets, which could be 12 times a year. Foundation funding timetables are much more favorable than government funding timetables, with which funding is made only once a year. If you a miss a federal government grant deadline or get turned down, you are out of luck for an entire year. If you miss a corporate or foundation deadline, you have an opportunity to apply in another month or two or to go to another funding agency with your request.

While I do not want to leave you with the impression that it is easy to obtain monies from corporations and foundations, I do want to point out that in my experience working in the public schools, I found that obtaining corporate and foundation funding was less demanding than obtaining government grants. I have also discovered that obtaining these grants takes more nurturing and personal contact. Some people like this, and others do not. Corporations and foundations want to feel that their money will be well spent if they award you a grant. Many of these funding agencies are becoming more and more interested in the evaluation component of your grant application and the evaluation results. They want to be able to report to their boards about the positive impact their funding has had on the schools. They desire to get to know you and want to feel confident in your proposed project and your school district's ability to deliver.

7

Strategies, Requests for Proposals (RFPs), and Resources for Winning Corporate and Foundation Funding

Over the years, I have gained experience in obtaining grants and gifts from corporations and foundations. Below you will find my 11-step strategy for winning corporate and foundation funding that has been refined and updated. Hopefully, you will find this to be of some assistance to you.

THE 11-STEP STRATEGY FOR WINNING CORPORATE AND FOUNDATION FUNDING

Step 1. Have an innovative idea and vision in mind. Use teams of two to five people to generate ideas. These teams should be made up of people having similar ideas and visions for funding. Obtain administrative support for your idea. Ask for release time to write your project if funds are available for this purpose.

Step 2. Begin to do prospect research by becoming familiar with corporate and foundation funding sources in your local area, the state, and the nation that are interested in funding K–12 education programs. It is usually easier to obtain monies from local and state foundations and corporations than from national foundations that traditionally fund projects having national implications and significance. However, if your project meets the criteria of any of the national foundations, go for it.

Step 3. Access the Foundation Center's Web site to locate corporations and foundations in your area, including community foundations that might be interested in making grants to the schools. The Foundation Center's Web site, for which access is free, is loaded with worthwhile information for people doing basic research on corporate and foundation giving. For a fee, people seeking more in-depth coverage can purchase the Foundation Center's database on a CD-ROM that features a comprehensive listing of active U.S. foundations and corporate giving programs and their associated grants. This database is also available for free through the Foundation Center's main cooperating collections located in New York City, Washington, DC, Atlanta, Cleveland, and San Francisco, and in smaller cooperating collections located all across the United States. You can find out where these locations are by accessing the Foundation Center's Web site. In addition to these programs, there are other materials that you can use to do prospect research. Some are hard-copy, more traditional types of books, and others are on CD-ROM. (See the bibliography for a list of these sources.)

In addition to studying these materials and locating foundations and corporations having the same interests as yours, also access the links from the Foundation Center's Web site that lead to the 990-PF forms to discover the giving patterns and trends of corporations and foundations in your area. Visit the fundraising resource libraries in your school, district office, county office, and the colleges and universities in your area. Before you know it, you are going to have many funding resources available to you.

Step 4. Once you have completed the prospect research phase, you are now ready to request the most recent information, yearbooks, and applications from the corporations and foundations that are potential funding sources for your school or district. This can usually be accomplished via e-mail, by telephone or fax, or by writing directly to the corporation or foundation. In school districts or counties where corporate and foundation files are kept up-to-date, contact the district or county person who is responsible for fundraising, and ask for assistance, or go onto the district Web site to look for grants and grantwriting links, if the district has moved in this direction.

Step 5. Make multiple copies of relevant applications and materials, and read and study them carefully. Reread several times. Check to see if there are any deadline dates of which you need to be aware. Discover how many public school projects were funded previously, including the amounts of funding. Pinpoint the deadline dates on your calendar.

Step 6. If possible, telephone the program officer at the foundation or corporation to discuss your ideas and to begin the nurturing process. Make certain that you are thoroughly familiar with your project and that you are able to discuss it with clarity, conviction, and strength. Also, be prepared to respond to any questions or concerns of the program officer, and incorporate into your proposal any relevant suggestions for improvement. For example, one question that is often asked is, "How are you planning to evaluate this project?" If it appears that the program officer is interested in your project and that monies are available to meet your needs based upon your prospect research, ask for an appointment to visit the foundation with your site- or district-level administrator. In instances where you are requesting a considerable amount of money, it is recommended that you invite your superintendent of schools and a board member to join you in meeting with the chief operating officer of the foundation. This person-to-person contact, especially with the heads of both organizations, could do wonders for your corporate and foundation fundraising effort. In fact, this approach is used on a continuing basis by private schools, colleges, universities, and nonprofit organizations. College and university presidents are on the road on a continuing basis soliciting funds. Why can't superintendents of schools make this part of their job description?

Step 7. If you are unable to visit the funding agency, invite the program officer and other staff members to visit your school. If there appears to be no interest in any visitations or in having you submit an application, go on to another funding agency with your ideas.

Step 8. If you are fortunate enough to have the funding agency indicate that it would like to make a site visit, then you are on the right track for getting funded. This is one of the key indicators that the funding agency is interested in your project. Sometimes a site visit might not be scheduled until after you submit an application. In either case, you have good reason to get a little excited. Determine how much time the program officer will spend in the school or district, including arrival and departure times. Prepare carefully for the visitation. Include an agenda that will be mailed out to the visitor and other invited guests ahead of time. Invite key people to the entrance and exit meetings, including the superintendent, principal(s), one or two board members, and representative parents and teachers. Meet the program officer at the airport, if this person is arriving by plane. Provide for food, snacks, lunch, and lodging, if appropriate. Your goal is to impress the visitor with your school or school district and proposed project.

Upon arrival at the entrance meeting, which could take place at the district office or at a school site, introduce the program officer and other visitors, if appropriate, to each person at the meeting, and then proceed to review the day's activities with everyone. Follow your time schedule and agenda very carefully, leaving time for classroom visitations and observations (if appropriate), lunch, follow-up, and the scheduled exit meeting.

The same people who were invited to the entrance meeting should be invited to the exit meeting. The goal of the exit meeting is to ascertain whether the program officer is impressed with what was seen and whether the program officer is ready to recommend the district for funding. In a number of instances, I have witnessed program officers at exit meetings tell district officials that they were so impressed with what they had seen that they were prepared to recommend the district for funding. In one exit meeting, a program officer requested that the district put together an application of three to five pages asking for $10,000, and the district got funded in that amount.

In instances when the program officer does not mention anything about funding your project, I believe it would be appropriate to ask the following questions: "What impressed you the most about your visit today?" "Do you have any suggestions for improvement?" "Are you planning to recommend us for funding?" "How much funding should we be requesting?"

Have a tentative budget available for the program officer to see if one is requested. The budget should be categorized and well thought out. Indicate in the budget how much the district is going to contribute to the project. This is referred to as an *in-kind* contribution and includes staff assigned to coordinate and facilitate the project at district expense; the cost of using district facilities for the project, including utility and custodial costs; and costs for materials and equipment paid for with district monies. (Several sample budgets are included with the sample grant proposals in Chapter 13).

Step 9. Whether you have arranged for a site visit or have been encouraged to submit an application without a site visit, begin to fill in the application, responding specifically to what the funding agency is asking. Note, however, that in some instances, the corporate or independent foundation does not provide an application. They merely will tell you to respond to their guidelines. If this is the case, it is recommended that you use a prototype application, making sure that you cover the needs, goals, objectives, activities, evaluation specifications, and budget of your project. Some states have a common application form that is recognized by most foundations in the state. If this is the case, obtain a copy of the application and study it carefully. Also, note that some corporations and foundations will ask for just a one- to two-page letter of request. This you will appreciate very much. Always give the funding agency exactly what it asks for, nothing more, nothing less. After you have responded to the funding agency's guidelines and have completed a first draft of the application or letter, go over it carefully to correct spelling, typographical errors, grammar, and word usage. (See Chapter 13 for several samples of complete grant proposals.)

Step 10. Have one or two persons who are not in your field of interest read the completed application for clarity and input. Also, have one or two persons in your field of interest read it as well. Ask for assistance when formulating your budget, including proper budget categorizing and cost breakdowns. In many school districts, the person to go to for help would be the business manager, district accountant, or site principal. It is essential to present to the funding agency a realistic, concise budget, providing explanations where appropriate.

Step 11. After you have completed Step 10 above, put together your final draft, including a cover letter that grabs the reader. The cover letter is usually one page and provides a brief summary of the project with all the necessary details. (See Resource C for a sample cover letter.) Obtain needed signatures and approvals, do necessary proofreading, and make final corrections. Mail your application to the funding agency using the U.S. Postal Service's "return receipt requested" service, or forward by another means in plenty of time to meet the funding deadline. Some funding agencies are now accepting proposals electronically, and others are providing applications online. Make certain that you are using the correct format for each funding agency to which you apply.

RESPONDING TO RFPS

Most corporations and foundations announce RFPs on their Web sites, in newsletters, and in their own publications. A number of education Web sites keep in touch with these funding agencies and also announce their RFPs. See the list at the end of this chapter, "101 Foundations Interested in Giving to K–12 Schools," and the bibliography for Web site addresses.

By announcing an RFP, the funding agency is pinpointing and targeting its monies in specific interest areas. Some agencies use this approach to ensure that they receive applications that respond to a specific need or concern of the agency. For a school or a school district, there are advantages and disadvantages in responding to an RFP. The first advantage is that you already know what the foundation is interested in from reading the materials that it provides in the RFP package. Second, the materials will probably indicate the size of grants to be made and how many grants will get funded. By contrast, one of the major disadvantages of responding to an RFP is that your focus will be narrowed down to the specific interest area of the funding agency. Of course, if your interests match the funding agency's interest area, this is not a problem. Another disadvantage is that you will probably have more competition in obtaining the grant if the foundation announces it to the world via its Web site and through other publications. More people respond to an RFP than make individual contacts with foundations. I would recommend that if you do respond to an RFP, follow the ideas and techniques recommended in this book and elsewhere, and your chances of getting funded will be enhanced.

Most grantseekers today are involved in accessing the World Wide Web to obtain needed information and applications. I have identified a list of 101 potential corporate and foundation funding resources and their Web addresses. These agencies have expressed an interest in funding prekindergarten through twelfth-grade programs; however, because funding priorities and interests change from time to time, it is very important to keep up-to-date and confirm with the agency what its interests are at the time of your investigation. It is also possible that some of the corporations and foundations listed here will change their funding priorities or their Web addresses by the time you read this book. It's also possible that some funding agencies listed here do not fund projects outside their state or geographical area or fund only private schools. For these reasons, make certain that your prospect research is current and that your school or school district is eligible for funding before wasting your time by applying for a grant that you are not qualified for. The list provided is not exhaustive by any means. It is rather a starting point to head you in the direction of potential funding sources. By accessing the Web sites below and the other Web sites, links, and resources listed elsewhere in this book, you will become familiar with the vast array of funding opportunities available to you.

101 FOUNDATIONS AND CORPORATIONS INTERESTED IN GIVING TO K–12 SCHOOLS

Funding Agency	Web Address
Abbott Laboratories	www.abbott.com
Andre Agassi Charitable Foundation	www.agassifoundation.org
J. A. & Kathryn Albertson Foundation, Inc.	www.jkaf.org

Paul G. Allen Family Foundations	www.pgafoundations.com
Allstate Foundation	www.allstate.com/foundation
Annenberg Foundation	www.annenbergfoundation.org
AOL Time Warner Foundation	www.aoltimewarnerfoundation.org
AT&T Foundation	www.att.com/foundation/
Bank of America Foundation	www.bankofamerica.com/foundation
BellSouth Foundation	www.bellsouthfoundation.org
Best Buy Children's Foundation	www.bestbuy.com
Boeing-McDonnell Foundation	www.boeing.com/
Lynde & Harry Bradley Foundation, Inc.	www.bradleyfdn.org
Broad Foundation	www.broadfoundation.org
Garth Brooks Teammates for Kids Foundation	www.planetgarth.com
Brown Foundation, Inc.	www.brownfoundation.org
J. Bulow Campbell Foundation	www.jbcf.org
Barbara Bush Foundation	www.barbarabushfoundation.com
Carnegie Foundation	www.carnegiefoundation.org
Annie E. Casey Foundation	www.aecf.org
Chevron Corporation	www.chevron.com/community
The Chicago Community Trust	www.cct.org
Cisco Systems Foundation	www.cisco.com/web/about
Citigroup Foundation	www.citigroup.com
Edna McConnell Clark Foundation	www.emcf.org
Coca-Cola Foundation	www.coca-cola.com
Corning Foundation	www.corning.com

Covenant Foundation, Inc.	www.covenantfn.org
Crail-Johnson Foundation	www.crail-johnson.org
Daniels Fund	www.danielsfund.org
Arthur Vining Davis Foundations	www.avdfn.org
John Deere Foundation	www.deere.com
Geraldine R. Dodge Foundation	www.grdodge.org
Dow Chemical Company Foundation	www.dow.com
Ford Foundation	wwwfordfound.org
GenCorp Foundation	www.gencorp.com
General Mills Foundation	www.generalmills.com
Bill & Melinda Gates Foundation	www.gatesfoundation.org
Hasbro Children's Foundation	www.hasbro.org
Charles Hayden Foundation	www.charleshaydenfdn.org
William & Flora Hewlett Foundation	www.hewlett.org
Hewlett-Packard Global Philanthropy	www.hp.com/hpinfo/grants
The Home Depot Foundation	www.homedepotfoundation.org
American Honda Foundation	www.hondacorporate.com
IBM Gives Grant Program	www.ibm.com/ibm/ibmgives/grant/
ING Foundation	www.ingchancesforchildren.com
Intel Foundation	www.intel.com
James Irvine Foundation	www.irvine.org
Ewing Marion Kauffman Foundation	www.kauffman.org
W. M. Keck Foundation	www.wmkeck.org/
W. K. Kellogg Foundation	www.wkkf.org
John S. & James L. Knight Foundation	www.knightfdn.org
Lilly Endowment, Inc.	www.lillyendowment.org

(Continued)

(Continued)

Lowe's Charitable and Educational Foundation	www.toolboxforeducation.com
Lucent Technologies Foundation	www.lucent.com/foundation
Lumina Foundation for Education	www.luminafoundation.org
John D. & Catherine T. MacArthur Foundation	www.macfound.org
Malone Family Foundation	www.malonefamilyfoundation.com
Milken Family Foundation	www.talentedteachers.org
Mockingbird Foundation	www.mockingbird.org
MBNA Foundation	www.mbnafoundation.net
Medtronic Foundation	www.medtronic.com/foundation
MetLife Foundation	www.metlife.com
Meyer Memorial Trust	www.mmt.org
Microsoft Corporation	www.microsoft.com/giving
National Geographic Society	www.nationalgeographic.com
NEA Foundation	www.neafoundation.org
NEC Foundation of America	www.nec.com/company/foundation
New York Community Trust	www.nycommunitytrust.org
Oberkotter Foundation	www.oraldeafed.org
Mr. Holland's Opus Foundation	www.mhopus.org
David & Lucille Packard Foundation	www.packard.org
William Penn Foundation	www.williampennfoundation.org
J.C. Penney Company	www.jcpenney.net
Peninsula Community Foundation	www.pcf.org
Prudential Foundation	www.prudential.com/community/
Qualcomm Corporation	www.qualcomm.com/community/

RGK Foundation	www.rgkfoundation.org
Rockefeller Foundation	www.rockfound.org
San Francisco Foundation	www.sff.org
Skillman Foundation	www.skillman.org
San Diego Foundation	www.sdfoundation.org
Sara Lee Foundation	www.saraleefoundation.org
Sea World Foundation	www.seaworld.org
Siemens Foundation	www.siemens-foundation.org
Alfred P. Sloan Foundation	www.sloan.org
Sprint Foundation	www.sprint.com
State Farm Foundation	www.statefarm.com
Stuart Foundation	www.stuartfoundation.org
Texas Instruments Foundation	www.ti.com
Toshiba America Foundation	www.taf.toshiba.com
Toyota Motor Sales	www.nsta.org/programs/tapestry
UPS Foundation	www.community.ups.com/
Verizon Foundation	www.verizon.com/foundation
Wallace Foundation	www.wallacefunds.org
Walton Family Foundation	www.wffhome.com
Harry & Jeanette Weinberg Foundation	www.hjweinbergfoundation.org
Wells Fargo	www.wellsfargo.com/wf/about/charitable
Weyerhaeuser Foundation	www.weyerhaeuser.com
Tiger Woods Foundation	www.twfound.org
Robert W. Woodruff Foundation	www.woodruff.org

Writing Winning Minigrants

I have been writing grant applications for years. More than 90 percent of my applications have been successful, but some have gone over like a lead balloon. I will focus in this chapter on first teaching you how to write a minigrant before moving on to writing major grants. Hopefully, the things that you will learn along the way will encourage a funding agency to part with their money in your behalf.

If you do not get funded the first or second time you apply for a minigrant, do not get discouraged. There are usually many more applicants than there are funds for projects. Keep plugging away, and the monies will start to flow in.

I think of a minigrant as any grant under $5,000, but you can use your own definition of a minigrant. Many schools, school districts, and school foundations have minigrant programs. Corporations and foundations have minigrant programs as well. Accessing Web sites that are listed in this book and elsewhere as well as contacting funding agencies in your city, county, and state will alert you to the funding opportunities that are out there for the asking.

SIX BASIC COMPONENTS

Regardless of the size of the grant opportunity, there are six basic components to any grant application:

1. **Needs assessment.** This section analyzes the extent of the problem (needs) and the conditions you wish to change. The statement of the problem or need is a representation of the reason for your proposal.

2. **Goals.** These are general in nature, broad based, and overarching. They summarize what you want to accomplish with your grant. It is recommended that you state just one or two goals in your application.

3. **Objectives.** When writing the objectives, divide them into *program objectives* and *process objectives*. Program objectives specify the outcomes of your project—the end product. Program objectives should be measurable and time specific and should become the criteria by which your program will be evaluated. Process objectives are also measurable and are written to ensure that the program objectives are carried out. Here are examples of each:

   – **Example of program objective.** At the conclusion of the project period, at least 80 percent of the target students will have gained at least one month academically for each month of instruction in reading vocabulary and reading comprehension, as measured by a standardized test selected by the school or district.

   – **Example of process objective.** During the project period, at least 80 percent of the target students will visit the school library at least once a week to select books for leisure reading. Visits will be measured by records kept by the school librarian.

4. **Activities.** The activities (methods) section of your application will explain in detail how you are going to achieve the desired outcomes stated in your objectives. Activities explain what will be done, who will do it, and when it will get done. Several activities are presented for each objective. The activities section should flow smoothly from the needs statement and the program objectives.

5. **Evaluation specifications.** This part of your application should help the funding agency determine the extent to which the objectives of your project will be met and the activities carried out. Be certain to describe your evaluation plan as clearly and succinctly as you can. First, take a look at the overall project. Study the goals, objectives, and activities. If the objectives written are truly measurable, then it should not be difficult to evaluate each objective. The objectives should have built-in evaluation criteria. (See objectives on page 53.)

6. **Budget.** The budget that you present to the funding agency delineates the costs involved in carrying out your project and expresses what you are trying to accomplish. It is important that you prepare this section carefully, because it has an impact upon your credibility with the funding agency. You might want to consult with your principal or district business manager on this section as you break out your costs. A number of funding agencies have their own budget pages that they want you to complete. Others ask you to prepare your own budget page. For a minigrant, the following budget categories will suffice with most funding agencies:

PROJECT BUDGET

1. Personnel

2. Fringe Benefits

3. Travel

4. Equipment

5. Supplies

6. Contracted Work

7. Other

8. Total Costs

Writing a successful grant application will excite and thrill you. It will bring you much recognition and acclaim. Once you learn how to write a minigrant, you should have little difficulty with major grants. Hopefully, the ideas presented in this book will assist in making this a reality.

PREPARING A WINNING MINIGRANT APPLICATION

Figure 8.1 provides you with a sample minigrant application to use to practice putting together a minigrant. It covers all the components that most funding agencies require. When applying for a minigrant from a funding agency, make certain that you request their application. While most agencies, including school districts, have similar minigrant applications, you will discover that there are slight differences in scope and content requirements. Follow the directions carefully, and make your grant application stand out among the crowd.

Figure 8.1   Sample Minigrant Program Application

CONTACT PERSON _____   **DATE** _____

SCHOOL OR SCHOOL DISTRICT _____

ADDRESS _____

TITLE OF PROJECT _____

_____

SUMMARY OF THE PROJECT (50 words or less)

_____

_____

_____

NEEDS ASSESSMENT DOCUMENTATION

_____

_____

_____

_____

OVERALL GOAL OF THE PROJECT

_____

_____

OBJECTIVES OF THE PROJECT (Write four measurable objectives.)

1. _____

_____

2. _____

_____

3. _____

_____

4. _____

_____

ACTIVITIES (Write at least two activities for each objective.)

1. a._____

   b._____

2. a._____

   b._____

3. a._____

   b._____

4. a._____

   b._____

EVALUATION SPECIFICATIONS (Describe how you will evaluate each objective.)

1. _____

_____

2. _____

_____

3. _____

_____

4. _____

_____

ESTIMATED BUDGET (By Category)

1. **Personnel**   _____
2. **Fringe Benefits**   _____
3. **Travel**   _____
4. **Equipment**   _____
5. **Supplies and Materials**   _____
6. **Contracted Work**   _____
7. **Construction**   _____
8. **Other**   _____
9. **TOTAL DIRECT COSTS**   _____
   (Total of lines 1–8)
10. **Indirect Costs**   _____
    (Use 6%)
11. **Training Stipends**   _____
12. **TOTAL COSTS** $ _____
    (Total of lines 9–11)

BUDGET JUSTIFICATION (Briefly justify the above budget figures and elaborate on any budgetary category that needs further elaboration.)

_____

_____

_____

WHY SHOULD THIS GRANT APPLICATION BE FUNDED? (In 50 words or less, justify why you think this grant application should be funded.) _____

_____

_____

_____

_____

_____

_____

_____

_____   _____   _____   _____
(Signature of Contact Person)   (Date)   (Signature of Principal)   (Date)

9

Writing Major Grant Proposals That Get Funded

S omeone once told me that the main difference between a minigrant and a major grant was just a few zeros added to the budget. The more zeros, the bigger the grant! I identify a major grant as any grant of $25,000 or more. You can set your own parameters for what is a major grant. I do know that when you start applying for grants of $25,000 or more, you begin to compete with some of the big boys and girls, and the competition gets a little keener. I am convinced, however, that if you have learned how to write successful minigrants, such as those discussed in the previous chapter, your chances of getting bigger grants approved become more favorable. As I mentioned before, don't be intimidated, and don't get discouraged if you are not funded the first time around. Hopefully, this book and the other books cited in the bibliography will help you raise your batting average.

I have been conducting grantwriting classes and workshops around the country for years. The most successful ones are those that are held in-house or at the university level, where teachers and others are given release time to attend. When this happens, participants understand that the school district is serious about training teachers for fundraising, because it is willing to spend district money for substitutes while teachers are being trained. I highly recommend release time for teachers and others, not only for training purposes, but also for those times when the teaching staff is asked to write grants. These dedicated staff members need a realistic amount of time to write grants and should receive release time to do it.

GOVERNMENT GRANTS

Most government grant opportunities would be considered major grants and are designed for schools and districts with large numbers of minority students, large numbers of non-English and limited-English speakers, serious academic and social needs, or large numbers of students eligible for the free or reduced-price lunch program. Government grants are usually offered once a year and have specific deadlines for the receipt of applications. In addition to programs funded by the U.S. Department of Education and the state departments of education, funding opportunities for public schools exist at the U.S. Department of Health and Human Services, the U.S. Department of Energy, the National Science Foundation, the National Endowment for the Humanities, and the National Endowment for the Arts.

Writing a major grant application is like writing a minigrant application with a few more zeroes added to the budget pages, and a little more meat on the bones. Just like a minigrant, a major grant comprises six basic components: needs assessment, goals, objectives, activities, evaluation specifications, and budget.

NEEDS ASSESSMENT

The validation of needs stated in the beginning of the grant application under the heading "Needs Assessment" or "Statement of Problem" analyzes the extent of the problem and the conditions you wish to change. The statement of the problem or need is a representation of the reason for your proposal. It should demonstrate a clear understanding of the need in human terms (e.g., student needs) and of the potential community benefits if your project is funded, and it should reinforce your credibility for investigating the problem. Adequate space should be devoted to reviewing the literature on the subject, including citing relevant research to justify why the problem should be investigated.

The needs statement should coincide with the interests and priorities of the funding agency. If the interests of the funding agency do not coincide with your needs, apply to another agency that has the same interests as yours. Do not waste your time or the funding agency's time if there is not a match between your needs and the funding agency's priorities or interests. Doing your homework to determine the funding agency's priorities and areas of interest, including grade-level interests, will save significant amounts of time, frustration, and energy and will increase your chances for success. This includes gathering information from funding agencies' Web sites, including those of the U.S. Department of Education, your state department of education, corporations, foundations, and others. Requesting relevant literature and publications on current grant opportunities from program officers and other contact people is also very helpful. Also, researching publications that announce grant opportunities on a continuing basis will provide you with relevant, timely information concerning grant opportunities (see bibliography).

Defining the General Nature of the Problem

The first step in doing a comprehensive needs assessment is to define the general nature of the problem in a clear and concise manner.

This is the most important step and should include the following:

- Who has the problem?
- How important and significant is the problem?
- What is causing the problem?
- What factors are presently aggravating the problem?
- Why should the problem be of special interest to the funding agency?

When gathering your needs assessment documentation, involve the total school community. This includes students, teachers, parents, administrators, and other stakeholders. Describe the needs in human terms. An example of a population with a specific need might be "the numbers of children who are limited- and non-English speakers." In so doing, you will connect with the reader and make a more compelling statement.

Gathering Data

There are two types of data that you will be gathering: *hard data* and *soft data*. Hard data is sometimes referred to as *cognitive data* and includes specific numbers and percentages gathered about a topic, such as grade levels, schools, ethnic makeup, gender, test scores, numbers of limited- and non-English speakers, languages spoken in students' homes, and education levels of parents and people in the community. Also, numbers reflecting instances of absenteeism; expulsions; juvenile delinquency; truancy; crime; divorce; vandalism; and alcohol, tobacco, and drug use can be used. Additionally, statistics on socioeconomic levels, numbers of children on free or reduced-price lunch programs, transiency rates, geographic location, average size and ages of family members, unemployment rates, poverty levels, and numbers of single parent households and unwed mothers are all examples of hard data.

Soft data is sometimes referred to as *affective data* and may provide information on attitudes, values, feelings, and self-concepts of a select population. The information is usually gathered through observations, surveys, interviews, and anecdotal records. For example, if you wanted to find out about student attitudes toward reading in ability groups, then you might want to develop an interview schedule to measure how the students feel about this grouping method for reading. If you want to find out how parents feel about not having computers in their homes, then you could develop a questionnaire to determine their feelings and send it home for completion. Observation checklists are also used to gather soft data about a particular classroom, subject area, or child. The checklists are usually developed by an external evaluator or curriculum specialist in cooperation with individual classroom teachers, parents, and administrators.

It should be mentioned that gathering soft data from students is sometimes considered controversial because of the personal nature of the questions asked. It is recommended that all instrumentation designed for this purpose first be approved by the school principal and then by the parents before being administered to the students.

Example of Needs Assessment Documentation for a Preschool Program

Following is a hypothetical example of how a needs assessment is reported in an application for federal assistance. The application is for a preschool program. The data can be expanded or cut back depending on the needs and desires of the funding agency.

XYZ School District

The XYZ School District, located in ABC County, Any State, encompasses preschool through Grade 12 in 15 schools serving approximately 9,800 students. More than 90 percent of the students are from minority groups and more than 75 percent are Hispanic. With an ethnically diverse population of approximately 100,000 and an average income that is less than half the national average, the XYZ School District ranks as one of the poorest urban districts in both the state and country. The median income for XYZ City last year was $32,000, adjusted for inflation. Thirty percent of the families of students attending schools in XYZ School District are on Aid to Families with Dependent Children (AFDC). Single parents account for 59 percent of the households, and 38 percent of that figure are female heads of household. Sixty percent of the female heads of household live below the federal poverty level. Over 40 percent of XYZ City's adult population lacks a high school diploma, and 50 percent of the families move at least once a year.

The XYZ School District has a total of 4,767 limited-English-proficient students. Overall, the district ranks 35th in the entire state in the numbers of limited-English-proficient students as a percentage of enrollment. Standardized test scores for the district indicate overall that students are below state norms in reading, writing, and mathematics.

XYZ School, the target site for the preschool program, is located on the east side of the school district and has an overall population of 750 students in preschool through sixth grade; 92 percent are minority students and 55 percent are limited-English-proficient. The Child Development Center located at XYZ School provides day-care services to 75 preschool-age children from low-income families in a state-subsidized program. The center has a waiting list of 415 children. Ninety percent of the families served at the Child Development Center fall below the state poverty level and do not pay a fee.

Last year, a community needs assessment was conducted to help identify the health and social service needs of the XYZ School families and to identify service inconsistencies. A broad-based participation survey was utilized that included input from parents, community members, agency workers, educators, and others. Sixty families were randomly selected to represent the school's ethnic and socioeconomic diversity. They were administered intensive one-on-one in-depth interviews in their dominant language. After the 60 families identified key areas of need, more than 35 community members participated in open forums, which were held at the school site, to assist in prioritizing and expanding the identified needs. Focus groups that included personnel from health, educational, and social-service agencies also provided input on community needs and barriers to existing services. The focus groups were organized in six different categories: public agencies, elementary and secondary schools, law enforcement, emergency services, mental health agencies, and community service agencies. The following needs were identified as being most critical to the school:

- Strengthened partnerships and relationships between parents, teachers, community members, and others regarding the preschool needs of children at XYZ School
- Strengthened partnerships with XYZ School staff related to parent education programs
- Ability for parents to access health and social-service information at the XYZ School site

GOALS AND OBJECTIVES

When a grant application asks for both goals and objectives, writers often confuse goals with objectives. It is important to be able to distinguish between the two. Once you understand the differences, you will not confuse them.

Goals

Goals are general in nature, broad-based and overarching. They summarize what you want to accomplish in your grant application. It is recommended that you state one to four goals in each application.

Some Examples of Goals

1. To have all students in Grades 1-6 working at grade level in mathematics

2. To support parents, including mothers, fathers, and guardians, in their role as primary caregivers and educators of their children

3. To provide a comprehensive two-way bilingual education program that includes listening, speaking, reading, and writing

4. To develop a highly trained, competent, and caring staff in the science and math departments of the high school

5. To introduce Microsoft Word to middle school students in Grades 6-8

Program Objectives

There are two types of objectives. Program (outcome) objectives specify the outcomes of your project—the end product. Each objective is related to a specific goal and is directly related to the needs statement. Program objectives are measurable and time-specific, and they become the criteria by which the effectiveness of your program is evaluated. They are quantifiable, and they define the population to be served in numerical terms. Sometimes referred to as *product objectives* or *behavioral objectives*, they are very important in the eyes of the agency staff that will read the application, because they are at the heart of the project and are directly related to the needs assessment.

Program objectives are more specific than goals. They do not describe the activities or methods. When agencies fund your project, they are actually buying your objectives. When evaluators evaluate your project, they are measuring whether you accomplished what you said you were going to do in your program objectives. When writing program objectives that are quantifiable, you are usually taking something negative and making it positive. Program objectives use phrases such as "to increase," "to decrease," "to reduce," or "to be able to" and indicate a specified amount of time in which these things will happen. An example is, "To increase reading comprehension skills at least one month for each month of instruction as measured by ___."

It is essential to write clear, concise, measurable program objectives, or you will probably not get funded.

To be useful, program objectives should

- Tell who is going to be doing what.
- Tell when it is going to take place.
- Describe how much change will be taking place.
- Tell how the change is going to be measured.

Process Objectives

Process objectives are measurable and are written to assist in ensuring that the program objectives are achieved. They are not program objectives, and they do not identify outcomes related to learning. Instead, process objectives support program objectives and are essential to providing for smooth program implementation. When writing process objectives, use terms such as "to provide," "to establish," "to create," "to schedule," "to assist," "to observe," "to meet," and "to visit." An example is, "To establish a Community Learning Center as of September 15 as evidenced by records available at the school office and verified by parent participants."

Some Additional Examples of Objectives

Program (Outcome) Objectives

1. At the conclusion of the project period, at least 80 percent of the target students will have increased their understanding of science concepts for their grade level as measured by a district-developed science rubric.

2. At the conclusion of the project period, at least 90 percent of the target students will express positive attitudes about the mathematics program for their grade level as measured by attitude surveys developed by the mathematics department and administered before and after the project period.

3. At the conclusion of the project period, at least 80 percent of the target students will be able to demonstrate increased growth at the .05 level or better in district reading and language arts assessments as measured by standardized tests for their grade levels.

4. At the conclusion of the project period, at least 80 percent of the target students will gain at least one month academically for each month of instruction in reading comprehension and reading vocabulary as measured by a standardized test.

Process Objectives

1. The school counselor will meet with each program participant at least once a week beginning on October 1 as indicated by logs kept by each counselor.

2. Beginning in September, the project will provide 30 laptop computers for students to take home as indicated by school records kept on file in the project director's office.

3. Each student participant will visit the school media center at least twice a week for 12 weeks beginning in October to do research and report back on the Civil War as indicated by records kept by the school librarian and the classroom teacher.

4. A parent advisory group of 25 parents will be established by September 15 and will meet at least once a month as indicated by logs kept by the community facilitator.

ACTIVITIES

The activities (methods) section explains in detail how you are going to achieve the desired outcomes stated in your objectives. Activities explain what will be done, who will do it, and when it will get done. Activities should be well thought out and related to each objective. The activities section should include a description of program staffing and the students to be served, as well as the rationale for selecting the students. It should flow smoothly from the needs statement and the program objectives. Several activities are usually presented for each objective.

The activity section in your application should answer the following questions:

- What are you going to do to meet the objectives of the project?
- What are the projected starting and ending dates?
- Who is going to be responsible to coordinate, direct, and evaluate the project?
- What kinds of facilities, materials, equipment, and capital improvements will be needed to implement the project?
- How will the participants and staff be selected?
- Who will be responsible to complete each activity?
- What evidence do you have that the activities selected will yield positive results? (Refer to research findings, expert opinion, and experience with similar programs.)
- Who will be responsible to ensure that the activities presented are reflected in the budget request?

A hypothetical example of an activities component for an Academy of the Arts project is displayed in the following box.

SAMPLE OF ACTIVITIES FLOWING FROM OBJECTIVES

Rising Star Academy of the Arts

Objective 1. Ninety percent of the middle school students participating in the Rising Star Academy of the Arts dance program will be able to satisfactorily focus attention on kinesthetic awareness in responding to a variety of stimuli and perform specific and repeatable movement sequences taught by the instructor as measured by teacher observation and an external evaluator.

Activities

- One hundred students will be selected for this program based upon interest, artistic talent, motivation, parent interest, and referrals from classroom teachers.

- Five dance teachers will be employed based upon their experience and training in working with middle school students.
- Academy dance classes will be held after school, during intersession, and during summer school.
- No tuition fees will be charged.
- Each class will be scheduled for six weeks.
- Students will be taught kinesthetic awareness exercises for dance, including musical beats and rhythms.
- Students will be taught how to manipulate forces and qualities of movement through active participation in dance and rhythms.
- Students will be asked to demonstrate the ability to rework dances as a result of class discussion, videotaping, peer responses, and self-evaluation.
- Teachers will be asked to complete an internal evaluation of the afterschool program every three weeks.
- An external evaluator will be asked to do an evaluation of the total program and to provide a written evaluation to the administration and to the funding source.
- Program will be revised and then recycle after six weeks.

For most proposals, it is a good idea to include a timeline to show when the activities will be carried out and who is responsible for carrying out each activity. I recommend using a triple-T chart (task, time, talent) for this purpose. Following is an example of a triple-T chart related to a health education program.

XYZ School District Health Education
Grant for Development of Curriculum Materials

Task	Time	Talent
Form curriculum development advisory group (CDAG).	July 1	Principal* Parents Teachers Community groups
Hire health education consultant and curriculum development team.	Aug. 1	Principal* CDAG
Begin to develop curriculum packets.	Aug. 15	Health education consultant* CDAG
Begin staff development program.	Sept. 15	Same as above
Begin field-testing curriculum materials.	Oct. 1	Same as above
Revise curriculum materials.	Nov. 1	Same as above
Conduct home visitation program.	Nov. 15–Apr. 15	Parent educators*
Complete internal evaluation.	May 1	Principal* CDAG Staff
Complete external evaluation.	June 1	External evaluator*
Revise and recycle for year two.	Aug. 1	Health education consultant* CDAG

NOTE: *Person primarily responsible for completing the task

10

Preparing the Evaluation Plan for Your Application

The evaluation plan determines the extent to which the objectives of your project are met and the activities carried out. It should demonstrate the effectiveness of your program and provide assistance to you in those areas that need improvement. Based upon the results of the evaluation, you can allocate resources better, improve your program offerings, and improve the overall effectiveness of your program. By completing a comprehensive evaluation of your program and making necessary changes for improvement, your chances for additional funding in ensuing years improve. If you have written measurable objectives and activities that are related to each objective, then it should be easy to write the evaluation plan.

There are two types of evaluations that are used in writing the evaluation component for your grant proposal. These are *internal* evaluation and *third-party* (external) evaluation, sometimes referred to, respectively, as *formative* and *summative* evaluation.

INTERNAL (FORMATIVE) EVALUATION

An internal or formative evaluation deals primarily with self-assessment as related to the proposed project. It addresses questions about implementation and ongoing planning related to the overall program. It could include self-assessments of the teaching-learning process, the school, the school district, and the school community. It is a structured way for the teachers, the staff, the administration, the parents, the school community, and the school board to assess progress and make changes in ways that lead to greater achievement of the goals and objectives of the program.

Evaluation is looked upon as an ongoing process. Information gathered should be shared internally and externally to assist in making individual and collective decisions that move your classroom, school, or school district to new levels of excellence. Internal evaluation should be nonthreatening; it includes asking good questions, collecting information, sharing information, and making decisions to achieve organizational effectiveness. In projects with budgets under $5,000, an internal evaluation alone is often sufficient to fulfill the requirements of the funding agency; however, some funding agencies might prefer that you also include an external evaluation.

EXTERNAL (SUMMATIVE) EVALUATION

While an internal evaluation is a positive force for change and empowerment, there are many funding agencies that look favorably upon, or require, a third-party (external) summative evaluation report. The report showcases outcomes associated with your program and offers suggestions for improvement. These agencies believe that a third-party evaluator will assure a candid and unbiased assessment of the project, will have knowledge and expertise in data-gathering techniques and instrumentation, and will report the findings in a clear and concise manner. It is recommended that a third-party evaluation be completed for all grant applications over $25,000, whether the funding agency requires it or not. I believe that employing an external evaluator is a positive step in getting your project approved for funding.

Corporations, foundations, and individual donors are placing more emphasis on the evaluation plan and the evaluation results than ever before. Additionally, wealthy individuals giving money to the schools want to be assured that their monies are being well spent. It is essential that you prepare a comprehensive evaluation plan that is clear, concise, and well thought out and that your evaluation results are positive and meaningful.

Using a Third-Party Evaluation Design

Use caution in employing an external evaluator. You want to be absolutely certain that the evaluator will not be biased in providing you with an honest, fair, and candid assessment of your program. Ask for a biographical sketch to be placed into the appendix of the application. The appendixes should also include examples of surveys, questionnaires, data-gathering instrumentation, data-analysis forms, and other relevant materials that will be used in the implementation of the project. This lends credibility and strength to your request for funding.

In large urban school districts, and in situations where you are going after big bucks, it is customary and sometimes required to go to bid on the utilization of third-party evaluators. If this is the case in your school district, make certain to check with the person at the district office who handles the bidding process.

The third-party evaluator is usually given the responsibility for completing the evaluation and reporting the results. It is absolutely essential that this person be in close contact with project participants, teachers, and administrators to keep lines of communication open and to develop credibility with the staff. It is not the role of the third-party evaluator to concentrate only on the negatives of the project, but rather to identify those areas that are being implemented successfully and to offer suggestions for refinement, revision, and improvement.

Preparing the Evaluation Plan

Presenting a Clear Strategy for Evaluating Program Objectives and Activities

If the objectives written are measurable and the activities describe how you are going to achieve the objectives, then it will be easy to present a clear and meaningful strategy for evaluating the program. In fact, most of the evaluation component will have been written if you do a good job with your objectives and activities. Developing a triple-T chart will also assist you in presenting a clear strategy for evaluating program objectives and activities.

Describing Which and How Many Participants Will Be Chosen

This section is one of the most important elements of your evaluation plan. Funding agencies base a lot of their budgetary decisions on this data. For example, projects involving many schools, many students, and many teachers cost more to implement than projects involving fewer schools, students, and teachers. These types of projects also impact more students than other projects. The funding agency needs to have this information to make a funding decision. Providing a realistic budget request in relationship to the size and scope of the project will help your chances of getting funded.

Explaining When the Evaluation Will Take Place

Explaining when the evaluation will take place and publishing the plan for all to see is essential. Is the evaluation going to include pre- and posttesting? If so, when will this testing take place? In addition, will there be continuous testing by classroom teachers? Will there be observations, questionnaires, or interviews? When will this testing take place? As mentioned above, if your objectives and activities are described properly and you develop a triple-T chart, then this section will not be difficult to write.

Describing the Design, Implementation, and Methods to be Used to Collect the Data

If your request is under $25,000, and your school plans to do its own evaluation, be certain to describe your evaluation plan as clearly and succinctly as you can. First, take a look at the overall project. Study the goals, objectives, and activities. If the objectives written are truly measurable, then it should not be difficult to evaluate each objective. Describe your design succinctly, tell how you are going to implement the project, and include the methods that you will use to collect and report the data.

Specifying Who Will Be Responsible for Completing the Evaluation and Reporting the Results

It will be easy to specify who will be responsible for completing the evaluation and reporting the results once you decide on whether you will be using a third-party evaluator. If the evaluation will be conducted internally, it is important to specify the person who will be responsible for this, as well. In smaller projects, the school principal or a district-level administrator is given the overall responsibility for completing the evaluation and reporting the results. At other times, specific teachers are assigned this task depending upon their interest, the size and scope of the project, and the time required to complete the task.

Utilizing the Evaluation Results for Program Refinement, Revision, and Improvement

Project participants, administrators, teachers, board members, and others should welcome an external evaluation of their program. Having the feedback of an outside resource person who is unbiased and who offers suggestions for refinement, revision, and improvement is a good thing for your project, and it could improve your prospects for getting continuation funding for years two and three.

Once the results are in for the midyear evaluation of your project, your entire staff and administration have time to make the needed changes to improve and refine program offerings; to acquire additional facilities, staff, and materials, if needed; and to do what it takes to improve the project during the second half of the school year.

The end-of-year evaluation report provides the school district with information concerning the entire year's results, including suggestions for improvement. It also provides the funding agency with a report to assist it in deciding whether to extend the funding for another year, and it helps to determine if the money was well spent.

SEVEN TIPS TO REMEMBER WHEN DESIGNING YOUR EVALUATION PLAN

1. Present a clear strategy for evaluating program objectives and activities (methods).

2. Specify who will be evaluated, what will be evaluated, how many participants will be evaluated, and how participants will be chosen.

3. Explain when the evaluation will take place.

4. Describe the design, instrumentation, and methods to be used to collect the data.

5. Specify who will be responsible for completing the evaluation and reporting the results.

6. Indicate how the results of the evaluation will be used for program refinement, revision, and improvement.

7. Utilize the services of a third-party (external) evaluator as appropriate.

11

Preparing the Application Budget

The budget that you present to the funding agency delineates the costs involved in carrying out your project and expresses what you are trying to accomplish. It is essential that you prepare this section with a great deal of care and competence, because it has an impact on your credibility with the funding agency. People reading your project will look very carefully at the budget figures you present to see if they reflect the activities that you describe in your narrative statement and the overall scope of the project. If you ask for too much money or too little money, or if your budget figures are unrealistic, the reviewers will usually recognize it. Additionally, if your budget format is unfamiliar to the reviewer, it probably says that you either did not follow directions or lack the experience necessary to fully carry out the project. It behooves you to get help from your school principal, the district accountant, or the business manager as you put together the budget piece. These people can also assist you with specific figures for salaries, fringe benefits, consultants, hourly rates for noncertificated personnel, materials, equipment, indirect costs, and other matters. They can also help you in formatting the material so that it is clear and understandable. Finally, do not put the budget off until the last minute, as the people you are going to seek help from are usually very busy and will need time to work it out with you.

THE APPLICATION BUDGET

When preparing a budget, answer the following questions. Does the budget

- Present a format that is consistent with the funding agency's requirements?
- Relate to the objectives and activities of the project?
- Provide the necessary resources to carry out the project?
- Provide necessary detail so that the reviewer understands how specific budget categories were calculated?
- Separate the indirect costs from the direct costs?
- Include a budget narrative explaining how you arrived at specific budget calculations for each budget category?

PRESENTING A BUDGET FORMAT

In preparing a grant application, the funding agency may ask you to complete a budget following a prescribed format. If the agency instead leaves it up to you to present your own format, you might include the following budget categories:

1. Personnel

2. Fringe Benefits

3. Travel

4. Equipment

5. Supplies

6. Contracted Work

7. Construction

8. Other

9. Total Direct Costs (sum of lines 1–8)

10. Indirect Costs

11. Training Stipends

12. Total Costs (sum of lines 9–11)

The budget categories above provide you with a format that you can use with corporate and foundation grant applications as well as with minigrant applications, unless the funding agency has their own format for you to complete. Of course, use only those categories that apply to your project.

Each budget category presented should relate to the objectives and activities of the project. This should be obvious to the reviewer. Nothing in the budget should stand out as being irrelevant, too costly, or not needed—these are red flags that you do not want to raise.

PROVIDING THE NECESSARY RESOURCES TO ADEQUATELY CARRY OUT THE PROJECT

While you do not want to propose anything that would be irrelevant, too costly, or not needed, you also want to make certain that you have enough resources delineated in the budget to adequately carry out the project. I have seen funding agencies turn down projects that do not ask for enough money to meet the objectives of the project. I have also seen funding agencies increase program budgets when they like a project and are convinced that the applicants did not ask for enough money. A funding agency might want you to beef up specific sections of the budget, might suggest increasing salaries for particular positions, or may request that you employ an external evaluator. If any of these suggestions are made, they will usually ask you to submit a revised budget.

Providing the necessary resources to adequately carry out the project is not a simple task. Asking for too much or too little money is not the way to go. Schedule time to do your homework, contact resource people both in the school district and outside the district, refer to this book as needed, and develop a budget request that is meaningful and meets the objectives and activities of your project head on.

PROVIDING THE NECESSARY DETAIL

When working on your itemized budget breakdown, sometimes referred to as a *line item budget,* provide the necessary detail to enable the reviewer to understand how specific budget categories were calculated. If, under Travel, you have a budget figure of $3,000, indicate how that money will be spent—for example, "one roundtrip to Washington, DC, for two staff members @ $500 each, includes per diem," or "ASCD conference in San Francisco for four staff members @ $125 each, includes per diem." You can elaborate further on each budget item in the Budget Narrative section.

Calculating the Direct Costs

Direct costs are those costs in items 1 through 8 above that are specifically related to the proposed project, such as personnel, fringe benefits, travel, supplies (materials), equipment, and contracted work. Each of these categories has a number of subcategories. For example, under Personnel, break out Certificated Personnel and Noncertificated Personnel. Under Fringe Benefits, do the same. For Travel, break out the number of trips, the destinations, and the number of staff traveling. For Supplies, specify what you intend to buy and how much each of the items is going to cost. For Equipment, do the same. Under Contracted Work, list any consultants that you are planning to bring in, such as an external evaluator at a daily rate—for example, "external evaluator, $4,000 (10 days @ $400 per day)." Note that most federal projects, corporations, and foundations do not provide monies for construction costs. They do provide funding at times for leasing office and classroom space. Check this out with your funding agency contact person.

The Other category in the program application is a catchall for all items that do not fit comfortably in the designated categories. For example, you might want to include budget figures for postage, mailings, publications, curriculum development, and duplication costs.

Calculating the Indirect Costs

Indirect costs are often referred to as administrative or overhead costs. These costs are difficult to quantify and pin down. Examples of indirect costs include the amount of time that the district accountant and other administrators spend on budgetary assistance such as payroll, accounting, and general project administration; the cost of utilities, custodial services, and facilities maintenance; and the use of district-owned materials and equipment such as copiers and computers.

Indirect costs are usually figured as a percentage of the grant by the federal government. Contact your principal or district office administrator to find out if you have an assigned indirect cost ratio for either federal and state grants. If you do not, five to six percent of the total grant request would be acceptable. Some corporate and foundation funding agencies allow you to use an indirect cost ratio, but the trend is moving in the direction of nonfunding of indirect and overhead costs. Make certain that it is permissible to use this figure before inserting it into a corporate or foundation grant request.

Writing the Budget Narrative

Whether it is required or not, it is a good idea to include a budget narrative explaining how you arrived at specific calculations for each budget category. This is usually accomplished through a narrative statement in paragraph form. If you do your homework, gather the needed data, talk to the right people, and get help as needed, the budget narrative should not be difficult to complete.

Writing the Dissemination Plan

Some funding agencies ask you to include a dissemination section in your application. This requires a plan to let others know about your accomplishments at the conclusion of the project year. Preparing a comprehensive dissemination plan will help generate positive publicity and recognition for your project and for the funding agency. Below are some approaches you can use to disseminate information about your project, both locally and nationally:

- Submitting press releases to local and national newspapers
- Appearing on local and national radio and television shows
- Providing information on the school district Web site
- Writing and distributing newsletters about the project
- Writing articles for publication in relevant educational journals
- Publishing a pamphlet or book about the project
- Speaking at local, state, and national conferences and conventions
- Speaking at local and national service organization meetings
- Visiting other school districts and reporting results
- Serving as a consultant to other school districts
- Conducting workshops and seminars at colleges and universities

I have found that providing a dissemination plan for your grant proposal (whether one is requested or not) will increase your chances of getting funded. Prepare the dissemination plan in paragraph form using some of the ideas above, and add additional ideas that are relevant.

Writing the Program Summary and Abstract

Most federal grant applications and some corporate and foundation grant applications require a one-page program summary and abstract. The abstract should briefly describe the needs being addressed in the project, including the numbers and types of participants to be served, the objectives and activities proposed to meet them, the intended outcomes, and the budget request. Because the reviewer will read this piece first, extreme care should be taken to carefully summarize the project in a clear and concise manner. Make certain that it is well written, truly reflects the essence of your project, and creates an immediate favorable impression. It is recommended that this section be written last, because you will have a clearer understanding of your total project after you have written the rest of the application.

FOURTEEN HELPFUL HINTS TO IMPROVE YOUR CHANCES OF GETTING FUNDED

1. Plan your writing schedule so that you have enough time to complete the task, gather signatures and approvals, and meet the deadline.

2. Do not send your project in early, because the more time you have with it, the more time you have to edit, revise, rewrite, reduce, and rearrange.

3. Make certain that you follow the exact guidelines of the funding agency. Go over the guidelines on a continuing basis to be sure that you are not leaving anything out.

4. Comply with the funding agency's instructions to use a specific font and type size (e.g., 12-point Times Roman with double spacing), and make sure your narrative is not longer than their stated maximum. Give it to the funding agency in exactly the form they have requested. If no form is specified, it is still a good idea to use a type font and size that are clear and understandable and to double-space the lines. This is particularly important if you will deliver the document electronically, because some fonts may look different on other computers than they look on yours. Times Roman and Arial are two that are reliably consistent from one machine to another.

5. Use lists and tables. They convey a lot of information in a small amount of space. They are also easy to read and present a welcome change for the reviewer.

6. Use bold type instead of underlining to emphasize key points or sections of the application. But be careful not to overuse it, because it can be distracting to the reviewer.

7. Use the same headings and subheadings in your application as the reviewers use in the evaluation form. Request a copy of the reviewers' evaluation form from the program officer for your project. If the form is not available, follow the application format exactly the way it is presented, and use the same headings and subheadings that appear in the application.

8. When putting your application together, include just the essentials in the appendixes. Check the program guidelines for any special requirements. Government grant applications sometimes ask that you place the following into the appendixes: letters of support, letters of commitment, the names of consortium members, resumes, job descriptions, and organizational charts.

9. Use a ragged right margin rather than a justified right margin, because it is easier to read.

10. Number your pages consecutively in the top right or center bottom of each page.

11. Prepare a table of contents that corresponds to your headings and subheadings.

12. Before submitting your proposal, proofread it over and over again. Have several other people proofread it as well. Look for any typographical errors, misspellings, and mistakes in punctuation, grammar, facts, figures, charts, graphs, phone numbers, Web addresses, and budget computations. Study the content carefully to make certain that it conveys what you are trying to say. Make changes as needed.

13. Make certain that you have made arrangements for duplication and collation of your application, allowing you enough time to make your final check of the application to see that pages are collated properly and that nothing is left out or misplaced. If time is available, make extra copies of the application for your own needs. Otherwise, keep at least one hard copy for yourself, and save the manuscript on the hard drive of your computer.

14. Deliver the completed application to the post office or another carrier in plenty of time to meet the deadline.

12

After You Receive the Grant, Then What?

ANNOUNCING YOUR GRANT AWARD TO THE WORLD

When you are notified of a grant award and have received the money, you have good reason to be elated. You also have an opportunity to enhance the image of your school or district by announcing the grant to the world. First, make certain that the funding agency agrees to allow you to make the announcement of the grant award. After you get the go-ahead, put together some press releases for the local newspapers and other media, and announce the grant on the district or school Web site. Second, take every opportunity to talk about the grant at conferences, workshops, and meetings of organizations like the PTA, Kiwanis, and Rotary.

It is enlightening to discover that once you start receiving grants and gifts, you begin developing a reputation for having quality programs. This in turn alerts other funding agencies about your school or school district and makes it easier for your school to get additional funding. School and district staff who know this phenomenon write grants and apply for monies on a continuing basis. As your school or district establishes a reputation for attracting money, using it effectively, and disseminating information that is useful to other schools, it will become ever more attractive as a grant recipient.

BEING GOOD STEWARDS
OF ALL GRANTS AND GIFTS

As big projects begin to be implemented, it is very important that you carry out your responsibilities in a professional manner and be good stewards of all monies received. This means setting up sound accounting practices for the actual expenditure of the funds. In many school districts, the accounting department or business office is assigned the responsibility to do the bookkeeping for all external grants and gifts. In other school districts, the individual school site principals are responsible for keeping track of all grants and gifts for their schools. As mentioned elsewhere, many funding agencies, including the federal government, allow you to use an indirect cost ratio to help defray some of the extra accounting and administrative costs brought on by the grant. The amount, usually about five to seven percent of the total grant, should be included when submitting your overall budget proposal. It would be difficult to negotiate an indirect cost ratio after the grant is approved.

Keeping in touch with your program officer at the funding agency is vitally important. Each approved project usually has a program officer (or someone else with a similar title) assigned to the project. Communicate with this person on a continuing basis. Let the program officer know how the project is progressing, and invite this person to visit your project along with other members of the agency staff. Be open and honest in your communication with the program officer, and talk about the problems as well as the successes you are having. Ask for assistance when you need it. Program officers know that everything is not going to run smoothly at first. They would rather you be honest with them than cover up any problems you are having.

The site principal is generally considered the instructional leader of the school. The principal is also one of the key players in the implementation of a successful project or program. Without the total support of the principal, your project will probably not succeed. Seek out the support of the principal and include this person in your planning, deliberations, and program evaluation. Develop a good relationship with the external evaluator as well. Communicate with this person both formally and informally during the implementation of the project. Ask for input and suggestions for improvement related to the overall progress of the project.

Communicate and ask for input from program participants, be they students, parents, teachers, or staff. Make certain that the participants play a major role in the evaluation of the overall program. Provide staff training and inservice training as described in your program proposal. If you have indicated in your proposal that you will have a project advisory group made up of community members, parents, teachers, and others that meets monthly, make certain that this takes place. It is critical that the services you promised in the program proposal are provided. Continue to assess your needs as the project progresses, and study the possibility of continuation funding for as many years as possible.

WHEN GRANT MONIES RUN OUT

Many administrators are concerned that when grant monies run out, programs will die on the vine.

While this is a legitimate concern, it shouldn't stop you from applying for grants for the following reasons:

1. Grants provide for the immediate needs of the school or district.

2. Many grants are awarded for multiple years, if you include this in your funding request.

3. Decisions concerning continuation funding are usually based on the needs of the school and school district and on successful implementation of the original grant.

4. When monies are no longer available from the original funding source, a request can be made to another funding agency to continue funding your project based upon your needs and successful implementation of the original grant.

5. Many school districts, with the recommendation of the superintendent of schools and the approval of the school board, use monies from the district's general fund to continue funding projects that have been previously funded by outside agencies. Most projects that get funded in this way after federal and corporate money runs out are projects that have been successful, meaningful, and needed by the total school community.

13

Some Examples
of Winning
Grant Proposals

Following are some examples of two winning minigrant proposals and one major grant proposal. The minigrants were written in the South Washington County Schools in Cottage Grove, Minnesota, and funded by the South Washington County Schools Education Foundation. Both winning minigrant proposals are published with the approval of the South Washington County Schools. Each minigrant presented is five pages long, and is provided to show you what a winning minigrant proposal looks like. While the content and writing style of the grant proposals is different, the format is the same and is based upon the requirements of the South Washington County Schools Education Foundation. It should be mentioned that minigrant program applications vary from district to district, state to state, and among corporations and foundations.

Also included in this chapter is an example of a successful Texas 21st Century Community Learning Center grant application. This application, which is very similar to an application to the U.S. Department of Education, is provided to give you some insights into how a major grant application looks and into the amount of work, time, and energy that it entails to put one together.

EXAMPLES OF WINNING MINIGRANTS

Teach, Assess, Support Kids (T.A.S.K.)

[PROP 1]

South Washington County Schools
7362 East Point Douglas Road South
Cottage Grove, MN 55016
South Washington County Schools Education Foundation
Written by – Norma Wilson, District Media Program Coordinator
Mini-Grant Application

1. Project Summary:

Media Specialists will create T.A.S.K. (Teach, Assess, Support Kids!) Packs to align Media outcomes with the classroom Balanced Literacy strategies, MAP vocabulary and Minnesota Academic Standards. These individual packets will include lessons, activities, and assessments based on the specific vocabulary, topics and literature genre that are found in their classroom Balanced Literacy focus lessons and the MAP assessments. The T.A.S.K. Packs will be formulated by three groups of Media Specialists, each with a clearly defined and measurable objective in Genre, Vocabulary, and Research.

2. Goal Statement:

The TASK is to improve student achievement in Balanced Literacy skills, to improve the partnership with classroom teachers in literacy strategies, and to provide additional support to students in their learning through implementation of Balanced Literacy T.A.S.K. packets.

3. Project Need: Describe your students and the needs that this project addresses.

The proposed activities are designed to help the district's Media Specialists address the following curriculum needs for children to improve their literacy skills.

Student/Instructional Needs:

    a. Media Specialists are in a unique position to support classroom learning in the reading/writing process. Best practice shows that students' knowledge gains are greater and more comprehensive when their learning is supported throughout the school day, not just in the designated learning period. Media and classroom partnerships do exist throughout our schools. However, Project LEAD has changed the way our teachers instruct the reading/writing process. This change has created a need for Media Specialists to re-align their curriculum and to make modifications to better support classroom learning and grade-level outcomes.

    b. After attending Balanced Literacy training in November by the District Literacy Coach, Media outcomes will need to be refined and aligned. Resources will need to be developed and put in a format that addresses the literacy skills children are striving to learn. The grant provides the needed funding, leadership and coordination to do so.

Supporting District Goals

The number one goal on the 2005-2006 Strategic Plan is to "be in the top 10% of all state school districts in MCA test results and ranked #1 among districts of comparable size and demographics." Through the grant Media Specialists will increase student knowledge and scores through their direct support to balanced literacy strategies.

Research/Best Practices

- Research found that "if a library acts as a curriculum partner with classroom teachers and is staffed with certified media specialists, students in that school will score higher on standardized tests regardless of socio-economic and educational levels." (T. Young)
- A state summary of School Library Programs found that "of schools with above-average scores on grade 3, 5, 8 reading tests, nearly 67 percent were schools with fulltime library media specialists." This indicates that classroom instruction aligned with support in media centers increases student achievement.

4. Describe Project Implementation.

TASK Development Teams:

Each of the three TASK development teams will include three Media Specialists and the District Media Program Coordinator. Three teams will be developed and Media Specialist volunteers will be recruited. The team structure allows the participation of ten Media Specialists who will use their expertise in curriculum development, knowledge of literature, and technology skills. Input and guidance will be provided by the district's Balanced Literacy Coach and the MAP Coordinator.

Project TASK:

The participants have a specific task with a specific outcome in three areas that are tested in the MCA's and MAP tests: Genre, Vocabulary, and Research. Within these topics the Media Specialists will develop a packet which includes a focus lesson, activity and assessment. Specific tasks will include the following.

Genre:

a. Align monthly classroom genre (literature topic) with Media Center instruction. (i.e. when Historical Fiction is studied in the classroom it is supported in the Media Center)
b. Prepare age appropriate lists of genre titles.
c. Select appropriate technology and non-fiction materials to support genre.
d. Develop a dual assessment in which (1) students can hear a passage read and state its genre and (2) students can list the characteristics of a certain genre.

Vocabulary:

a. Identify the vocabulary assessed in the reading MAP test and align it with the grade level instruction in the Media Center.
b. Prepare lesson packets to introduce or review the vocabulary word using examples of literature. (i.e. simile, metaphor, compare/contrast etc.)
c. Develop assessments appropriate to age level and the terminology used. (i.e. multiple choices for 'either/or' words, Venn diagrams for compare/contrast, illustrate an example of....)

Research:

a. With input from the District Balanced Literacy Coach, determine significant vocabulary so that the same terminology is presented from both the classroom teacher and the Media Specialist. (i.e. matrix, personal narrative)
b. Prepare lesson packet to introduce or review research vocabulary using non-fiction books. (i.e. table of contents, glossary, almanac)
c. Develop variety of assessment that students can indicate knowledge of research skills, i.e. :
   1. Paper pencil to label parts of a book as title page, index, glossary and their purpose.
   2. Active participation: using almanacs, encyclopedias, atlases, websites etc. and selecting the best choice to locate information.
   3. Completing a computer designed test where they select the correct vocabulary from choices.

5. **Project Timeline:**

The framework to begin the project will be in place by the end of November as it is critical to student needs to begin alignment as soon as possible.

November 15, 2005 – Attend mandatory <u>Balanced Literacy Instruction in the Media Center</u> training.
   (This is separate from the grant but the basis for which the grant is needed. It is directed by the District Balanced Literacy Coordinator.)
December 2005 - Media Specialists develop T.A.S.K. Packs with Genre Focus
January 2006 – Share materials with Media Staff and begin implementation with students
February 2006 – Two Media Specialists groups develop TASK Packs: Vocabulary and Research focus
February 2006 - Share materials with Media Staff and begin implementation with students
April 2006- Evaluation of program

6. **Three Measurable Project Outcomes:**
   a. 100% of the students will demonstrate understanding of the intended outcomes at 90% or more.
   b. Anecdotal assessments with teachers will indicate 100% of the teachers observe an increased understanding of content in their students.
   c. Student performance in reading/writing assessments will increase as demonstrated in district MAP and MCA testing.

7. **Project Evaluation:**
   a. The data will be collected from the formal and informal assessments in the T.A.S.K. Packs. This will occur monthly. Student performance on the assessments will indicate if the children are successful in their learning. Learning will be modified for non-achieving students and reassessed.
   b. Informal discussions and formal surveys with teachers will indicate if integrated instruction is impacting learning.
   c. Analysis of standardized testing will occur when MAP and MCA results are returned. MAP results are available directly after testing mid-winter in some schools and in spring testing in all schools. MCA results and analysis will be available in June.

8. **School Partners, Organizations and Volunteers:**
   a. The District Balanced Literacy Coach will provide input and guidance to the Media Staff.
   b. The District MAP coordinator will provide vocabulary and in-service to Media staff in determining vocabulary and understanding test results.
   c. Follett Company will in-service online use of collections of literature, book leveling, and selecting books that focus on literary devices used in reading.
   d. Media Center volunteers will locate and compile the materials in the library from lists provided by the Media Specialist.

9. **Sharing Information:**
   a. Information will be shared with all Media Specialists at District level meetings.
   b. Information will be shared at the District Curriculum Department meetings and on the District Curriculum Drive.
   c. Information will be presented to each building staff, to reading specialists at department meeting, and to principals individually and at administrative meeting, and to community through newsletters.

10. Detailed Project Budget

Expense Item	Detailed Description	Foundation Grant Request	School/Other Contributions
Extended Hours: District Media Specialist	12 hours x 22 = 264; $264.00 x .1265 = $33.396 Total amount = $297.40	$297	
Substitute Teachers $113.25 per day	9 substitutes, 3 days each: 27 @ $113.25 = $3057.75 Fringe benefits: $3057.75 x .1265 = $386.80 Total amount: $3444.55	$3445	
Paper/Copying Each building will cover their own expense in paper and copying (1.5 cents per page)	37 cases paper @ 22.10 = 817.70		$818
Packet Containers: Hold T.A.S.K. Packs	300 Packs Office Max: 12 X 19.99 = $239.88	$240	
Substitute Teachers $113.25 per day from Media Services budget to plan for T.A.S.K. development teams	2 substitutes @ $113.25 = $ 226.50 Fringe benefits: $226.50 x .1265 = $28.65 Total amount: $255.15		$255
Substitute Teachers $113.25 per day from Curriculum Department budget to pay for substitutes so Media staff can attend the mandatory Balanced Literacy/Media training. This is part of the complete project but not requested in the grant.	19 substitutes @113.25 = $2151.75 Fringe benefits: $2151.75 x .1265 = $272.20 Total amount: $2423.95		$2424
	Total Expenses	$3,982	$3,497

[PROP 2]

Concepts About Print Come Alive (Cap)

South Washington County Schools
7362 East Point Douglas Road South
Cottage Grove, MN 55016
South Washington County Schools Education Foundation
Written by – Ann Mulvey, Reading Specialist, Hillside Elementary School

Mini-Grant Application

---

1. Project Summary: (100 word maximum)

Our early literacy project called "Concepts About Print Come Alive" is designed to improve pre-reading and reading skills of kindergarten and first grade students, particularly students who are at risk. Helping students learn the Concepts About Print (CAP) will improve their reading and writing abilities. CAP includes skills such as knowledge of proper direction to read, difference between word and letter, and 1:1 word matching. This project will include time for teachers to interpret CAP scores and to improve CAP instruction. Our project will provide materials to teach Concepts About Print to whole groups and small groups of children.

2. Goal Statement:
- Our goal is identify children with low CAP scores in Kindergarten and provide them with intense CAP instruction.
- Our goal is to reduce the number of students who need reading intervention in first grade.
- Our goal is to meet district and state literacy standards for kindergarten and first grade.
- Our goal is for Kindergarten and First Grade students to improve as readers and writers.

3. Project Need:

Children who have been read to daily and encouraged to handle books since infancy acquire Concepts About Print skills more readily. Since many Hillside Elementary (HE) students lack rich preschool interaction with books, kindergarten and first-grade teachers at Hillside must spend a great deal of time on CAP instruction to make up for years of literacy deprivation.

Several years ago, the Reading Specialists in the district noticed that the children with low kindergarten CAP scores were often the same children being considered for Reading Recovery one year later when they entered first grade. It appeared that kindergarten students who scored 9 points or less on the CAP assessment were very likely to be considered for Reading Recovery. Therefore, by using CAP scores teachers can identify the children who may be at risk for learning to read. Teachers can intervene immediately by offering CAP instruction during reading and writing time.

Hillside Elementary literacy scores from the past three years have been studied. This analysis indicates that 45% to 50% of all kindergarten students score 9 points or less on the CAP assessment given each September. Therefore, almost half of all Hillside kindergarten students may be at risk for learning to read. The study also shows that 30% to 35% of first grade students are assessed for Reading Recovery. This indicates that one-third of HE first grade students are at risk for learning to read. It is imperative that we focus on these at-risk kindergarten and first grade students to improve their reading and writing abilities early in their education. Unfortunately at HE, kindergarten and first-grade teachers do not have enough materials to meet the needs of these at-risk students.

Teaching CAP is one of many State and District reading and writing expectations. State reading expectations list CAP under the headings of Word Recognition, Analysis and Fluency, and Comprehension. State Writing expectations list CAP under the headings of Elements of Composition, Spelling, and Handwriting.

4. Describe Project Implementation.
- Kindergarten teachers, first-grade teachers, and the Reading Specialist will meet to discuss CAP scores from the 2004-05 and 2005-06 school year. During this discussion a scope and sequence for teaching CAP will be developed. Specific reading and writing lessons will be planned using the new materials during monthly meetings.
- During daily-shared reading lessons, kindergarten and first grade classroom teachers will use Big Books to teach targeted CAP skills. Shared reading lessons will be taught as whole group lessons during which the teacher does a "Think-Aloud" and eventually a "Think-Together" with the students.
- Kindergarten and first-grade teachers will also teach CAP during Writing Workshop focus lessons, thus, connecting CAP skills to writing.
- During guided reading lessons the kindergarten and first grade classroom teachers will use sets of books to teach CAP skills to small groups of students. These homogeneous groups will be formed in order to meet the needs of those students who are most at risk for learning to read. The teacher will use direct instruction during these small group guided reading lessons. This small group time provides the children with guided practice of the newly acquired CAP skills. Guided Reading time offers a gradual release of responsibility from teacher to student.

5. Project Timeline: (Give a chronological timeline for major activities from Jan. 2005 – June 2006.)
- January–The project team will meet to interpret CAP scores and to develop CAP scope and sequence.
- January–Reading Specialist will review possible book selections with the project team to make the best choices. Book sets and Big Books will be ordered.
- February–Reading Specialist and PTA volunteers will process books.

- February–Team will develop lesson plans to meet the CAP goals.
- February to June–Teachers will use the Big Books daily for shared reading lessons. Guided reading books will be used daily with small groups of students. All books will be shared by four sections of kindergarten and five sections of first grade.
- February to June–Teachers will assess CAP growth by gathering anecdotal information during Guided Reading and during Writer's Workshop.
- May–The project team members and the principal will discuss CAP scores and DRA scores to see if the project met its goals. The team will plan how to teach CAP during the 2006-2007 school year.

6. Project Outcomes:
- The most notable outcome will be the improvement that students make in their acquisition of CAP skills. Growth in CAP acquisition can be measured with the formal kindergarten CAP assessment. Students will be more comfortable handling little books, and their awareness of how books work will improve.
- If students are provided with meaningful experience with books, such as focused CAP instruction, their reading ability may improve. Teachers can compare the January DRA scores to the May DRA scores to prove if students are able to read books with a higher level of text difficulty.
- The writing of kindergarten and first grade students will reflect how well they grasp CAP skills. In addition to showing growth in CAP acquisition, student writing will improve in quantity and clarity.

7. Project Evaluation:
- All kindergarten students are given the Concepts About Print assessments in September, January, and May. We have reached our goal if 90% of all kindergarten students score 13 out of 15 points on the CAP assessment given in May.
- All first grade students are given the reading assessment called the Developmental Reading Assessment (DRA). The DRA shows the level of text difficulty that is just right for each child. Teachers can compare the January DRA scores to the May DRA scores. The kindergarten DRA average will improve from Level 2 in January to Level 5 in May. The first grade DRA average will improve from Level 16 in January to Level 24 in May.
- Teachers can evaluate CAP growth in reading by analyzing running records. Teachers can refer to running records taken once a week during guided reading lessons to note CAP growth.
- Teachers will collect writing samples every week and evaluate them every month. Writing samples will show student growth in CAP skills over four months time. In addition to CAP growth, students will also meet District writing standards.
- Teachers can also track CAP improvement in student writing by analyzing the anecdotal evidence recorded on the "Prompt and Praise" records gathered during Writer's Workshop time.

8. Identify school or community partners/organizations and volunteers involved in the project and roles.
- Hillside Elementary has a wide network of volunteers including parents, grandparents, business partner volunteers, high school student volunteers, and upper grade buddies. Kindergarten and first grade students will read their guided reading books to many of these volunteers.
- The HE Reading Specialist, kindergarten teachers, and first-grade teachers will donate time to preview and order the proper books. This team will also donate time to plan lessons when the materials arrive. This team will also donate time to evaluate student growth.
- The HE Literacy team will donate time to formulate long-term literacy goals and how to meet the needs of early readers.
- Parent volunteers organized by the Hillside Elementary PTA will tape, stamp and level the books. Financial support and other donations are being considered by the HE principal, literacy team, Student Council, PTA and by Rigby Publishing.

9. Sharing Information:
Information will be shared in a variety of ways. First, the Hillside Elementary Literacy team will be involved with long term literacy goals. A staff meeting in February will be devoted to informing the entire staff of the project including how it will be implemented and how to measure its success. The Reading Specialist and principal will share project information at reading specialist and principal meetings. Each month from January until June teachers in kindergarten and first grade will meet monthly to reflect on how the project is working and how to improve student achievement using the project materials.

10. Detailed Project Budget – Show Budget Calculations.

Expense Item	Detailed Description	Foundation Grant Request	School/Other Contributions
Extended Hours—For coordination/planning time needed beyond contract. If extended pay is not requested, list the estimated number of staff hrs @ $22/hr that the school will contribute to the project/program.	School contributions include: 38 hours × $22.00 = $836.00 $836.00 × .1265 = $105.75 $836.00 + 105.75 = $941.75 Total		38 hrs × $22 = $836.00 $836 × .1265 = $105.75 $836.00 + 105.75 = $941.75 Total
*Substitute Teacher(s) $113.25 per day Benefits must be included below.			
Contracted Personnel/Stipend			
Software			
Conference/Workshop Registration Fees			
Instructional Supplies and Materials	Guided reading books Rigby PM Levels 1 to 6 6 each of 112 titles = 672 books Rigby shipping $200.00 Big Books 20 titles Big Book shipping	$3015.00 $ 200.00 $ 700.00 $ 70.00	Book tape and stickers $49.00
Equipment (Grant request cannot exceed 50% of the total Foundation request)			
Printing/Copying			Kindergarten and Grade One newsletter 400 sheets × $.03 = $12.00
Other *(Field trip & travel are not allowed.)*			
	Total Project/Program Costs	**$3985.00**	**$1,002.75**

If needed, provide additional narrative explanation of budget request below.

EXAMPLE OF A WINNING MAJOR GOVERNMENT GRANT

Texas 21st Century Community Learning Center

The following winning grant application for a Texas 21st Century Community Learning Center was submitted to the Texas Education Agency, Austin, Texas, and is printed with permission from Dr. Gary Lee Frye, director of development / special student programs for the Lubbock-Cooper Independent School District, Lubbock, Texas. Because of the length of the application, certain sections have been excluded.

For TEA Use Only	TEXAS EDUCATION AGENCY	
Adjustments and/or annotations made on this have been confirmed with	**Standard Application System (SAS)** **Texas 21st Century Community Learning Centers, Cycle 3** Spring, Summer, and Fall of 2005, 2006, and 2007	**152-906** County-District No. 75-1360736 9-Digit Vendor ID# 17
_____ by telephone/FAX on_____ by _____ of TEA.	-- SCHEDULE #1 General Information	ESC Region _____ NOGA ID/Project No. (Assigned by TEA)

1. Applicant Agency: (Name, Address, City, State, Zip) Lubbock-Cooper ISD 16302 Loop 493 Lubbock, TX 79423-7805 If Open Enrollment Charter School, Name of Sponsoring Entity:	**2. Applicant Contact Person:** (Name, Title, Address [if different]): Gary Lee Frye, Ed.D. Director of Development / Special Student Programs Phone (806) 863-2282 x 112 FAX (806) 863-2397 E-Mail glfrye@lcisd.net	**3. Purpose of Application:** [x] Application ☐ Amendment No. _____ (The last day to submit an amendment is 90 days prior to the ending date of the grant.) RFA # 701-04-025

4. Use of the Standard Application System: This system provides a series of standard schedules to be used as formats by applicants who apply for funds administered by the Texas Education Agency. If additional clarification is needed, please call 512-463-9269.

5. Program Authority: PL107-110. Title IV, Part B-21st Century Community Learning Centers
Year 1 Project Beginning Date: October 1, 2004   Year 1 Project Ending Date: December 31, 2005

6. Index to this Application: An X has been placed in the New Application column to indicate each schedule that **must** be submitted as a part of the application. The applicant must place an X in this column for each additional schedule submitted to complete the application. For amendments, the applicant must place an X in the Amendment Application column next to the schedule(s) being submitted as part of the amendment.

Sch No.	Schedule Name	New Applic.	Amend Applic.	Sch No.	Schedule Name	New Applic.	Amend. Applic.
1	General Information	X	X	4A	Program Abstract	X	☐
2	Certification for Shared Services Arrangements	X	☐	4B	Program Description	X	☐
3	Budget Summary	X	X	4C	Program Evaluation Design	X	☐
3A	Purpose of Amendment	N/A	X	4D	Equitable Access and Participation	X	☐
	Support Schedules for—			4E	(Other Program Schedules)		
3B	Payroll Costs 6100	X	☐	5	Private Nonprofit Schools	X	☐
3C	Professional and Contracted Services 6200	X	☐	5A	(Other Supplemental Schedules Specify)		
3D	Supplies and Materials 6300	X	☐	6A	General Provisions and Assurances	X	
3E	Other Operating Costs 6400	X	☐	6B	Debarment and Suspension Certification	X	
3F	Debt Service 6500	N/A	N/A	6C	Lobbying Certification	X	
3G	Capital Outlay 6600 (Exclusive of 6619 and 6629)	X	☐	6D	Disclosure of Lobbying Activities		
				6E	NCLB Provisions and Assurances	X	
3H	Building Purchase, Construction or Improvements 6629	N/A	N/A	6F	Program-Specific Provisions and Assurances	X	

Certification and Incorporation

7. I hereby certify that the information contained in this application is, to the best of my knowledge, correct and that the local education agency named above has authorized me as its representative to obligate this agency. I further certify that any ensuing program and activity will be conducted in accordance with all applicable Federal and State laws and regulations, application guidelines and instructions, the Provisions and Assurances, Debarment and Suspension, lobbying requirements, Special Provisions and Assurances, and the schedules attached as applicable. It is understood by the applicant that this application constitutes an offer and, if accepted by Agency or renegotiated to acceptance, will form a binding agreement.

Typed **Name** of Authorized Official Pat Henderson	Telephone Number (806) 863-2282	Date Signed 06/04/2004	
Title of Authorized Official Superintendent			Original Authorized Signature (blue ink preferred)

6 complete copies of the application, at least 3 with original signature(s),
must be received by 5:00 p.m., Thursday, June 10, 2004 in the:
  Texas Education Agency
  William B. Travis Bldg.
  Document Control Center, Room 6-108
  1701 North Congress Avenue   _____
  Austin, Texas 78701-1494   TEA DOCUMENT CONTROL NO.

<table>
<tr><td colspan="2">

For TEA Use Only

Adjustments and/or annotations made on this have been confirmed with

_____

by telephone/FAX on_____

by _____ of TEA.

</td><td colspan="2">

TEXAS EDUCATION AGENCY
Standard Application System (SAS)
Texas 21st Century Community Learning Centers,
Cycle 3
Spring, Summer, and Fall of
2005, 2006, and 2007
--
SCHEDULE #2
Certification for Shared Services Arrangements

</td><td>

__152-906__
County District No.
Lubbock-Cooper ISD
Applicant Agency

</td></tr>
</table>

Program Authority: PL 107-110, Title IV, Part B-21st Century Community Learning Centers

I, as one of the undersigned, certify that to the best of my knowledge, the information contained in this application is correct and complete, that the local education agency (LEA) that I represent has authorized me to file this application, and that such authorization action is recorded in the minutes of the agency's board meeting. The participating or intermediate education agency named below has been designated as the administrative and fiscal agent for this project and is authorized to receive and expend funds for the conduct of this project. The fiscal agent is accountable for all shared services arrangement activities and is therefore responsible for ensuring that all funds including payments to members of shared services arrangements are expended in accordance with applicable laws and regulations. All participating agencies have entered into a written shared services agreement which describes the responsibilities of the fiscal agent and SSA members, including the refund liability that may result from on-site monitoring or audits and the final disposition of equipment, facilities, and materials purchased for this project from funds specified below. It is understood that the fiscal agent is responsible for the refund for any exceptions taken as a result of on-site monitoring or audits; however, based upon the **SHARED SERVICES AGREEMENT**, which must be on file with the fiscal agent for review, the fiscal agent may have recourse to the member agencies where the discrepancy(ies) occurred. All funds arerel eased when the tentative entitlement is released, i.e., any additional funds that result from the maximum entitlement or from reallocation will not require additional signatures. **Each member identified below acknowledges accountability for the requirements contained in Schedules #6A through #6E as applicable.**

Line #	County District Number (A)	Typed Legal Name of Agency (B)	Typed Name and Title of Authorized Representative (C)	Signature (D)	Amount of Funds Designated for Member Use (If Applicable) (E)
01	152-906	Designated Fiscal Agent: Lubbock-Cooper ISD	Pat Henderson, Superintendent		$ 524,700
02	083-902	Member Districts: Loop ISD	Phil Mitchell, Superintendent		$ 41,919
03	153-903	O'Donnell ISD	Dale Read, Superintendent		78,276
04	083-901	Seagraves ISD	Wynn Robinson, Superintendent		107,309
05	110-906	Smyer ISD	Dane Kerns, Superintendent		122,796
06					
07					
08					
09					
10					
11					
12					
13					
14	**TOTAL AMOUNT**				$ 875,000

For TEA Use Only
Adjustments and/or annotations made on this have been confirmed with
_____
by telephone/FAX on_____
by _____ of TEA.

TEXAS EDUCATION AGENCY

Standard Application System (SAS)
Texas 21st Century Community Learning Centers,
Cycle 3
Spring, Summer, and Fall of
2005, 2006, and 2007
--
SCHEDULE #3   Budget Summary
Administrative Costs

____152-906
County District No.
Lubbock-Cooper ISD
Applicant Agency

TEXAS EDUCATION AGENCY

Program Authority: PL 107-110, Title IV, Part B-21st Century Community Learning Centers, Cycle 3

Fund Code/Shared Services Arrangement Code: 265/352

Year 1 Project Period: October 1, 2004 through December 31, 2005

Line No.	Class/Object Description	Schedule Number	C/Object Code	Budgeted Expenditures- Year 1		
				Program	Administration	Total
01	Payroll Costs	3B	6100	$ 376,761	$ 27,009	$ 403,770
02	Professional and Contracted Services	3C	6200	91,500		91,500
03	Supplies and Materials	3D	6300	266,989	1,770	268,759
04	Other Operating Costs	3E	6400	101,137		101,137
05	Debt Service	3F	6500			
06	Capital Outlay (Exclusive of 6619 and 6629)	3G	6600	0		0
07	Building Purchase, Construction or Improvements	3H	6629			
08	Total Direct Costs (Sum of lines 1-7)			836,387	28,779	$ 865,166
09	Indirect Costs LCISD 1.929 only			0	9,834	9,834
10	Total Costs			$ 836,387	$ 38,613 (2)	$ 875,000

11	Payments to Member Districts of Shared Services Arrangements*(3)		6493	$ 350,300	$ 0	$ 350,300

(3)* These costs must be included in lines 01-10 as applicable and must be reflected in the appropriate support schedules.

Administrative Cost Calculation

Enter total amount from Schedule #3
-Budget Summary, Line 10, Last $875,000
—

Multiply by 0.05 (5% limit)   X 0.05

** Enter Maximum Allowable for
   Administration $43,750
____

The amount in Line 10, Administrative Costs, may
 not exceed this amount.

(1) Limited to 5%, or the restricted indirect cost rate, whichever is less if not claiming direct administration costs.

(2)** Districts receiving funds under this initiative must limit administrative expenses, including indirect costs, in each fiscal year to five percent (5%) of the total amount received under this application.

TEXAS EDUCATION AGENCY
Standard Application System (SAS)
Texas 21ˢᵗ Century Community Learning Centers,
Cycle 3
Spring, Summer, and Fall of
2005, 2006, and 2007
--
SCHEDULE #3B   Payroll Costs 6100

__152-906__
County District No.

Lubbock - Cooper ISD
Applicant Agency

Line No.	Description of Payroll Costs (Include gross salaries, wages, and benefits)	Number of Positions	Estimated Percent of Time Charged to Grant	Admini-stration	Total Payroll Costs
01	Program Coordinator	1	10%	$ 6,000	$ 6,000
02	Program Director	1	100%		50,850
03	Technologist	1	100%		29,500
04	Center Coordinator	5	25%	2,500	50,000
05	Grant management support staff	2	20%	9,850	9,850
06	Clerical support staff	1	20%	5,700	5,700
07	**Employee Benefits for Personnel Listed Above (6140)**			2,959	18,145
08	**Substitutes** for Public School **Personnel** (6112) (Explain purpose:) Training on various software and other programs used in the out-of-school-time programs Three days of training @ $55 per day for subs	65	100%		10,725
09	**Extra-Duty Pay**/Beyond Normal **Work Hours** (6119/6121) (Explain purpose:) To operate out-of-school-time programs during the staff's none contracted time –before school, after school, summer school, etc.	75	100%		223,000
10	**TOTAL COSTS**			$ 27,009	$ 403,770

For federally-funded projects, charges to payroll must be documented according to the requirements in the applicable OMB cost principles. Refer to the SAS instructions for Schedule #3B for a summary of these requirements.

<table>
<tr><td colspan="2">

For TEA Use Only

Adjustments and/or annotations made
on this have been confirmed with

_____

by telephone/FAX on_____

by _____ of TEA.
</td><td colspan="2">

TEXAS EDUCATION AGENCY
Standard Application System (SAS)
Texas 21st Century Community Learning Centers,
Cycle 3
Spring, Summer, and Fall of
2005, 2006, and 2007
--
SCHEDULE #3C   Professional and Contracted
Services 6200
</td><td>

<u>152-906</u>
County District No.
Lubbock-
Cooper ISD
Applicant Agency
</td></tr>
</table>

Line No.	Description of Expense Items	ADMINI-STRATION	TOTAL AMOUNTS
01	<u>Contracted Services provided by ESC (6230)</u> (Specify <u>type(s)</u> of services):	$	$
02	<u>Professional/Consulting Services (6210)</u>: (Enter the topic and the total amount to be paid to each consultant/contractor. Include travel costs for consultants and materials provided by consultants in the budgeted amount. Travel costs include reasonable airfare, lodging, meals, and mileage not to exceed 35 cents per mile, etc. Attach separate page if more space is needed.) A. Consultant A Topic: ___Lubbock Community Theatre_____ $ 4,000___ B. Consultant B Topic: ___Outside Program Evaluation_____ $ 9,000___ C. Consultant C Topic: ___TTU staff development programs_____ $ 5,000 _ D. Consultant D Topic: ___Writers author's program_____ $ 2,400___ E. Consultant E Topic: ___SPACLC Programs_____ $ 2,000___ F. Consultant F Topic: ___Stretch-n-Grow preK Program_____ $ 15,000___ 125 preK Students @ $12 per month for 10 months (For each consultant/contractor receiving more than $10,000, attach a budget by cost category and line item to this schedule.)		$ 37,400 _____ (Enter the total amount for professional/ consulting services.)
03	Contracted <u>maintenance and repair</u> of equipment purchased with grant funds (6240)		
04	<u>Utilities (6250)</u>, including telephone, FAX charges, and telecommunication services. Also includes water, electricity, and gas for heating/cooling for grant activities conducted before school, after school, or during the summer		24,700
05	<u>Rental or lease of equipment or building space (6260)</u> (specify type and purpose):		
06	<u>Audit fees/expenses</u> (allowable only for audits of **federal** grant programs conducted in accordance with the requirements in OMB Circular A-133, Audits)		
07	<u>Services provided by an Internal Service Fund. Identify types of services:</u>		
08	TA/RA positions (2 half-time) at Texas Tech University College of Education to allow for the coordination and recruitment of mentors along with staff development activities and research programs to determine the effectiveness of the program activities.		29,400
09	<u>Tuition</u> Services (6220) Not for staff. **See instructions**: (Explain purpose:)		
10	**TOTAL COSTS**	$	$ 91,500

All contracted services must be provided by persons not employed by the applicant. The applicant shall not use or pay any consultant if the services could have been rendered by applicant's employees. "Honorariums" are not allowable expenditures. Refer to the SAS Instructions. **Copyright/Ownership**: The grantee must ensure that the Texas Education Agency retains copyright and ownership of any and all materials/products conceived or developed under the grant by any and all contractors. Grantee must ensure that such copyright/ownership is clearly stated in any and all written agreements/contracts for services.

For TEA Use Only		
Adjustments and/or annotations made on this have been confirmed with		

_____

by telephone/FAX on_____

by _____ of TEA.

TEXAS EDUCATION AGENCY
Standard Application System (SAS)
Texas 21st Century Community Learning Centers,
Cycle 3
Spring, Summer, and Fall of
2005, 2006, and 2007
--
SCHEDULE #3D—Supplies and Materials 6300

__152-906__
County District No.
Lubbock-Cooper
ISD
Applicant Agency

Line No.	Description of Expense Items	ADMINI-STRATION	TOTAL AMOUNTS
01	General supplies and materials (6390), including consumable teaching and office supplies; workbooks; audio-visual aids, such as filmstrips, VCR tapes, CD-Rom disks, diskettes, computer tapes; and supplies for technology	$	$ 135,815
02	Textbooks and other reading materials (6320) (includes textbooks and magazines, periodicals, newspapers and reference books placed in the classroom or in an office. Also includes library books and media that are not capitalized and/or that have a useful life of one year or less. (Subscriptions to periodicals/magazines must be in the name of the organization and not in the name of an individual)		50,300
03	Testing materials (6330) (does not include scoring of tests)		
04	Computer hardware (not capitalized) (List hardware requested and the estimated quantity for each. Describe the use/purpose of the hardware in accomplishing the objectives of the project. Attach an additional page if necessary. An amendment is required if the use/purpose of the hardware changes, if the estimated quantity increases by more than 20 percent, or if a new item is requested.) 1 Laptop for Program Director @ 1,770 to allow the director to have access to information at each of the centers 35 Desktop computers @ 1,150 to allow the students to have access to computers that will be able to operate the extra instructional software to provide other methods of instruction for the students	1,770	42,020
05	Computer software (not capitalized) (List software requested and the estimated quantity for each. Describe the use/purpose of the software in accomplishing the objectives of the project. Attach an additional page if necessary. An amendment is required if the use/purpose of the software changes, if the estimated quantity increases by more than 20 percent, or if a new item is requested.) PLATO, Lexia, Kurzweil Language Lab, Failure Free, Accelerated Reader, Success For All, and teacher selected software for the 35 computers to allow the students to have additional instructional programs to expand the methods for instruction that are different from the normal classroom instructional methods		40,624
06	Other equipment not capitalized (List equipment requested and the estimated quantity for each. Describe the use/purpose of the equipment in accomplishing the objectives of the project. Attach an additional page if necessary. An amendment is required if the use/purpose of the equipment changes, if the estimated quantity increases by more than 20 percent, or if a new item is requested.)		
07	Supplies/materials for maintenance and/or operations (6310), including gasoline/fuel for transportation, janitorial supplies, building maintenance supplies, and supplies for upkeep of equipment		
08	Food Service (6340) (supplies and materials for the district food service program). Identify purpose of district food service costs:		
09			
10	**TOTAL COSTS**	$1,770	$ 268,759

All costs include shipping and handling costs.

<table>
<tr><td colspan="2">

For TEA Use Only

Adjustments and/or annotations made
on this have been confirmed with

_____

by telephone/FAX on_____

by _____ of TEA.
</td><td colspan="2">

TEXAS EDUCATION AGENCY
Standard Application System (SAS)
Texas 21st Century Community Learning Centers,
Cycle 3
Spring, Summer, and Fall of
2005, 2006, and 2007
--
SUPPORT SCHEDULE #3E--Other Operating Costs
6400
</td><td>

152-906
County District No.
Lubbock-Cooper
ISD
Applicant Agency
</td></tr>
</table>

Line No.	Description of Expense Items	ADMINI-STRATION	TOTAL AMOUNTS
01	Travel Costs for Employees, Students, and Non-Employees (6410), including: a. In-State Travel, which includes lowest available airfare; actual cost for lodging not to exceed $80/day (not including tax), meals not to exceed $30/day, and mileage not to exceed 35 cents per mile or local policy, whichever is less. b. Out-of-State Travel, which includes lowest available airfare; actual cost of lodging and meals not to exceed maximum allowable federal government rates for the locale or local policy, whichever is less; and reimbursement for mileage not to exceed 35 cents per mile or local policy, whichever is less. c. Conference/Workshop/Seminar Registration Fees (Topics must be directly related to the purposes of the grant.) SEDL and other 21st Century grant training programs.		(Enter the estimated amount for each) a. $8,500 b. $ c. $ 4,500
02	Membership Dues (6499) in Professional Organizations (membership must be in the name of the grantee organization and not in the name of an individual).		
03	Awards for Recognition/Incentives for Participation (6499) (nominal in cost). Identify types of awards/incentives to be provided:		
04	~~Reimbursement of tuition (6499) and fees for staff completing university/college courses directly related to grant. Not Allowable with these grant funds.~~		
05	Insurance (6420). Identify purpose:		
06			
07	Transportation costs other than those incurred for the purpose of transporting students to and from the regular school day. Please refer to SAS Instructions. Explain purpose: Afterschool and summer buses for students		63,637
08	Food and Beverage Costs (not provided by the district food service program) (6499). Refer to instructions for allowable food and beverage costs. Explain purpose: Lite-snacks for after school and summer programs		9,500
09	Stipends to Non-employees (6413). Explain purpose: Pre-service mentors, parental training, and educational programs for students.		15,000
10	**TOTAL COSTS**	$	$ 101,137

Refer to the SAS instructions for Schedule #3E for additional explanation and requirements.

For TEA Use Only
Adjustments and/or annotations made on this have been confirmed with
_____
by telephone/FAX on _____
by _____ of TEA.

TEXAS EDUCATION AGENCY
Standard Application System (SAS)

Texas 21st Century Community Learning Centers, Cycle 3
Spring, Summer, and Fall of 2005, 2006, and 2007
-- SUPPORT SCHEDULE #4A—Program Abstract
(Including Needs and Objectives)

152-906
County District No.

Lubbock-Cooper ISD
Applicant Agency

PART 1: CENTER INFORMATION

Part 1: Center Information Each Center must have a completed Center Information Form.

Center #1 1. Name: __Lubbock-Cooper__	3. Physical Street Address, including City, Texas, ZIP 16302 Loop 493 Lubbock, TX 79423	5. Estimated number of students to be served: ___1679
2. Number of Participating schools:_4__	4. Center Phone Number (806) 863-2282	6. Estimated number of adults to be served: _325_
7. Age range of students (not including adults) Youngest: _3_____ Oldest: __15___	8. Grade range of students (not including adults) Lowest Grade: preK Highest Grade: _8th___	9. Identify Adjunct Site, if applicable: _North Elementary Campus
10. a. Summers 2005 Days per week: __5_____ Hours per day: __8_____ Weeks per summer: _5	10. b. Summer 2006 Days per week: ___5_____ Hours per day: ___8_____ Weeks per summer: _5	10. c. Summer 2007 Days per week: ___5_____ Hours per day: ___8_____ Weeks per summer: _5
11. a. Spring School Year 2004-2005 and Fall 2005-2006 Days per week: __4_____ Hours per day: __3_____ Weeks per school year: __28_____	11. b. Spring School Year 2005-2006 and Fall 2006-2007 Days per week: ___4_____ Hours per day: ___3_____ Weeks per school year: __28_____	11. c. Spring School Year 2006-2007 and Fall 2007-2008 Days per week: ___4_____ Hours per day: ___3_____ Weeks per school year: 28

Center #2 1. Name: _Loop_	3. Physical Street Address, including City, Texas, ZIP Hwy 303 Loop, TX 79342	5. Estimated number of students to be served: ___134_____
2. Number of Participating schools: _1__	4. Center Phone Number (806) 487-6411	6. Estimated number of adults to be served: _20__
7. Age range of students (not including adults) Youngest: _4___ Oldest:__19__	8. Grade range of students (not including adults) Lowest Grade: _preK_ Highest Grade:12	9. Identify Adjunct Site, if applicable: _____
10. a. Summers 2005 Days per week: ___5_____ Hours per day: __8_____ Weeks per summer: _5	10. b. Summer 2006 Days per week: ___5_____ Hours per day: __8_____ Weeks per summer: _5	10. c. Summer 2007 Days per week: __5_____ Hours per day: __8_____ Weeks per summer: _5
11. a. Spring School Year 2004-2005 and Fall 2005-2006 Days per week: __4_____ Hours per day: __3_____ Weeks per school year: ___34_____	11. b. Spring School Year 2005-2006 and Fall 2006-2007 Days per week: ___4_____ Hours per day: __3_____ Weeks per school year: __34_____	11. c. Spring School Year 2006-2007 and Fall 2007-2008 Days per week: __4_____ Hours per day: __3_____ Weeks per school year: ___34_____

For TEA Use Only
Adjustments and/or annotations made on this have been confirmed with _____ _____   by telephone/FAX on_____ by _____ of TEA.

TEXAS EDUCATION AGENCY
Standard Application System (SAS)
Texas 21ˢᵗ Century Community
Learning Centers, Cycle 3
Spring, Summer, and Fall of
2005, 2006, and 2007
SUPPORT SCHEDULE #4A—
Program Abstract
(Including Needs and Objectives
continued)--

152-906
County District No.
Lubbock-Cooper
ISD
Applicant Agency

Part 2: Participating Campus Name(S) And Information.

Each campus may only be in one center and in one application.

*Copy as many pages as needed to complete the listing of all participating campuses in all Centers included in the application. **Be sure to read and carefully follow the instructions (Part II RFA, pages 35-36) prior to completing the schedule.**

---

1. Check the box to indicate the correct center number for each participating campus.

[x] Center #1; ☐ Center #2;

☐Center #3; ☐Center #4;

☐ Center #5

---

4. Title I Schoolwide Campus 2003-2004:

[x] Yes or ☐ No
(must be 40% or greater economically disadvantaged)

_____
2003-2004 Receiving funds Part A, Title I:

[x] Yes ☐ No

---

7. Percentage LEP Students:

2003-2004: ___3.9___ %

---

2. Campus Name:

North Elementary - LCISD

Street Address:
3202 108ᵗʰ

City: Lubbock, Texas

ZIP Code: 79423

9 digit Campus Number:
152-903-103

---

5. Title I-Part A Campus in Need of Improvement for 2003-2004:

☐ Yes or [x] No

_____
It Yes, check applicable year

☐ Year 1 or ☐ Year ☐.
:

---

8. Academic Performance: Spring 2004 Administration of TAKS

8. A. Enter the percent of students that Met Standard on all tests taken:	81
8. B. Enter the percent of students that Met Standard In Reading:	91
8. C. Enter the percent of students that Met Standard in Mathematics:	84
8. D. Enter the percent of students that Met Standard in Science:	n/a

---

3. Total Enrollment:

2002-2003: ___436___

2003-2004: ___501___

---

6. Campus Receiving Title I -Part A funds 2003-2004:

[x] Yes or ☐ No

---

9. Percentage Economically Disadvantaged:

2002-2003: ___50.7___ % (AEIS Report)

2003-2004: ___51.2___ %

---

9. RISKY BEHAVIORS
Enter by school-year indicated from PEIMS 425 Report
A. number of incidents in each category for each year as indicated and
B. the percentage of students involved:

Category of Referral: School Year:	Non-Criminal 2002-2003		Criminal 2002-2003		Check the appropriate response: 1. Did the number of non-criminal referrals
	A. # of Incidents	B. % of Students	A. # of Incidents	B. % of Students	☐ increase [x] remain the same or ☐ decrease during 2003-2004? 2. Did the number of criminal referrals
	38	8	0	0	☐ increase [x] remain the same or ☐ decrease during 2003-2004?

Limited to the space provided.   **Retain the format given.**

For TEA Use Only
Adjustments and/or annotations made on this have been confirmed with
_____
by telephone/FAX on_____
by _____ of TEA

TEXAS EDUCATION AGENCY
Standard Application System (SAS)

Texas 21st Century Community Learning Centers,
Cycle 3
Spring, Summer, and Fall of
2005, 2006, and 2007
SUPPORT SCHEDULE #4A—Program Abstract
(Including Needs and Objectives continued)--
(page 1)

__152-906__
County District No.

__Lubbock-Cooper ISD__
Applicant Agency

Over the last few years Lubbock-Cooper ISD (LCISD), Loop ISD, O'Donnell ISD (OISD), Seagraves ISD (SeISD) and Smyer ISD (SmISD) have joined together in applying for grants. The five school districts have received several grants that have helped them more quickly achieve their long-range goals that have resulted in the improvement of all students' educational outcomes. The Long Range Performance Plan (LRPP), District Improvement Plan (DIP) and Campus Improvement Plans (CIP) of the five districts align in the sense that the goals of developing programs, that more fully meet the life long learning needs of students and other community members, was a theme contained within each school district's plans. The leadership of each of these school districts sees the role of the school going beyond the basic 8 to 4 education for normal school age children, to one where the school district must make its resources available to everyone within the community to promote a general improvement in each community.

The community members of Loop (location of LISD in Gaines County), O'Donnell (location of OISD in Lynn County), Seagraves (location of SeISD in Gaines County), Smyer (location of SmISD in Hockley County), and Woodrow (location of LCISD in Lubbock County) have joined together in developing this 21st Century Community Learning Centers grant (see attached letters of commitment). They have done this because of unique resources that each school and community brings to the grant and to make the program more cost effective.

Demographic and TEA Rating Needs Information:

LCISD – located in the un-incorporated community of Woodrow, Texas, population 120 and serves 2,409 students preK-12. These students have the following characteristics: 69% are Anglo, 30% are Hispanic, and 1% are African American: of these students, 41.1% qualify for the free/reduce lunch program, 14.6% qualify for special education services, and 3% are LEP students. TEA has classified the two zip codes that LCISD serves as areas of high juvenile crime. LCISD is 9 miles south of Lubbock, Texas. Lubbock County's unemployment rate is 2.9% (37% below state average). The per capita income is $23,451 or 7.56% below state average. 27.1% of persons 0-17 years of age live below the poverty level or 15% above the state average. The number of births to persons below the age of 17 is 8.7% or 43% above the state average. The number of reported STD's (sexually transmitted diseases) is almost double the state average and Lubbock County is ranked 5th in STD's. Lastly, the Intermediate campus has been designated by TEA as "Needs Improvement" based on the 2003 TAKS test. (four of five the campuses qualify for inclusion in this grant)

LISD – located in the incorporated community of Loop, Texas, population 178 and serves 138 students preK-12. These students have the following characteristics: 51% are Anglo and 49% are Hispanic, 53.6% qualify for the free/reduce lunch program, 13.8% qualify for special education services, and 11.6% are LEP students. LISD is 54 miles southwest of Lubbock, Texas. Gaines County's unemployment rate is 5.4% (17.4% above state average). The per capita income is $18,191 or 28.29% below state average. 20.5% of persons 0-17 years of age live below the poverty level or 22% above the state average. The number of births to persons below the age of 17 is 5.7% or 7% below the state average. The number of reported STD's is almost the state average. The K-3 students were identified as Low-performing under Title I, Part A and the 9-12 students were identified as being on a Low-performing campus for 2003 TAKS scores.

OISD – located in the incorporated community of O'Donnell, Texas, population 1,011 and serves 318 students preK-12. These students have the following characteristics: 39% are Anglo, 60% are Hispanic, and 1% are African American: of these students, 79.5% qualify for the free/reduce lunch program, 14.6% qualify for special education services, and 12% are LEP students. OISD is a State of Texas and a National Title 1 Select award winner. OISD is 41 miles south of Lubbock, Texas. Lynn County's unemployment rate is 4.4% (4% below state average). The per capita income is $17,743 or 30.06% below state average. 32.9% of persons 0-17 years of age live below the poverty level or 39% above the state average. The number of births to persons below the age of 17 is 8.2% or 34% above the state average. The number of reported STD's is almost the state average. The K-3 students were identified as Low-performing under Title I, Part A.

SeISD – located in the incorporated city of Seagraves, Texas, population 2,334 and serves and serves 648 students preK-12. These students have the following characteristics: 23% are Anglo, 66% are Hispanic, 9% are African American and 2% are Native American: of these students, 69.9% qualify for the free/reduce lunch program, 15.1% qualify for special education services, 13.3% are LEP students and 1% have had disciplinary placements. SeISD is 62 miles southwest of Lubbock, Texas. Gaines County's unemployment rate is 5.4% (17.4% above state average). The per capita income is $18,191 or 28.29% below state average. 20.5% of persons 0-17 years of age live below the poverty level or 22% above the state average. The number of births to persons below the age of 17 is 5.7% or 7% below the state average. The number of reported STD's is almost the state average. The K-3 students were identified as Low-performing under Title I, Part A and the 9-12 students were identified as being on a Low-performing campus for 2003 TAKS scores.

SmISD – located in the incorporated city of Smyer, Texas, population 480 and serves 349 students preK-12. These students have the following characteristics: 69% are Anglo, 28% are Hispanic, and 3% are African American: of these students, 50.8% qualify for the free/reduce lunch program, 8.6% qualify for special education services, and 6% are LEP students. SISD is 21 miles west of Lubbock, Texas. Hockley County's unemployment rate is 6.8% (48% above state average). The per capita income is $18,516 or 27.01% below state average. 25.5% of persons 0-17 years of age live below the poverty level or 8% above the state average. The number of births to persons below the age of 17 is 10.9% or 79% above the state average. The number of reported STD's is almost the state average. The Elementary campus was designated as "Needing Improvement" under Title I. Lastly, the High School campus has been designated by TEA as "Needs Improvement" based on the 2003 TAKS test.

The basic needs of the general demographic information can be summed up as being ones related to the following: lower income for the parents which results in more children living in poverty; higher rates for underage sexual activity as measured by 'under 17 years old birth rates' and STD's; less opportunity for educational experiences; and higher crime rates in the LCISD area. These items have been exacerbated by the fact that in 4 of the last 6 years all of these counties have been declared federal disaster areas due to weather related destruction of crops. This last fact has greatly limited the ability of the local community to provide "extra" programs.

Academic Needs: Detailed information from the AEIS and TAAS/TAKS scores for each grade tested, exhibit a major problem in addition the specific lower performance ratings stated above. This problem is that there is a discrepancy between the Anglo and Hispanic students. In every case the

<table>
<tr><td colspan="2">For TEA Use Only</td></tr>
</table>

For TEA Use Only

For TEA Use Only
Adjustments and/or annotations made on this have been confirmed with

_____

by telephone/FAX on_____

by _____ of TEA

TEXAS EDUCATION AGENCY
Standard Application System (SAS)

Texas 21ˢᵗ Century Community Learning Centers,
Cycle 3
Spring, Summer, and Fall of
2005, 2006, and 2007
SUPPORT SCHEDULE #4A—Program Abstract
(Including Needs and Objectives continued)--
(page 2)

152-906
County District No.

Lubbock-Cooper ISD
Applicant Agency

Hispanic students' performance on these measures of academic skills is lower than the Anglo students. This means that, though the students receive the same instruction from the same teacher in the same class, they are not effectively having their educational needs met. We find this an unacceptable condition. We believe that we are "Building the future…One student at a time!" Therefore, we cannot accept lower performance of this group of students. Additionally, there are a much larger percentage of Hispanic students who are behind their age-peers in graduation from high school. This is why a major focus of this grant is improving the Hispanic students' access to multi-forms of educational experiences (along with LEP students who tend to be Hispanic). This is also why we have looked at building a leadership core of Hispanic students who are not just expected to go to college, but to go to the nation's leading colleges and universities. We believe that this change in mind-set for the staff, students, and parents will cause all of our students to see what is possible if they dream big enough. (This problem does extend to Economically Disadvantaged students.) The general scores on the TAKS for all students have deceased for all students but the above sub-group students have declined proportionally more.

These sub-group students' parents also tend to have less formal education experience. This caused LCISD to develop an adult education program, linking the education of the students to that of the parents in an after school setting that will be used as the model for developing the community education aspects of this 21ˢᵗ Century grant proposal. The benefits have been great for both these students and their parents. The students report that they never knew their parents thought school was important enough to give up their time to increase their education. The students have subsequently done better in their classes. The parents have been making progress towards obtaining GED, but more importantly, they now report they feel they can take a more active role in their children's education. These parents are now also coming to the campuses and helping teachers, which rarely occurred before the program. The parents reported that before the program they did not feel that they knew enough to help at school. Now they report that feel that the school's staff want and benefit from their help.

Lastly, several of the campuses have been designated by TEA for Needing Improvement. These are – 1) Seagraves Elementary and Junior High for Title I – Part A; and Smyer Elementary for Title I – Part A; 2) Loop, O'Donnell, and Seagraves preK-3 for Texas Reading First Initiative, and 3) Lubbock-Cooper Intermediate, Loop 9-12, Seagraves High School, and Smyer High School for TAKS testing results. These designations qualify this proposal for the 10 Federal Priority point under schools identified as in need of improvement under Title I, section 1116 School Improvement. Taken with the differences in TAAS/TAKS performance of our Hispanic and Economically Disadvantaged when compared to our Anglo student again points out the need for our Learning Center proposal because we are targeting these students for inclusion in these out-of-school-time learning programs. Further, since we will use the intergenerational model that LCISD has developed to link the learning of parents and their children, we will be able to target the population at the school districts that are in the most need of support.

Community Needs: With the drop in farm income related to the drought disaster conditions; there are not enough available funds to establish "extra" programs. These counties have been declared disaster areas in four years of the last six years. During the last several years because of other grants, LCISD, LISD, OISD, SeISD, and SmISD surveyed their community stakeholders to determine needs in the community. From these surveys, it was determined that there were the following needs: 1) increase the early intervention in at-risk students' education; 2) provide before-school, after-school, summer programs, and Saturday school for the education and supervision of students; 3) provide adult education for GED preparation, English Language Arts skills, and technology skills; 4) provide training in parenting skills and special population issues; 5) provide methods to increase parental involvement with the school district in their children's education; 6) provide methods for integrating technology into the curriculum; 7) develop a program to integrate other methods of instruction for the most at-risk students; 8) provide methods for character education; 9) provide a location for broadband width access to the Internet and other forms of technology training for the entire community; 10) develop a health and fitness program that can improve the general health within each of the communities and 11) to develop methods to integrate all of the community stakeholders into a reform process of restructuring within these five school districts.

Instructional Staff Needs: One of the current facts-of-life in times of reducing budgets is that, programs that the instructors determine that would be effective in meeting the needs of specific students cannot be purchased unless they are already in the budget. This greatly limits the ability of teachers - who are the first line in educating the students - to obtain programs that they know would benefit their student(s). We must have funds to allow teachers to purchase programs that they feel will help their students. We feel that the small amount of funds that we have built into this proposal for these types of purchases will provide large returns for our students. We also feel that by having the TTU graduate research student connection, we could research the effects of this program on our student learning to establish best practices. Also, this TTU connect will promote all teachers being aware of current educational research. Further, because of the use of technology to disseminate information about what the staff is doing that is working, other teachers will be able to develop a system by which they determine the best practices for teaching our at-risk and other targeted students. The two TTU professors who will be heading this area are recognized national experts of Hispanic Student Studies (full resumes in appendix).

Required Statements and Why 21ˢᵗ Century Grant is Needed: All of the campuses being served have at least 40% of the students identified as being economically disadvantaged. Each of the campuses has seen a decrease in the level of student performance on the new TAKS test as compared to the TAAS. Also, each of the campuses saw sub-group students' performance lower. The before, after, and summer school type programs have been seen to decrease this gap in sub-groups' scores and increase the TAAS/TAKS performance of other students who were members of groups that other grants have provided these supportive types of programs. Without the funding of the 21ˢᵗ Century grant none of the school districts are going to be able to create a general broad based before, after, and summer school program that will allow all students to have access to these programs. The community stakeholders have shown their support for the development of this general out-of-school-time program (letters in appendix) but funding caps will not allow new programs to be started (though the local budgets would allow for them to be maintained). Lastly, by having a 21ˢᵗ Century grant funded that links this many communities and their stakeholders, we believe that at the end of state funding many of the mentoring and community linked programs will be a part of the culture of each of the schools and therefore will be maintained. This will allow us to develop the culture of Life-Long-Learning that will promote success for all students. To assure that our programming decisions are driven by student data we are using an outside evaluator who has served this role in federally funded 21ˢᵗ Century programs (resume in appendix). The program coordinator holds 19 certifications from TEA which allows him to assure that effective instruction is occurring and that the out-of-school-time programs are linked to the regular day instruction (resume in appendix).

For TEA Use Only
Adjustments and/or annotations made on this have been confirmed with
_____
by telephone/FAX on_____
by _____ of TEA.

TEXAS EDUCATION AGENCY
Standard Application System (SAS)

Texas 21st Century Community Learning Centers,
Cycle 3
Spring, Summer, and Fall of
2005, 2006, and 2007
SUPPORT SCHEDULE #4A—Program Abstract
(Including Needs and Objectives continued)--

__152-906__
County District No.

Lubbock-Cooper ISD
Applicant Agency

From the above needs assessments, the following broad objectives were developed. The West Texas Community Learning Centers will: 1) reduce risk for educational failure for all children by providing extended-day and extended-year integrated activities which promote academic excellence in a safe and drug-free environment, 2) reduce risk of educational failure for younger children by providing additional preK activities during the regular school day along with establishing a fitness program for these students and their parents, 3) increase the level of knowledge and quality-of-life for all community members through the adult education activities and community fitness programs, and 4) develop a large non-partisan constituency that will hold the school districts accountable for high academic standards and promote the goals of the 21st Century grant while providing the base to continue these programs after funding ends.

The extended-day and extended-year activities will be used to increase the general academic performance of all of the students. The anticipated results for the students from this part of the program are: 1) increase academic performance as measured by grades, 2) gains in promotion and graduate credits with a goal of 100% promotion and graduation with age-peers, 3) increased scores on TAKS with the goal of 100% pass rate, and 4) increase enrollment in AP and other higher level courses where students can obtain college credits. We expect that due to nature of this programming to have student attendance at the programs over 80% at the end of the first year. The anticipated results for the parents and other community stakeholders are: 1) increased number of parents and other stakeholders mentoring at the campuses, 2) increased use of the campus technology infrastructure to allow these stakeholders to gain abilities to use technology, and 3) increased intergenerational literacy programs from using the campus libraries as a literacy center for the community. The center will actively recruit students from the targeted populations set forth in the RFA but all students enrolled at each of the campuses will have access to these programs. The community mentors will be recruited from the various community groups who have stated they will support the program in this manner. The activities will build on programs that have been proven to work at one or more of the school districts in the consortium. The upper level students will have access to credit recovery programs that are technology based which will allow them to rejoin their age-peers for graduation. Additionally, teacher directed academic programs, UIL based activities, accelerated reader and special needs student activities will be included. The summer program will provide field based learning activities to extend the regular school curriculum and provide the targeted students with the background knowledge to be effective in a normal educational setting. The effects of these programs will be to increase the passing rates of students on TAKS, assure that they have the academic skills to be promoted, provide a base for increasing student performance in all core (reading, math, science, and social studies) content area and ultimately produce high school graduates who have the skills to become life long learners.

The preK program will extend the current curriculum and parental involvement to provide a solid base for all subsequent educational activities for these stakeholders. The community members and school district staff felt that providing a base program at this level would allow LEP and Hispanic students to obtain a much better start in school and living a healthy life style (Stretch-n-Grow program) which is a concern of this sub-group's students' parents. This program can and will be done during the regular school day which will help develop in these students' parents the mind-set that we want them at school and involved with their children's education. We believe that this form of early intervention will allow these students to have the extra exposure to academic activities that will allow them to effectively bridge the gaps that we see in upper level students from similar backgrounds. We believe that this focus will also increase parental involvement with the school and the literacy of their young children. This statement is made because of all the schools' experience with the full day preK program and LCISD's parent/student program.

The learning centers will use the program that LCISD has seen to be effective in helping the parents of the targeted students increase their general level of education. We will use a combination of technology based and other trainings to help the centers become a place where all community members feel they can come to find information, improve their level of knowledge, and have access to training that leads to GED or other forms of certification. We will open the libraries of the schools during the afterschool programs. Each library has full access to the Internet that is screened according to Child Protective Code contained in the e-rate plans. The librarians will help the parent/community member mentors make effective use of the resources of the libraries and the Internet in extending the mentoring of their students. This will also assist these stakeholders in becoming life long learners and see that the schools have something to offer them even if it has been years since they graduated from high school.

We will use the training and activities of several organizations to promote the community taking a more active role with each school - WTSO and SPACLC. We believe that increasing the involvement of all community members with the schools will increase understanding among the groups within each community. Further, this will promote use of the schools' resources in a manner that extends the benefits beyond just providing preK-12 education to becoming a general community asset. This will allow the community members to develop new ways of looking at their community with a focus that links groups together who then can have a greater effect on the quality of life. The learning centers will become a key to future development in each of the communities. All of these programs will allow the consortium to develop programs that can request funds from other sources to continue the program once this grant ends along with building the community support to continue the successful program with other local funds. We will be able to use the technology infrastructure of the schools to provide access to educational opportunities that would not be possible without the formation of community learning centers through the funding of the 21st Century program. We will use this technology infrastructure to support staff development and dissemination of information about the programs both within the community and through the TTU link to the world. The academic programs developed will increase our students' proficiency in the core content areas and allow them to exceed Adequate Yearly Progress to gain more then one year's growth for each year's education which will allow students that are behind age-peers to rejoin them. The methods of evaluation of these programs will provide us with data, through pre/post testing that the vender academic software and other academic programs that will allow our staff to make informed determination of the most effective methods of instruction for each student. We will be able to use the power of the Internet to access the knowledge of the world and provide resources to our community stakeholders that they might not otherwise be able to access. The quality of the programs will cause students, parents, and other community stakeholders to want to come to the afterschool programs so we can meet the objective of the RFA for at least 80% attendance of students choosing to come to the program. We will be able to "Build the future…One person at a time!" and by viewing the centers in this manner we will be able to build communities where life long learning is the norm and all community members see the value of working together to better the lives of everyone - we will be able to create 21st Century Community Learning Centers.

For TEA Use Only
Adjustments and/or annotations made on this have been confirmed with
_____
By telephone/FAX on _____
by _____ of TEA.

TEXAS EDUCATION AGENCY
Standard Application System (SAS)

Texas 21st Century Community Learning Centers, Cycle 3
Spring, Summer, and Fall of
2005, 2006, and 2007
TEXAS EDUCATION AGENCY

152-906
County District No.

Lubbock-Cooper ISD
Applicant Agency

SCHEDULE #4B--Program Description - Part 2
Program Strategies

Limit to 9 pages. Arial or Times New Roman; Front only, size not less than 9 point. (Exclusive of Sustainability Chart)

Introduction:

"Partnerships must be viewed as an essential component of school organizations that influence student development and learning, rather than as an optimal activity or matter of public relations." (Epstein, Coates, Salinas, Sanders, and Simon, 1997) Effective school-community partnerships can:

- Extend learning opportunities for students and staff (Otterbourg, 1986);
- Assist students to succeed in school and life, support staff in their work, and improve school programs and school climate (Institute for Responsive Education, 1996);
- Positively impact student attendance, aspirations for post-secondary education, enrollment in challenging high school curriculum, and successful transitions from special education to regular classes (Jordan, Orazco, and Averett, 2002);
- Provide mutually beneficial resources to schools and community partners (U.S. Department of Education, 1993); and
- Enable schools to become assets for community and economic development (Cahill, 1996).

The process of developing a community learning centers grant proposal lends itself to the creation of these partnerships in that at each of the five communities, the school staff works with various community stakeholders to form the programs that are presented in this proposal. At several points in the process of developing this proposal various groups had input into the design of the program. In "Help at Last: Developing Effective School-Community Partnerships" a basic roadmap is given for methods of teaming the community and the school that was used in the creation of the centers and the obtaining of the input (RMC Research Corporation, 2002). Because of these school districts working together in the past on other grants and developing this proposal, we have been able to develop a shared vision among the schools that can be extended by the funding of this grant which will supplement all of the school districts' current programs. To this end we are forming the West Texas Community Learning Centers Consortium (WTCLCC) which will allow the five school districts to work with local Community and Faith Based Organizations to form a total program which meets the needs of each of the communities, these community's stakeholders, the students and the parents, the staff of the school districts and the goals of the 21st Century Grant. The single most important factor in remediating risk factors of our targeted students, their parents and other community members is that this grant will create an integrated complete life long learning program for improving the quality of life in each of the communities. For the student we will extend this concept to be based in the TAKS assessments so that we can assure that every student will make adequate yearly progress and graduate with their age-peers. This type of program is beyond the normal function of school districts because we are attempting to develop Life Long Learners, and not just graduating students from high school when the learning of all community members is factored into the program. **Supplement-Not-Supplant:** The programs developed will supplement the current education of our students and none of the current programs will supplant any of the current programs at any of the school districts. Each school district will assure this by continuing to fund any similar program to the 21st Century Programs at the same level. The services to the students and the community will be expanded. We are looking at developing the infrastructure within each community so that all members of the community can benefit from the programs. None of the programs required by law will be done with 21st Century funds.

Program Activities:

There will be four main programs. These programs were developed from the need analysis and input from staff, students, parents, and community stakeholders. This data has been collected over the last four years and specifically for the 21st Century over the last year. The needs and related objectives can be broken down in the following: 1) reduce risk for educational failure for all children by providing extended-day and extended-year integrated activities which promote academic excellence in a safe and drug-free environment, 2) reduce risk of educational failure for younger children by providing additional preK activities during the regular school day along with establishing a fitness program for these students and their parents, 3) increase the level of knowledge and quality-of-life for all community members through the adult education activities and community fitness programs, and 4) develop a large non-partisan constituency that will hold the school districts accountable for high academic standards and promote the goals of the 21st Century grant while providing the base to continue these programs after funding ends.

The first of these four objectives we are calling *Enrich Me* because the programs related to the extended day and extended year times will "enrich" the education of the students. WTCLCC will provide extended-day and extended-year activities for the *Enrich Me* program will include: 1) expanded academic instruction before-school, after-school and on weekends directly related to current curriculum to help all students exceed state educational standards; 2) enrichment academic instruction before-school, after-school, on weekends, and during the summer designed to expand the life experiences of the students, their parents, and other community members; 3) technology and telecommunication education programs before-school, after-school, on weekends, and during the summer for individuals of all ages; 4) before-school, after-school, weekend, and summer recreational and cultural programs for individuals of all ages; 5) health and nutrition programs for individuals of all ages; 6) expanded library service hours since none of the communities currently have public libraries; 7) direct and integrated services for individuals with disabilities that use technology and other programs to meet these community members' special needs; 8) adult English Language Arts for English Language Learners (formally known as English as a Second Language) and GED preparation programs; 9) college course exploration and/or dual credit programs; 10) parenting skill development programs; 11) community member training on 21st Century goals, developing community capacity, developing community leaders, and academic standards; 12) training for community members on special populations individuals' unique needs; 13) training on how to create and maintain intergenerational programs; 14) training on how to create safe and drug free communities; 15) special preK program for early intervention; and 16) a general method of researching all of these activities to modify the program to improve it on an ongoing basis.

The *Enrich Me* programs will be designed to use a combination of technology based, hands-on materials, and life-experiences to increase the student's knowledge base so that regular academic instruction will be more effective. We will also include specialized service programs to serve our

For TEA Use Only
Adjustments and/or annotations made on this have been confirmed with
_____
By telephone/FAX on _____
by _____ of TEA.

TEXAS EDUCATION AGENCY
Standard Application System (SAS)

Texas 21st Century Community Learning Centers, Cycle 3
Spring, Summer, and Fall of
2005, 2006, and 2007
TEXAS EDUCATION AGENCY

SCHEDULE #4B--Program Description - Part 2
Program Strategies

152-906
County District No.

Lubbock-Cooper ISD
Applicant Agency

special population students. We will use UIL academic activities as another linkage to the current curriculum and method for assuring that TAKS goals are met. We will include programs that are designed to meet these special students' needs - Dyslexia software, Lexia, Failure Free, Bridges, Locan, SOI, Kurzweil Language programs, etc. We will integrate all students together in these programs so that they can learn that everyone has problems and/or handicaps that must be overcome. We will model the after-school and summer enrichment program that LCISD has developed over the last five years because it has proven to be effective at increasing student academic performance. We will use the HOSTS (Language arts, Math, and ESL) and PLATO programs to allow for additional instructional methods to be employed. Also, we will integrate the education of English as a Second Language (ESL) parents into this program. We are doing this because LCISD has had great success in getting both the parents and their children to come to these programs. This program allows for adult educational activities to be done in a manner that links the parent and the student. We will have multi-programs that last from one to twelve weeks that teach fun art and other cultural programs along with specially designed teacher programs. These programs are being included as a method to encourage students and the parents to attend the learning centers. All of these programs will be tied to TAKS/TEKS objectives so that these programs will improve student performance on this standardized measure of academic performance. We will use the specialized skills of current community member in some of this instruction. We will also use the people in the communities to provide other recreational activities for the students. The remediation of risk factors that this program will provide a safe place for the students outside of the normal school hours by: providing physical fitness training for all the students; providing extra curriculum activities that are designed to be fun – art, music, dance, etc. – that will keep the students coming to the program; providing extra academic enrichment programs that will allow us to accelerate students and provide additional learning opportunities; and providing activities that integrate students, parents, staff, and other community members so that a greater sense of community is developed. Within these programs we will develop an extended preK program that greatly increases the ability of the preK teachers to meet the needs of the targeted students. All of the schools currently have preK programs and the funds from this proposal will allow the teachers of these students to increase the effectiveness of their respective programs. The preK program will also have a fitness program that will provide this positive lifestyle for our youngest students. We are hoping that this program, with the other community fitness activities, will cause our communities to become healthier.

The next program to meet our goals is the *Community Technology Center* will become a single location where all members of the community can have broadband width access to the Internet. We will use current facilities that TIF grants, E-rate, other TEA grants, and local funds have provided. This will allow greater supplementation of these programs and help provide other ongoing funding streams that will allow the community learning centers to be maintained at the end of this grant's funding. The *Community Technology Center* will serve as a training location for technology and support other software. It will support software designed to provide the students with graduation credits, academic skills development, and a place to produce multi-media presentations. It will support software designed to provide community members with GED classes, adult academic and English Language skills, college credit courses, and multimedia presentations production. It will support software, designed to be used by individuals with special needs to overcome handicapping conditions through the use of technology. We will be able to develop technology training that is geared to the needs of our community members. The remediation of risk factors will be to provide more educational opportunities to the students, staff, parents, and other community stakeholders. The *Community Technology Center* will become the center for the development of Life Long Learners within each of the communities because we are providing for the technology and technology training to access the resources of the Internet. We will use each school district's current technology infrastructure to support the development of web based staff development and information dissemination web-pages concerning the programs. The *Community Technology Center* will use the current technology labs, libraries, and other facilities of the school districts to maximize the use of current resources in these grant funded activities. The consortium will hire a technologist to assist the current technology staff of each of the schools. This technologist will also help maintain web-pages and listserv's for the consortium so that the instructional staff can share methods that work with the targeted students and that other school districts along with community members can access information about our projects. The consortium will use hardware purchased will supplement and extend the current level of technology.

Homework Helpers will become a program where every student who is not making adequate academic progress can get extra assistance on missed academic skills. This will also be a program that other community stakeholders, regardless of having children enrolled, can become involved within the 21st Century Learning Center programs. This program will allow community members of all generations to interact. Texas Tech University (TTU) pre-service education students will serve as the core of the mentor/tutoring volunteers. We will use the HOSTS mentor training system and English Language Arts program to provide part of the materials for instruction of the students. We will also have other English Language Arts programs based on technology (Lexia, Success For All, Failure Free, Visagraph, Bridges, Locan, SOI, and Kurzweil Language programs) because we have seen that many student academic problems are based on reading skill problems. We will also provide transportation home to all students in the program either through late buses or mileage reimbursements to parents. The remediation of risk factors will be that students will receive extra instruction on any academic skills that they are missing as soon as the classroom teacher sees any drop in performance. Also, students who are lacking academic concepts that regular classroom instruction did not provide can come to receive training on these skills. This will allow the student's academic skill acquisition to be accelerated instead of just remediated. The PLATO software will be used to provide another method for instruction in all of the content areas tied to the TAKS/TEKS.

The last program, *Acceleration Academy* will be modeled off the 9th Grade grants that LCISD and OISD have received. Many 9th grade students have benefited from this program and have been able to obtain additional credits towards graduation. This program has "caught up" many students with their age peers for graduation. Both of the school districts have determined that if this program was extend to higher and lower grade level students the benefits would be even greater. The reason for this statement is that this extension would allow the process of allowing students to rejoin their age peers to be done in earlier grades and continue the process after the 9th grade. The PLATO software is tied to the TAKS and will allow pre/post measures on all of the content areas that the students study. The expanded PLATO software also has a "GED-prep" section that will allow the parents of the targeted

TEXAS EDUCATION AGENCY
Standard Application System (SAS)

Texas 21ˢᵗ Century Community Learning Centers, Cycle 3
Spring, Summer, and Fall of
2005, 2006, and 2007
TEXAS EDUCATION AGENCY

SCHEDULE #4B--Program Description - Part 2
Program Strategies

152-906
County District No.

Lubbock-Cooper ISD
Applicant Agency

students to have another method of preparing for this specific test. Also, the expanded PLATO software has pre-college sections which will allow parents of the targeted student who might wonder if they have skills to attend college to "see" what the work would be like. This program is also designed to provide instruction in a manner that is not the same as the normal instruction that is currently being done in the classroom so that the students will be willing to attend the out-of-school-time programs.

The above programs translate into the project goals. These goals are as follows:

Project Goal 1: The West Texas Community Learning Centers Consortium (WTCLCC) will reduce risk for educational failure for children by providing extended-day and extended-year integrated activities in a safe and drug-free environment

Objective 1: To improve academic achievement of all students

    Strategy 1: provide before-school, after-school and Saturday tutoring and homework assistance on all content areas with the PLATO, HOSTS, and teacher created programs using a variety of vender software
    Strategy 2: provide extended hours of access to technology to improve academic skills and knowledge concerning the use of technology
    Strategy 3: provide students with strategies for career planning and goal setting
    Strategy 4: provide special needs students with support through technology and special programs that allows them to achieve to their maximum abilities and in manners that would not be possible without this technology
    Strategy 5: provide special population students (ESL, LEP, At-risk, preK etc.) with support through technology and special programs that meet their unique educational needs
    Strategy 6: provide community and TTU students as tutors/mentors to work with students
    Strategy 7: provide summer field based learning experience programs

Anticipated measurable outcomes:
- Improved six-weeks grades
- Improved individual TAKS scores
- Lowering of the differences in TAKS scores between Hispanic and Anglo students
- Improved student abilities to use technology to advance their educational outcomes
- Improved goal setting as measured through career planning activities
- Special needs students are able to work more independently
- Attendance in the extra-hours and extra-days increases as students and parents see their extra value
- Student 'academic drop' during the summer months will be lowered
- Increased community and parental involvement with the school districts

Objective 2: To provide increased supervision for students during out-of-school hours

    Strategy 1: provide before-school, after-school, Saturday-school, and summer-school programs
    Strategy 2: provide extend library hours of operation
    Strategy 3: provide organized recreational activities for both regular and special population students that promote healthy lifestyle choices
    Strategy 4: provide a system to involve community members as mentors to students
    Strategy 5: provide a system to involve senior citizens and local city government officials in activities that promote the linking of students to these groups
    Strategy 6: provide cultural enrichment activities for students

Anticipated measurable outcomes:
- Lowering of juvenile referrals to local law enforcement agencies
- Increased involvement of the youth in after school programs
- Lowering of school discipline referrals
- Increased involvement of community members with the school district and the students
- Increased intergenerational activities within the community
- Increased community service projects

Objective 3: Increased knowledge concerning drug and safety issues

    Strategy 1: Community development training from TTU, SPACLC, WTOS, and others that provide the community with the knowledge to develop programs that will positively affect the quality-of-life within each community
    Strategy 2: School-based programs that promote positive character development
    Strategy 3: School-based programs that show the dangers of drugs
    Strategy 4: School-based programs that show what can happen when a student becomes involved with the juvenile justice system
    Strategy 5: School-based programs that promote the development of refusal skills and alternative methods for dealing with violence for students

Anticipated measurable outcomes:
- Increased level of knowledge concerning drug and safety issues within the community
- Increased awareness of positive character traits and students being reminded of how their actions relate to these positive character traits
- Decreases in the number of discipline referrals

For TEA Use Only	TEXAS EDUCATION AGENCY	152-906

<table>
<tr>
<td>For TEA Use Only
Adjustments and/or annotations made on this have been confirmed with

_____

By telephone/FAX on _____

by _____ of TEA.</td>
<td>TEXAS EDUCATION AGENCY
Standard Application System (SAS)

Texas 21st Century Community Learning Centers, Cycle 3
Spring, Summer, and Fall of
2005, 2006, and 2007
TEXAS EDUCATION AGENCY

SCHEDULE #4B--Program Description - Part 2
Program Strategies</td>
<td><u>152-906</u>
County District No.

<u>Lubbock-Cooper ISD</u>
Applicant Agency</td>
</tr>
</table>

- Decreases in the number of students in the juvenile justice system
- Increases in the ability of the students to handle conflicts in a positive manner

Project Goal 2: The WTCLCC will reduce risk for educational failure for younger children by providing a school-day based preK program that provides expanded learning opportunities for these students

Objective 1: To improve academic readiness for preK students

   Strategy 1: expand each school's current preK curriculum to better meet the educational needs of these at-risk students

   Strategy 2:   provide a system for increasing the linkage of these students' parents to the schools

   Strategy 3:   provide the parents with increased knowledge to become more effective at being their "Child's First Teacher"

Anticipated measurable outcomes:

- Improved academic readiness of these students
- Improved later year academic success because of the 'head-start' that these students received
- Lowering of the differences in TAKS scores between Hispanic and Anglo students because of the 'head-start'
- Increased parental involvement with the school districts because of the 'head-start'

Project Goal 3: The WTCLCC will increase the level of knowledge and quality-of-life for all community members

Objective 1: Develop a system to create a community of life long learners

   Strategy 1: Provide for technology training for the community

   Strategy 2:   Provide for general academic training ranging from GED to college for the community members

   Strategy 3:   Provide for links among the different community stakeholders to integrate community activities

   Anticipated measurable outcomes:

- Community members use the technology learning center
- Community members become involved with the school district
- Community members obtain GED's and/or further their education using the technology center
- Community members develop programs that extend the 21st Century concept into other programs for the communities

Objective 2: Develop other social and culture activities within and for the communities

   Strategy 1: Develop Internet tours of the community's points-of-interest

Strategy 2: Develop other social and cultural activities for all ages of community members

Anticipated measurable outcomes:

- O'Donnell's Dan Blocker Museum "Hoss Cartwright from *Bonanza*" is placed on-line
- City "pro-mo's" are developed and placed on-line
- Student and other community member performances are staged

Project Goal 4: The WTCLCC will develop a large non-partisan constituency that will hold the school districts accountable for high academic standards, promote the goals of the 21st Century grant, and provide the base to continue these programs

   <u>Objective 1: Community members trained on academic standards</u>

   Strategy 1: WTOS and SPACLC provide training to community members

   Strategy 2: Staff members from each school district provide AEIS training

Anticipated measurable outcomes:

- More community members understand high academic standards
- More community members understand how TEA measures academic standards
- More community members become involved with the school districts

Objective 2: Community members understand and promote the goals of the 21st Century grant

   Strategy 1: TTU, SPACLC, and WTOS provide training to community members

   Strategy 2: Community member become involved in the 21st Century Leadership team

Anticipated measurable outcomes:

- Community members understand the goals of the 21st Century grant
- Community members join the leadership team

Objective 3: Methods of obtaining continuing funding are sought

   Strategy 1: LCISD's grant writer works with the 21st Century Leadership team to develop an ongoing grant writing program for this project (No cost to this grant – funding from LCISD's local funds)

Anticipated measurable outcomes:

- A system for seeking additional continuing funding is developed
- Grants and/or local funding for the program are obtained
- Other community resources are found and blended with this program to provide ongoing support for the programs

Management Plan:

   Partnership / Involvement of Others: WTCLCC grant proposal is unique in that five school districts, 48 CBO/FBO, and numerous other adults came together to create this basic plan. Each of the groups or people brought a unique and diverse perspective to the grant development process. If

<table>
<tr><td colspan="2">

For TEA Use Only

Adjustments and/or annotations made on this have been confirmed with

_____

By telephone/FAX on _____

by _____ of TEA.
</td><td>

TEXAS EDUCATION AGENCY
Standard Application System (SAS)

Texas 21ˢᵗ Century Community Learning Centers, Cycle 3
Spring, Summer, and Fall of
2005, 2006, and 2007
TEXAS EDUCATION AGENCY

SCHEDULE #4B--Program Description - Part 2
Program Strategies
</td><td>

152-906
County District No.

Lubbock-Cooper ISD
Applicant Agency
</td></tr>
</table>

LCISD is funded these groups will then working in the mentoring program and other school related activities so that the teachers have extra help in meeting their students' needs. This table shows the CBO/FBO who will be working in some aspect of the program. The following listing of collaborating partners shows the initial community planning in the grant proposals and the support that we currently have to develop these learning centers. Most CBO/FBOs are providing mentors to the programs but some are doing other activities.

Collaborating Community Partners (letters in appendix)		
Faith-Based Organizations **First Baptist Church of O'Donnell** **Catholic Family Services** **Loop Baptist** **Loop Church of Christ** University **Texas Tech University - College of Education** Parent / Teacher Groups **O'Donnell CAFÉ** **Cooper CARE** **Smyer PTA** **Loop PTO** **Seagraves PTA** Law Enforcement Agencies **LCISD Police Force** **Gaines County Sheriff Department** **City of O'Donnell Police Department** **Hockley County Sheriff Department**	Private for profit businesses **HOSTS Corporation** **PLATO Corporation** **Tri County Tribune** **1,2 Buckle My Shoe Childcare** **Teacher's Touch Daycare** Health and Fitness Organizations **O'Donnell Little League** **Smyer Little League** **Cooper Little League** **Stretch-n-Grow** **Seagraves Little Dribbler's** **Smyer Little Dribbler's** **Cooper Little Dribbler's** Arts Organizations **Lubbock Community Theatre** **Little Eagle Publications**	Community-Based Organizations **O'Donnell Girl Scouts** **Neighborhood Missions** **Senior Citizen Centers** **West Texas Organizing Strategies** **Lion's Club of Woodrow** **O'Donnell Museum** **South Plains Area Community Leadership Counsel** **Loop Booster Club** **Gaines County Library** **Seagraves Chamber of Commerce** **City of Seagraves** **Teamkid Organization** **Woodrow Lion's Club**

Management of Grant Activities: The first aspect of the management of the grant was to develop a basic timeline for the first year of the grant. In doing this table we thought about what items needed to be done in what order to provide for an effective start to the program since school had already started. The following table will be used by the project coordinator (Gary Frye), project director (To Be Hired; see job qualifications with resumes), campus leadership team, district leadership team, and 21ˢᵗ Century leadership team (To Be Selected by staff and community members on all of the campuses) as an operational base for the grant. The specific items may need to be modified but the general template will serve as a guide. LCISD is the fiscal agent for the grant and will use its general accounting system to track all the funds of the grant. Each of the school districts will track the funds that they receive through their business office. All school districts will use acceptable TEA accounting procedures to track funds. The CBO (community) and FBO (faith) groups who receive any funds from the grant will use their account procedures to track this money.

Timelines and Milestones for First Year

September 2004	Announcement award of grant; form Leadership Board for Consortium and Districts; begin community training; place orders for instruction materials for October, software, hardware, engage in basic student enrichment and acceleration programs, form management team for the grant
October 2004	Hire consortium staff positions; hire instructional staff; start community development training; bring Leadership Boards and Directors 'up-to-speed' on current school district after-school, summer, and enrichment programs; develop preliminary schedule of student, parent, and community member activities; prepare advertisements for newspapers and develop information for campus notification of parents about the programs that will be available; schedule staff development for vender programs. All training programs continue; learning centers provide for unique learning setting for students and community members; all extra day and extra year programs are operating; first six-week grades of students are reviewed and students needing extra assistance are recruited for the programs, TTU forms links with all campuses
November 2004	Have training for instructional staff on vender programs; recruit and train community members for mentoring; begin extended day and year programs; TTU, WTOS, SPACLC and other training programs; have 1st quarter formative evaluation; make corrections and/or modify programs based on this evaluation; plan summer programs; Intergeneration instruction programs started; students in need of academic acceleration identified and start programs; students selected for leadership training; continued staff develop training; contracted service providers begin programs; student baseline data is collected
December 2004	All training programs continue; learning centers' unique possibilities for instruction are integrated into current curriculum lessons; all extra day and extra year programs are operating; evaluation and student input is integrated into modifying the programs; student academic achievement in terms of first semester grades is collected; contract service providers collect data on the effectiveness of their programs, TTU linkage prepares to recruit pre-service students to work with the schools in the spring
January 2005	WTOS training of community members to hold school accountable for high academic standards begins; TTU, SPACLC, and other community training on leadership development continues; develop program evaluation; continue to recruit mentors; satellite learning centers are connected to the school district's T-1 system; expand staff development; evaluate the effects of the summer programs; extend summer health programs; expand library and technology hours, TTU pre-service students used in the programs

For TEA Use Only
Adjustments and/or annotations made on this have been confirmed with
_____
By telephone/FAX on _____
by _____ of TEA.

TEXAS EDUCATION AGENCY
Standard Application System (SAS)

Texas 21st Century Community Learning Centers, Cycle 3
Spring, Summer, and Fall of
2005, 2006, and 2007
TEXAS EDUCATION AGENCY

152-906
County District No.

Lubbock-Cooper ISD
Applicant Agency

SCHEDULE #4B--Program Description - Part 2
Program Strategies

February 2005	All training programs continue; satellite learning centers' unique possibilities for instruction are integrated into current curriculum lessons; all extra day and extra year programs are operating; TAKS prep programs are begun, Leadership Board meet to determine if any changes in programs are needed to benefit the goals of the grant, students in danger of failing for the year are recruited and parents are involved in the program, the mentoring system focuses on these most at-risk students to provide them with greater support
March 2005	All training programs continue; learning centers' unique possibilities for instruction are integrated into current curriculum lessons; all extra day and extra year programs are operating; quarterly evaluation done; current LRPP, DIP, and CIP evaluations begun in relationship to the grant programs; news releases developed for newspapers; TAKS prep programs continued
April 2005	Leadership Boards evaluate evaluations of the first 7 months of programs and make recommendations for program changes; these evaluation are integrated into LRPP and CIP's; plans are made for summer programs; students who may be in danger of failing a grade are recruited for intensive acceleration programs
May 2005	Initial AEIS evaluation done; all training programs continue; satellite learning centers' unique possibilities for instruction are integrated into current curriculum lessons; all extra day and extra year programs are operating; data collected on student academic performance, data collected on student; staff, parent, and community members opinions and suggestions for the programs; collect information for year end evaluation; summer programs planning done, teachers recommend students for summer program
June 2005	All training programs continue; satellite learning centers' unique possibilities for instruction are integrated into current curriculum lessons; all extra day and extra year programs are operating; year end evaluation results are given to Leadership Boards; District and Consortium Leadership Boards meet to determine any changes to the program;, news releases are prepared, summer fun programs done to promote at-risk students coming to the program, field-based learning experiences are developed that will promote attendance at the program and extend the educational activities of the students, staff will schedule joint events so that the students from the various school districts can interact.
July 2005	All training programs continue; learning centers' unique possibilities for instruction are integrated into current curriculum lessons; all extra day and extra year programs are continuing; quarterly evaluation done; alignment of the 21st Century grant goals to Long Range Performance Plans (LRPP), District Improvement Plan (DIP) and Campus Improvement Plans (CIP) are begun; students in the programs are surveyed about the programs and what they would like to see added or changed; news releases are prepared, a formative evaluation is done so that methods of changing the program can be integrated into each CIP and DIP
August 2005	Contact service providers for additional materials and training, and CIP committees determine the effects for the first eleven-months of the program; all training programs continue; satellite learning centers' unique possibilities for instruction are integrated into current curriculum lessons; all extra day and extra year programs are operating, develop news releases for parents through the campus newsletters; students with academic problems recruited; mentors recruited; links between the parents and staff increased by expanding the home liaison home visits, school district and others fine arts programs began
September 2005	Have management team link 21st Century data to each school district's CIP and DIP by formally including them in the school board approved plans; begin evaluation of the academic effects of the programs; have community meetings to inform each of the communities of the progress and obtain their input into improving the program; begin the formal evaluation process; establish methods of integrating the out-of-school-time programs to the needs of the students, TTU researcher begin to submit papers for publication
October 2005	Develop the methods for expanding the out-of-school-time programs to meet the needs of the students and other community members; begin fine art extended programs; management team integrates the various programs across the communities; TAKS testing scores evaluated in terms of the students who came to the program versus students who did not attend, work with staff to determine what they thought was effective over the last year

<table>
<tr><td colspan="2">For TEA Use Only</td></tr>
<tr><td colspan="2">Adjustments and/or annotations made on this have been confirmed with

_____</td></tr>
<tr><td colspan="2">
By telephone/FAX on _____</td></tr>
<tr><td colspan="2">
by _____ of TEA.</td></tr>
</table>

TEXAS EDUCATION AGENCY
Standard Application System (SAS)

Texas 21st Century Community Learning Centers, Cycle 3
Spring, Summer, and Fall of
2005, 2006, and 2007
TEXAS EDUCATION AGENCY

152-906
County District No.

Lubbock-Cooper ISD
Applicant Agency

SCHEDULE #4B--Program Description - Part 2
Program Strategies

The second aspect of the management of the grant was to break this year long program down to specific day activities. The pattern for each day is as follows:

Proposed School Year Daily Schedule

7:00am-7:45 am	Community technology center opens, parents can bring children to the center to be supervised in Safe Places Program
7:45am-8:15 am	Students are served breakfast
8:00am-3:45pm	Community Technology Center is open for use by community members
8:00am-3:45pm	Students are in regular education classes and special extend preK (with fitness and other grant activities)
4:00pm-4:20pm	Students staying for after-school programs are given snacks
4:30pm-6:30pm	Community Technology Center; Homework Helpers; "Enrich Me" Before-School, After-School, Saturday, and Summer Enrichment; and Acceleration Academy
4:30pm-6:30pm	Intergenerational ESL instruction program at the centers with a base number of ESL parents

Proposed Saturday Daily Schedule

9:00am	Students arrive

For TEA Use Only		
Adjustments and/or annotations made on this have been confirmed with _____ By telephone/FAX on _____ by _____ of TEA.	**TEXAS EDUCATION AGENCY** **Standard Application System (SAS)** **Texas 21st Century Community Learning Centers, Cycle 3** **Spring, Summer, and Fall of** **2005, 2006, and 2007** **TEXAS EDUCATION AGENCY** **SCHEDULE #4B--Program Description - Part 2** **Program Strategies**	**152-906** County District No. **Lubbock-Cooper ISD** Applicant Agency

9:15am-11:45	Students work on special academic programs, high school graduation credit programs, use technology based instruction, etc. using the Community Technology Center and Acceleration Academy
12:00am	Students leave

Proposed Summer Daily Schedule

8:30am	Students arrive at school – transportation provided
8:30am-9:15am	Students given breakfast and allowed to play in organized activities
9:30am-10:30am	Reading time
10:45am-11:30am	Writing time
11:45am-12:45pm	Lunch with nutrition programs
1:00pm-2:00pm	Organized physical games
2:15pm-2:45pm	Sharing with small groups on what they had learned and how the field based educational experience relates to what they have learned during the regular school year
3:00pm	Students return home – transportation provided
9:00am-2:45pm	On field based educational experiences days – students at the sites

The project coordinator and project director will be the staff members that manage and monitor on a day-to-day basis the programs at the five school districts and coordinate the activities among all of the stakeholders. They will solicit feedback from all of the stakeholders and with the assist of the outside evaluator will use these data to ensure that the basic programs outlined above are improved on a continuous basis so that stakeholder needs are better met and the information gained is integrated into each CIP and DIP.

Internal Communication, Coordination and Reporting: Several staff members will travel among the school districts. These are the project coordinator, project director, and technologist. These staff members will assist in providing regular and frequent communication among all stakeholders in a face-to-face manner. Additionally, the Internet will be used to provide this type of communication among all staff and community stakeholders because there will be a central listserv that anyone from these communities can post to all the other people on the list. Also, monthly reports will be given at the school board meetings so that the management staff of each of the school districts is aware of all WTCLCC programs and activities. Lastly, the data from the yearly summative evaluation of the program will be incorporated into the CIP and DIP at each campus and school district which again will be shared with the larger community during the campus/district report card meetings. Since a large portion of each campus's students will be in the program on a daily basis, we will use notes home and newsletters to inform the community stakeholders. These will be sent home at least every six-weeks.

Grant Project management and Personnel: The project coordinator will be Gary Lee Frye, Ed.D. He will have coordination of this program as part of his other duties for LCISD where he is Director of Development / Special Student Programs. He holds 14 teacher and 5 professional certifications from TEA - this allows him to teach all required courses preK-12, along with all special education courses and ESL courses. Further, he is a certified special education and regular counselor, educational diagnostician, mid-management, and superintendent. In his development work he has funded over ten million dollars in programs. His resume is in the appendix. The project director will be hired from grant funds. His/her qualifications will be to hold at least one certification in a teaching field and have a masters. S/he will have technology skills and the ability to communicate effectively with others. The technologist will be hired from grant funds. S/he will be able to repair, train staff on software, and manage a listserv. S/he will either have the certifications and/or real world experience in working with technology. David Gerabagi, Ph.D. will be the outside evaluator (resume in appendix). He was selected because he is doing several 21st Century evaluations currently and has done other program evaluations. Eva Midobuche, Ed.D. and Alfredo Benavides, Ph.D. are the lead Texas Tech University (TTU) professors. This husband and wife team are internationally known experts in the field of Hispanic studies. They, with Graduate Assistants to be hired, will provide research studies and a research base for the programs selected. They will also provide "just-in-time" staff development through e-mail and other professional development trainings. Their complete vitas are in the appendix.

Management team and Resource Management: The Management Team, composed of consortium staff, school district site-based team members, and other community members, will oversee all components at all of the learning centers. The local learning centers will have center based management teams that will use the current site-based system of each of the school districts. The Program Director will meet with all of these management team levels to assure that there is coordination among the various sites and programs. The management team will be responsible for assuring that grant requirements listed on pages 28 and 29 are met. Because each of the centers is located on school district campuses, the sites are ADA compliant, safe, and are easily accessible to the community. The management team, through the school districts and other partners, will provide information about the learning centers to each of the communities by having meetings at the schools and the director scheduling presentations to community groups. Where other communication media is available, it will be used as another method to inform the community members. Given the rural nature of all of these areas we will also make use of the farming co-op as a method to publicize what the centers can do for the communities. The various letters of support (see table above for community partners) showed the broad range of support that we have been able to obtain in just the planning phase of this grant. We expect that this will increase once funding of this proposal is received. These organizations at the community and consortium level had input into the design of these programs (many offering to assist with volunteer mentors to work with the students).

We have linked this proposal to the normal funding streams of the school districts. All of the programs developed by this grant proposal will be used to supplement current programs and no current programs will be supplanted. In addition to this funding stream, we will use the infrastructure that

TEXAS EDUCATION AGENCY
Standard Application System (SAS)

Texas 21st Century Community Learning Centers, Cycle 3
Spring, Summer, and Fall of
2005, 2006, and 2007
TEXAS EDUCATION AGENCY

SCHEDULE #4B--Program Description - Part 2
Program Strategies

152-906
County District No.

Lubbock-Cooper ISD
Applicant Agency

several grants the school districts have received have developed. Resources developed by TIF grants, Technology Renovation Grants, 9th Grade Success Grants, After-school grant, Read First grant, and Accelerated Reader grants will be linked to this program. (Many of these programs were eliminated and without funding of the 21st Century proposal the services would not be continued.) All of the school districts will continue to provide related Title programs to the students and the funding of this program will allow the service to the students to be expanded. This integration of programs allows the funds and current programs to be leveraged and build a learning center concept that will allow life long learning to be developed.

During the planning process of this proposal, the community groups were given notice of intent to submit the proposal and were instrumental in development of several aspects of the program. The community groups saw this grant as a method to bring together several programs into a coordinated effort to meet specific school district needs along with providing general community education opportunities that would not be possible without these funds. They saw the desire for continued community input as a method by which the communities and the school districts could form even closer working relationships to support the goal of developing communities where life long learning was the norm instead of just a goal.

Current and future funding sources:

Funding Source	LCISD	LISD	OISD	SeISD	SmISD
TIF Grant	X	X	X	X	X
After-school grant	X				
9th Grade Success Grant	X		X		
Technology Renovation Grant	X				X
Read First Grant		X	X	X	
Texas High School Completion and Success Grant Program		X		X	X
Community Resources and Support with funds and/or mentors	X	X	X	X	X
Local Funds	X	X	X	X	X
Title Funds	X	X	X	X	X
Ongoing Proposal Development from local funds	X	X	X	X	X
E-Rate discount program	X	X	X	X	X

We will use these other funding sources to extend the 21st Century program and to build ongoing support for the program so that when these funds end the programs can continue. The ongoing program to seek other funding is having a positive effect on the community because they are see that the school districts are attempting to create world class programs for life long learning without just raising taxes.

The full resources of five school districts, several CBO/FBO's, and many community stakeholders are being integrated into the full program. This will assist the schools in maintaining the program after TEA funding ends. The costs per student in higher than what would be seen in Houston because of numbers, but the level of support and the potential to impact five West Texas communities is well worth the increased costs per student in our opinion because of our total community approach.

Jointly Submitted Application:

This application meets this requirement by having five school districts and 48 CBO/FBO's in the five communities working together to develop, design, implement and then seek ways to continue the program. The West Texas Community Learning Centers Consortium (WTCLCC) is a true consortium in the sense that the impact on the five communities of Loop, O'Donnell, Seagraves, Smyer, and Woodrow will extend to every part of the communities not just the school district. We are looking at the funding of this grant as a method to increase the academic level of everyone because of the involvement of so many stakeholders with the school based programs.

Unique features of our program:

We have developed our programs in close cooperation with each of the communities. This is allowing for each school district and community to meet its unique needs in the framework that only this type of consortium can provide. The management team that has

For TEA Use Only
Adjustments and/or annotations made on this have been confirmed with
_____
By telephone/FAX on _____
by _____ of TEA.

TEXAS EDUCATION AGENCY
Standard Application System (SAS)

Texas 21st Century Community Learning Centers, Cycle 3
Spring, Summer, and Fall of
2005, 2006, and 2007
TEXAS EDUCATION AGENCY

152-906
County District No.

Lubbock-Cooper ISD
Applicant Agency

SCHEDULE #4B--Program Description - Part 2
Program Strategies

already been developed could not have been created at any one of the school districts because most are too small to have these experts within their areas. By bring together five rural communities we are able to overcome the cost factor to a degree (the cost of the program is higher but this is because of the rural nature of the school districts). By linking the community learning centers to Texas Tech University College of Education we will be able to research the effectiveness of our programs to a degree that would be impossible. Also, by having mentors from the college in each of the programs as HOSTS mentors our students will have role models that they normally do not see because they are not near a college. These students will be able to relate to the students in a way that others cannot and will help all of our students see that they could go on to college.

The use of the school districts' current technology infrastructure (supplemented by the requested hardware and software) will allow us to develop a system by which the community members can have access during the day with training provided by the technologist and the students can have access at night. We will use the technology backbone of each school district to form a virtual community that is formed for the five communities that would not be possible without the use of the technology. We will also expand the use of the school districts' technology into the community. Through the development of "Senior Projects" modeled after the High Schools That Work programs that LCISD has we believe that students will be able to help business and the communities have a presence on the Internet that would not normally be possible. We feel that this could be the start of a system that allows these community members to enter into e-commerce that would allow these communities to reverse the declines that they have seen for the youth to live and work in the area after gradation.

The out-of-school-time programs will allow the students to have another form of instruction that extends the normal classroom instruction. This will promote life long learning for the students and the linkage to the parents will allow for the educational needs of the communities to be met in a unique manner only possible through the use of mentors and technology. The students will also be exposed to a vast array of field based learning experience that would not be possible within the normal school day which will again increase the probability that they will become life long learners.

This program when funded will allow the communities to build the "learning infrastructure" needed to promote life long learning and new thinking in the communities. Much as the TIF grants built the technology infrastructure that we will use in this proposal, the funding of this grant proposal will allow all of the communities to "Build the Future . . . One Person at a Time!"

DESCRIBE ON THIS SCHEDULE ONLY THOSE ACTIVITIES TO BE PAID FROM THESE GRANT FUNDS. GRANT FUNDS WILL BE USED TO PAY ONLY FOR ACTIVITIES BUDGETED ON SCHEDULES #3 – 3

<table>
<tr><td>

For TEA Use Only

Adjustments and/or annotations made on this have been confirmed with

_____

by telephone/FAX on_____

by _____ of TEA.

</td><td>

TEXAS EDUCATION AGENCY
Standard Application System (SAS)

Texas 21st Century Community Learning Centers, Cycle 3
Spring, Summer, and Fall of 2005, 2006, and 2007
SCHEDULE #4B-- Program Description - Part 2
Program Strategies
Sustainability of Center(s)

</td><td>

152-906
County District No.

Lubbock-Cooper ISD
Applicant Agency

</td></tr>
</table>

Part 1. (The chart may not exceed the space provided. *Note: **You may adjust the row height and column width to accommodate the text, but you may not exceed the limit of one page.**) Font size no smaller than 9 point, Arial or Times New Roman

Year:	A. Infrastructure Provided with Grant Funds	B. Sustainability from Other Fund Sources	
		(1) Major Activities/Expenditures/ Human Resources	(2) Strategies and Potential Sources
1	Conduct research on best -practice sustainability models.

Begin the process for Sustainability plan.

Link these grant activities with the ongoing programs that have developed over the last four years.

An advisory committee comprised of project staff, parents, business community, and decision makers will be formed. | Developmental work done by project coordinator

Forming linkages among all the stakeholders linked by the funding of the grant

Advisory committee list.
Research findings analyzed.
Groundwork for sustainability laid out.

Other grant, foundation, and community funding sources are developed. | Other state and federal grants

Increases in local budget due to ADA increases

Begin the development of West Texas Community Area Foundation

We will attempt to address the foundation for our sustainability efforts during the first year of the project. |
| 2 | Develop a vision statement for our sustainability plan.

Outline activities that must be undertaken.
Identify key benefits of the project that will benefit the community.

Develop methods by which community stakeholders can support the program | Developmental work done by project coordinator

Forming linkages among all the stakeholders linked by the funding of the grant

Vision statement developed.

Expected results are numerated.

Benefits identified. | Other state a federal grants

Increases in local budget due to ADA increases

Chartering of West Texas Community Area Foundation

Our first step will be what unifies all of our programs' sustainability efforts and will serve as the focal point that will bring program staff, partners, participants and supporters together. |
| 3 | Designate key program partners.

Identify key resources each partner will bring to the program.

Assign roles and responsibilities of each partner.

Establish a communication process to keep partners informed.

Develop an educational foundation that the consortium members can work through | Developmental work done by project coordinator

Forming linkages among all the stakeholders linked by the funding of the grant

Key partnerships secured.

Communication mechanisms are in place.

Educational foundation is developed. | Other state a federal grants

Increases in local budget due to ADA increases

West Texas Community Area Foundation seeks funding though other non-tax or normal school district funding sources

Collaboration is a key ingredient for sustainability. Community partners each possess unique skills and resources to contribute to the program and expand its support base. |

For TEA Use Only	TEXAS EDUCATION AGENCY	152-906
Adjustments and/or annotations made on this have been confirmed with _____ by telephone/FAX on _____ by _____ of TEA.	Standard Application System (SAS) **Texas 21st Century Community Learning Centers, Cycle 3 Spring, Summer, and Fall of 2005, 2006, and 2007 SCHEDULE #4B-- Program Description - Part 2 Program Strategies Sustainability of Center(s)**	County District No. **Lubbock-Cooper ISD** **Applicant Agency**

Part 1. (The chart may not exceed the space provided. *Note: **You may adjust the row height and column widthto accommodate the text, but you may not exceed the limit of one page.**) Font size no smaller than 9 point, Arial or Times New Roman

Year:	C. Infrastructure Provided with Remaining Grant Funds	D. Major Activities Needing Support from Supplementary Sources	E. Strategies and Potential Sources
Year 4 **20% less than Year 1 Funds**	Clarify what our program supporters need to advocate for. Identify who program advocates are. Determine which ones have influential connections that can be tapped. Determine which decision makers program advocates are to approach.	Developmental work done by project coordinator Forming linkages among all the stakeholders linked by the funding of the grant Advocacy tactics and targets identified. Campaign for sustainability started.	Must replace 20% of Year 1 Funding Increases in local budget due to ADA increases West Texas Community Area Foundation seeks funding though other non-tax or normal school district funding sources Advocates for our program will be parents, business leaders, Community-based organizations, public agency representatives and youth for our community.
Year 5 **20% less than Year 4 Fund**	Maximize existing resources, assign responsibilities to identify and pursue other funding opportunities and create new sources by strategically using community partners.	Developmental work done by project coordinator Forming linkages among all the stakeholders linked by the funding of the grant Funders approached. Funding for sustainability secured.	Must replace 20% of Year 4 funding Increases in local budget due to ADA increases West Texas Community Area Foundation seeks funding though other non-tax or normal school district funding sources We will clearly identify what is needed to sustain program and systematically analyze the feasibility of a range of public and private financing options based on our resource needs.
Year 6 & Beyond **No grant funds**		Developmental work done by project coordinator Forming linkages among all the stakeholders linked by the funding of the grant Funders approached. Funding for sustainability secured. Various community stakeholder have gone through grant development training and are seeking grants for various aspects of the programs	Must replace all 21st CCLC grant funds Increases in local budget due to ADA increases West Texas Community Area Foundation seeks funding though other non-tax or normal school district funding sources Successful programs total integrated into the CIP and DIP and have access to local budget funds

For TEA Use Only

Adjustments and/or annotations made
on this have been confirmed with

by telephone/FAX on _____ of TEA.
by _____

TEXAS EDUCATION AGENCY
Standard Application System (SAS)
Texas 21st Century Community Learning Centers, Cycle 3
Spring, Summer, and Fall of
2005, 2006, and 2007
SCHEDULE #4B–Program Description - Part 3
Program Activities/Budget Year 1: October 1, 2004 - December 31,
2005

(Enter Component Area if applicable)

Use as Many Pages as Necessary, front only, font size not less than 9 point.

LOCAL PROGRAM OBJECTIVE
The West Texas Community Learning Centers will reduce risk for educational failure for children by providing extended-day and extended-year integrated activities in a safe and drug-free environment.

STRATEGY
To improve academic achievement of all students by providing after-school and Saturday tutoring and homework assistance on all content areas with the PLATO, HOSTS, and teacher created programs

The goals of the program are:
The purpose of 21st Century Community Learning Centers, Cycle 3, is to provide opportunities for communities to establish or expand activities in community learning centers that—
(1) provide opportunities for academic enrichment, including providing tutorial services to help children, particularly students who attend low performing schools, to meet State and local Student academic achievement standards in core academic subjects, such as reading and mathematics
(2) offer students a broad array of additional services, programs and activities, such as youth development activities, drug and violence prevention programs, counseling programs, art, music, and physical education and fitness programs, and technology education programs that are designed to reinforce and complement the regular academic program of participating students; and
(3) offer families of students served by community learning centers opportunities for literacy and related educational development.

Activities to Be Carried Out to Accomplish Strategy	Positions Responsible	Timeline	Effectiveness Indicators
1. Instructional staff at each of the learning centers assist in the creation of unique learning programs that best meet the educational needs of their students	Instructional staff Director	Ongoing	The instructional staff created specific programs designed to meet their students' unique needs.
2. Develop unified procedures to assess student needs: a) Running records b) Benchmark student testing (TAAS/TAKS and retention) c) Assessment review (TAAS, IQ, other standardized, end-of-course, or state/district mandated tests) d) Practice TAAS testing e) Screening of transfer students	Aides Teachers Counselors	October	Students selected for the programs Classroom records. Student's permanent files.
3. Conduct before, during, and after school tutorial program.	Aides Teachers	October	Classroom records; grade reports; program attendance records.
4. Conduct individualized mentoring activities (homework tutorials, computerized instruction, class work tutorials)	Aides; Upper level high school students; community volunteers	October	Classroom records; grade reports; program attendance records.

GRANT FUNDS WILL BE USED TO PAY ONLY FOR ACTIVITIES OCCURRING BETWEEN THE BEGINNING AND ENDING DATES OF THE GRANT AS SPECIFIED ON THE NOTICE OF GRANT AWARD.

For TEA Use Only

Adjustments and/or annotations made
on this have been confirmed with

by telephone/FAX on _____
by _____ of TEA.

TEXAS EDUCATION AGENCY
Standard Application System (SAS)
Texas 21st Century Community Learning Centers, Cycle 3
Spring, Summer, and Fall of
2005, 2006, and 2007
SCHEDULE #4B--Program Description - Part 3
Program Activities/Budget Year 1: October 1, 2004 - December 31,
2005

Use as Many Pages as Necessary, front only, font size not less than 9 point   *(Enter Component Area if applicable)*

LOCAL PROGRAM OBJECTIVE
The West Texas Community Learning Centers will reduce risk for educational failure for children by providing extended-day and extended-year integrated activities in a safe and drug-free environment.

STRATEGY
To improve academic achievement of all students by providing after-school and Saturday tutoring and homework assistance on all content areas with the PLATO, HOSTS, and teacher created programs

The goals of the program are:
The purpose of 21st Century Community Learning Centers, Cycle 3, is to provide opportunities for communities to establish or expand activities in community learning centers that—

(1) provide opportunities for academic enrichment, including providing tutorial services to help children, particularly students who attend low performing schools, to meet State and local Student academic achievement standards in core academic subjects, such as reading and mathematics

(2) offer students a broad array of additional services, programs and activities, such as youth development activities, drug and violence prevention programs, counseling programs, art, music, and physical education and fitness programs, and technology education programs that are designed to reinforce and complement the regular academic program of participating students; and

(3) offer families of students served by community learning centers opportunities for literacy and related educational development.

Activities to Be Carried Out to Accomplish Strategy	Positions Responsible	Timeline	Effectiveness Indicators
5. Utilize computer labs for enhancement of basic skills.	Aides Teachers	October	Classroom records, student grade reports; program attendance records.
6. Emphasize problem solving activities for students.	Teachers Aides	October	Student grade reports.
7. Identify students in need of summer school.	Principal; Counselors	May	Identified students scheduled for summer school.

GRANT FUNDS WILL BE USED TO PAY ONLY FOR ACTIVITIES OCCURRING BETWEEN THE BEGINNING AND ENDING DATES OF THE GRANT AS SPECIFIED ON THE NOTICE OF GRANT AWARD.

TEXAS EDUCATION AGENCY
Standard Application System (SAS)
Texas 21st Century Community Learning Centers, Cycle 3
Spring, Summer, and Fall of
2005, 2006, and 2007
SCHEDULE #4B--Program Description - Part 3
Program Activities/Budget Year 1: October 1, 2004 - December 31, 2005

(Enter Component Area if applicable)

Use as Many Pages as Necessary, front only, font size not less than 9 point

LOCAL PROGRAM OBJECTIVE
The West Texas Community Learning Centers will reduce risk for educational failure for children by providing extended-day and extended-year integrated activities in a safe and drug-free environment.

STRATEGY
To improve academic achievement of all students by providing after-school and Saturday tutoring and homework assistance on all content areas with the PLATO, HOSTS, and teacher created programs

The goals of the program are:
The purpose of 21st Century Community Learning Centers, Cycle 3, is to provide opportunities for communities to establish or expand activities in community learning centers that—
(1) provide opportunities for academic enrichment, including providing tutorial services to help children, particularly students who attend low performing schools, to meet State and local Student academic achievement standards in core academic subjects, such as reading and mathematics
(2) offer students a broad array of additional services, programs and activities, such as youth development activities, drug and violence prevention programs, counseling programs, art, music, and physical education and fitness programs, and technology education programs that are designed to reinforce and complement the regular academic program of participating students; and
(3) offer families of students served by community learning centers opportunities for literacy and related educational development.

Activities to Be Carried Out to Accomplish Strategy	Positions Responsible	Timeline	Effectiveness Indicators
1. Identify students needing homework assistance.	Teachers	Each grading period.	All eligible students have a place in the Learning Center.
2. Canvas classroom teachers to determine homework assignments to be addressed in the assistance sessions.	Teachers	Weekly, November	Current homework assignments are secured for each student; the number of students earning passing grades in the core curriculum increases by 5%.
3. Conduct homework assistance sessions.	Teachers Mentors/Tutors	Weekly, October	The number of students earning passing grades in the core curriculum increases by 5%.
4. Review student performance in class to determine effectiveness of the homework assistance sessions.	Teachers	Weekly, October	The number of students earning passing grades in the core curriculum increases by 5%.

GRANT FUNDS WILL BE USED TO PAY ONLY FOR ACTIVITIES OCCURRING BETWEEN THE BEGINNING AND ENDING DATES OF THE GRANT AS SPECIFIED ON THE NOTICE OF GRANT AWARD.

112

TEXAS EDUCATION AGENCY
Standard Application System (SAS)
Texas 21st Century Community Learning Centers, Cycle 3
Spring, Summer, and Fall of
2005, 2006, and 2007
SCHEDULE #4B--Program Description - Part 3
Program Activities/Budget Year 1: October 1, 2004 - December 31,
2005

(Enter Component Area if applicable)

Use as Many Pages as Necessary, front only, font size not less than 9 point

LOCAL PROGRAM OBJECTIVE

The West Texas Community Learning Centers will reduce risk for educational failure for children by providing extended-day and extended-year integrated activities in a safe and drug-free environment.

STRATEGY

To improve academic achievement of all students by providing summer programming

The goals of the program are:
The purpose of 21st Century Community Learning Centers, Cycle 3, is to provide opportunities for communities to establish or expand activities in community learning centers that—

(1) provide opportunities for academic enrichment, including providing tutorial services to help children, particularly students who attend low performing schools, to meet State and local Student academic achievement standards in core academic subjects, such as reading and mathematics

(2) offer students a broad array of additional services, programs and activities, such as youth development activities, drug and violence prevention programs, counseling programs, art, music, and physical education and fitness programs, and technology education programs that are designed to reinforce and complement the regular academic program of participating students; and

(3) offer families of students served by community learning centers opportunities for literacy and related educational development.

Activities to Be Carried Out to Accomplish Strategy	Positions Responsible	Timeline	Effectiveness Indicators
1. Integrate all academic vender programs into a field based experience summer program	Director Teachers Principals	June	The consortium members have a summer program that extends the current learning for targeted students.
2. The staff selects field based extended learning experiences that allow for the school based learning activities to be extended	Teachers Director	June	The field based activities extend the classroom learning and provide the students with unique TAKS based learning activities.
3. The staff integrates physical activities into the summer program so that the fitness of the students is increased and so that the students will want to come to the summer program.	Teachers	June	The students report that the summer program is "fun" and something that they want to do.
4. The effects of the summer program are evaluated	Outside evaluator Director	August	The data from the summer is used to improve the program.

GRANT FUNDS WILL BE USED TO PAY ONLY FOR ACTIVITIES OCCURRING BETWEEN THE BEGINNING AND ENDING DATES OF THE GRANT AS SPECIFIED ON THE NOTICE OF GRANT AWARD.

TEXAS EDUCATION AGENCY
Standard Application System (SAS)
Texas 21st Century Community Learning Centers, Cycle 3
Spring, Summer, and Fall of
2005, 2006, and 2007
SCHEDULE #4B--Program Description - Part 3
Program Activities/Budget Year 1: October 1, 2004 - December 31, 2005

152-906
County District No.
Lubbock-Cooper ISD
Applicant Agency

Amendment No. _____

(Enter Component Area if applicable)

Use as Many Pages as Necessary, front only, font size not less than 9 point.

LOCAL PROGRAM OBJECTIVE
The West Texas Community Learning Centers will reduce risk for educational failure for children by providing extended-day and extended-year integrated activities in a safe and drug-free environment.

STRATEGY
To improve academic achievement of all students by increasing their attendance at the programs and in school in general

The goals of the program are:
The purpose of 21st Century Community Learning Centers, Cycle 3, is to provide opportunities for communities to establish or expand activities in community learning centers that—
(1) provide opportunities for academic enrichment, including providing tutorial services to help children, particularly students who attend low performing schools, to meet State and local Student academic achievement standards in core academic subjects, such as reading and mathematics
(2) offer students a broad array of additional services, programs and activities, such as youth development activities, drug and violence prevention programs, counseling programs, art, music, and physical education and fitness programs, and technology education programs that are designed to reinforce and complement the regular academic program of participating students; and
(3) offer families of students served by community learning centers opportunities for literacy and related educational development.

Activities to Be Carried Out to Accomplish Strategy	Positions Responsible	Timeline	Effectiveness Indicators
1. Develop and communicate procedures to personnel.	Principal,	May	Written communication with faculty and staff.
2. Systematically communicate with and update parents and students on attendance status and expectations.	Attendance Officer	October	Improved student attendance.
3. Conduct home visits.	Attendance Officer	October	Improved student attendance.
4. Conduct student and parent conferences regarding attendance.	Attendance Committee	October	Improved student attendance; copies of correspondence with parents.

GRANT FUNDS WILL BE USED TO PAY ONLY FOR ACTIVITIES OCCURRING BETWEEN THE BEGINNING AND ENDING DATES OF THE GRANT AS SPECIFIED ON THE NOTICE OF GRANT AWARD.

152-906
County District No.

Lubbock-Cooper ISD
Applicant Agency

Amendment No. _____

TEXAS EDUCATION AGENCY
Standard Application System (SAS)
Texas 21st Century Community Learning Centers, Cycle 3
Spring, Summer, and Fall of
2005, 2006, and 2007
SCHEDULE #4B--Program Description - Part 3
Program Activities/Budget Year 1: October 1, 2004 - December 31, 2005

(Enter Component Area if applicable)

Use as Many Pages as Necessary, front only, font size not less than 9 point

LOCAL PROGRAM OBJECTIVE
The West Texas Community Learning Centers will reduce risk for educational failure for children by providing extended-day and extended-year integrated activities in a safe and drug-free environment.

STRATEGY
To improve academic achievement of all students by developing a preK program the meets the targeted students' unique early educational needs

The goals of the program are:
The purpose of 21st Century Community Learning Centers, Cycle 3, is to provide opportunities for communities to establish or expand activities in community learning centers that—
(1) provide opportunities for academic enrichment, including providing tutorial services to help children, particularly students who attend low performing schools, to meet State and local Student academic achievement standards in core academic subjects, such as reading and mathematics
(2) offer students a broad array of additional services, programs and activities, such as youth development activities, drug and violence prevention programs, counseling programs, art, music, and physical education and fitness programs, and technology education programs that are designed to reinforce and complement the regular academic program of participating students; and
(3) offer families of students served by community learning centers opportunities for literacy and related educational development.

Activities to Be Carried Out to Accomplish Strategy	Positions Responsible	Timeline	Effectiveness Indicators
1. Developing of a unique preK program that is designed to increase these students' ability to benefit from school based educational activities	Lead preK teacher	October	The staff develops a system by which information and activities from the various programs are used to create a unique preK program.
2. Developing a system by which all content areas (art, music, core curriculum, etc.) are blended into a program that allows for these children's parents to be their first teacher	Lead preK teacher PreK staff Director Principal	October	The program developed will lend itself to the creation of a total educational activity that allows parents, teachers, and students to develop a well rounded outlook on future school activities.

GRANT FUNDS WILL BE USED TO PAY ONLY FOR ACTIVITIES OCCURRING BETWEEN THE BEGINNING AND ENDING DATES OF THE GRANT AS SPECIFIED ON THE NOTICE OF GRANT AWARD.

TEXAS EDUCATION AGENCY
Standard Application System (SAS)
Texas 21ˢᵗ Century Community Learning Centers, Cycle 3
Spring, Summer, and Fall of
2005, 2006, and 2007
SCHEDULE #4B--Program Description - Part 3
Program Activities/Budget Year 1: October 1, 2004 - December 31,
2005
(Enter Component Area if applicable)

Use as Many Pages as Necessary, front only, font size not less than 9 point.

LOCAL PROGRAM OBJECTIVE
The West Texas Community Learning Centers will reduce
for educational failure for children by providing extended
and extended-year integrated activities in a safe and drug
environment.

STRATEGY
To improve academic achievement of all students by
integrating the Character Counts program into the
educational activities.

The goals of the program are:
The purpose of 21st Century Community Learning Centers, Cycle 3, is to provide
opportunities for communities to establish or expand activities in community learning
centers that—

(1) provide opportunities for academic enrichment, including providing tutorial services to
help children, particularly students who attend low performing schools, to meet State and
local Student academic achievement standards in core academic subjects, such as
reading and mathematics

(2) offer students a broad array of additional services, programs and activities, such as
youth development activities, drug and violence prevention programs, counseling
programs, art, music, and physical education and fitness programs, and technology
education programs that are designed to reinforce and complement the regular
academic program of participating students; and

(3) offer families of students served by community learning centers opportunities for
literacy and related educational development.

Activities to Be Carried Out to Accomplish Strategy	Positions Responsible	Timeline	Effectiveness Indicators
1. Using the school districts' Character Counts program as a means to teach wise lifestyle choices	Principals Counselors	June	The number of Office referrals shows a 5% decrease

GRANT FUNDS WILL BE USED TO PAY ONLY FOR ACTIVITIES OCCURRING BETWEEN THE BEGINNING AND ENDING DATES OF THE GRANT AS SPECIFIED ON THE NOTICE OF
GRANT AWARD.

116

For TEA Use Only

Adjustments and/or annotations made
on this have been confirmed with

by telephone/FAX on _____ of TEA.
by _____

152-906
County District No.

Lubbock-Cooper ISD
Applicant Agency

Amendment No. _____

TEXAS EDUCATION AGENCY
Standard Application System (SAS)
Texas 21st Century Community Learning Centers, Cycle 3
Spring, Summer, and Fall of
2005, 2006, and 2007
SCHEDULE #4B--Program Description - Part 3
Program Activities/Budget Year 1: October 1, 2004 - December 31, 2005

(Enter Component Area if applicable)

Use as Many Pages as Necessary, front only, font size not less than 9 point

LOCAL PROGRAM OBJECTIVE
The West Texas Community Learning Centers will reduce for educational failure for children by providing extended and extended-year integrated activities in a safe and drug environment.

STRATEGY
To improve academic achievement of all students by increasing these students' ability to use technology

The goals of the program are:
The purpose of 21st Century Community Learning Centers, Cycle 3, is to provide opportunities for communities to establish or expand activities in community learning centers that—
(1) provide opportunities for academic enrichment, including providing tutorial services to help children, particularly students who attend low performing schools, to meet State and local Student academic achievement standards in core academic subjects, such as reading and mathematics
(2) offer students a broad array of additional services, programs and activities, such as youth development activities, drug and violence prevention programs, counseling programs, art, music, and physical education and fitness programs, and technology education programs that are designed to reinforce and complement the regular academic program of participating students; and
(3) offer families of students served by community learning centers opportunities for literacy and related educational development.

Activities to Be Carried Out to Accomplish Strategy	Positions Responsible	Timeline	Effectiveness Indicators
1. The students use the various vender software programs	Teachers Venders' staff Mentors/tutors	October	The number of times that the students use computers in their lessons increase
2. The parents of the targeted students come to the learning centers to learn how to use technology	Director Students Teachers	May	The number of parents coming to the centers to use technology increases
3. The special needs parents and students come to the learning centers to use technology	Teachers Director Director of Sp.Ed.	April	The number of special needs students and their parents using the learning centers increases
4. The community in general increases their use of the learning center technology	Teachers Community mentors	May	The number of community members using technology increases

GRANT FUNDS WILL BE USED TO PAY ONLY FOR ACTIVITIES OCCURRING BETWEEN THE BEGINNING AND ENDING DATES OF THE GRANT AS SPECIFIED ON THE NOTICE OF GRANT AWARD.

152-906
County District No.

Lubbock-Cooper ISD
Applicant Agency

Amendment No. _____

TEXAS EDUCATION AGENCY
Standard Application System (SAS)
Texas 21st Century Community Learning Centers, Cycle 3
Spring, Summer, and Fall of
2005, 2006, and 2007
SCHEDULE #4B--Program Description - Part 3
Program Activities/Budget Year 1: October 1, 2004 - December 31,
2005

(Enter Component Area if applicable)

Use as Many Pages as Necessary, front only, font size not less than 9 point

LOCAL PROGRAM OBJECTIVE
The West Texas Community Learning Centers will reduce
for educational failure for children by providing extended
and extended-year integrated activities in a safe and drug
environment.

STRATEGY
To improve academic achievement of all community
members by having access to the learning centers

The goals of the program are:
The purpose of 21st Century Community Learning Centers, Cycle 3, is to provide
opportunities for communities to establish or expand activities in community learning
centers that —
(1) provide opportunities for academic enrichment, including providing tutorial services to help
children, particularly students who attend low performing schools, to meet State and local
Student academic achievement standards in core academic subjects, such as reading and
mathematics
(2) offer students a broad array of additional services, programs and activities, such as youth
development activities, drug and violence prevention programs, counseling programs, art,
music, and physical education and fitness programs, and technology education programs that
are designed to reinforce and complement the regular academic program of participating
students; and
(3) offer families of students served by community learning centers opportunities for literacy
and related educational development.

Activities to Be Carried Out to Accomplish Strategy	Positions Responsible	Timeline	Effectiveness Indicators
1. The general level of community stakeholder interaction with the learning centers is enhanced by having the programs available	Director Teachers	May	The number of community members using any aspect of the learning centers
2. The community members come to the centers	Director Teachers Outside evaluator	April	The surveys of use of the centers by community members. The evaluation of the effects of the center.

GRANT FUNDS WILL BE USED TO PAY ONLY FOR ACTIVITIES OCCURRING BETWEEN THE BEGINNING AND ENDING DATES OF THE GRANT AS SPECIFIED ON THE NOTICE OF
GRANT AWARD.

TEXAS EDUCATION AGENCY
Standard Application System (SAS)
Texas 21st Century Community Learning Centers, Cycle 3
Spring, Summer, and Fall of
2005, 2006, and 2007
SCHEDULE #4B--Program Description - Part 3
Program Activities/Budget Year 1: October 1, 2004 - December 31,
2005

Use as Many Pages as Necessary, front only, font size not less than 9 point

(Enter Component Area if applicable)

LOCAL PROGRAM OBJECTIVE
The West Texas Community Learning Centers will increase the level of knowledge and quality-of-life for all community members

STRATEGY
The learning centers become a focus point for the community

Activities to Be Carried Out to Accomplish Strategy	Positions Responsible	Timeline	Effectiveness Indicators
The goals of the program are: The purpose of 21st Century Community Learning Centers, Cycle 3, is to provide opportunities for communities to establish or expand activities in community learning centers that— (1) provide opportunities for academic enrichment, including providing tutorial services to help children, particularly students who attend low performing schools, to meet State and local Student academic achievement standards in core academic subjects, such as reading and mathematics (2) offer students a broad array of additional services, programs and activities, such as youth development activities, drug and violence prevention programs, counseling programs, art, music, and physical education and fitness programs, and technology education programs that are designed to reinforce and complement the regular academic program of participating students; and (3) offer families of students served by community learning centers opportunities for literacy and related educational development.			
1. Students, parents, and staff can use the centers to further their education	Teachers Center Technologist TTU mentors	March	The number of people using the various software programs, accessing the Internet, and generally reporting the value of the centers
2. The Libraries are used to increase the general literacy of the communities	Staff	May	The number of books checked out and special programs attended
3. Technology training on the various software programs	Center Technologist	April	The number of community members trained on the technology and the software

GRANT FUNDS WILL BE USED TO PAY ONLY FOR ACTIVITIES OCCURRING BETWEEN THE BEGINNING AND ENDING DATES OF THE GRANT AS SPECIFIED ON THE NOTICE OF GRANT AWARD.

For TEA Use Only

Adjustments and/or annotations made
on this have been confirmed with

by telephone/FAX on _____
by _____ of TEA.

Use as Many Pages as Necessary, front only, font size not less than 9 point

TEXAS EDUCATION AGENCY
Standard Application System (SAS)
Texas 21ˢᵗ Century Community Learning Centers, Cycle 3
Spring, Summer, and Fall of
2005, 2006, and 2007
SCHEDULE #4B--Program Description - Part 3
Program Activities/Budget Year 1: October 1, 2004 - December 31,
2005

(Enter Component Area if applicable)

LOCAL PROGRAM OBJECTIVE
The West Texas Community Learning Centers will develop a large non-partisan constituency that will hold the school districts accountable for high academic standards and promote the goals of the 21ˢᵗ Century grant while providing the base to continue these programs after Federal funding ends

STRATEGY
Training provided by WTOS, SPACLC, and TTU on understanding educational goals

The goals of the program are:
The purpose of 21st Century Community Learning Centers, Cycle 3, is to provide opportunities for communities to establish or expand activities in community learning centers that—
(1) provide opportunities for academic enrichment, including providing tutorial services to help children, particularly students who attend low performing schools, to meet State and local Student academic achievement standards in core academic subjects, such as reading and mathematics
(2) offer students a broad array of additional services, programs and activities, such as youth development activities, drug and violence prevention programs, counseling programs, art, music, and physical education and fitness programs, and technology education programs that are designed to reinforce and complement the regular academic program of participating students; and
(3) offer families of students served by community learning centers opportunities for literacy and related educational development.

Activities to Be Carried Out to Accomplish Strategy	Positions Responsible	Timeline	Effectiveness Indicators
Recruit staff, parents, and other community stakeholders for WTOS training	Counselor Principal WTOS staff TTU staff	30 days after notification with the training occurring throughout the year	Number of these individuals who complete training along with the resulting development of a larger non-partisan constituency to hold the school accountable for high academic standards.
WTOS, SPACLC, TTU and others provide local training on special population students' needs	WTOS Staff TTU staff and students Contracted individuals LCISD staff members	Every 6-weeks (or more often) as determined by stakeholders	Number of individuals who attend local training along with the resulting development of a larger non-partisan constituency to hold the school accountable for high academic standards.

For TEA Use Only

Adjustments and/or annotations made
on this have been confirmed with

by telephone/FAX on _____ of TEA.
by _____

TEXAS EDUCATION AGENCY
Standard Application System (SAS)
Texas 21ˢᵗ Century Community Learning Centers, Cycle 3
Spring, Summer, and Fall of
2005, 2006, and 2007
SCHEDULE #4B--Program Description - Part 3
Program Activities/Budget Year 1: October 1, 2004 - December 31, 2005

Use as Many Pages as Necessary, front only, font size not less than 9 point   (Enter Component Area if applicable)

LOCAL PROGRAM OBJECTIVE
Training of the staff on the use of the Science, Social Studies, PLATO, HOSTS, Kurzweil, Reading Plus, Lexia, Failure Free, and Visagraph programs

The goals of the program are:
The purpose of 21st Century Community Learning Centers, Cycle 3, is to provide opportunities for communities to establish or expand activities in community learning centers that—

(1) provide opportunities for academic enrichment, including providing tutorial services to help children, particularly students who attend low performing schools, to meet State and local Student academic achievement standards in core academic subjects, such as reading and mathematics

(2) offer students a broad array of additional services, programs and activities, such as youth development activities, drug and violence prevention programs, counseling programs, art, music, and physical education and fitness programs, and technology education programs that are designed to reinforce and complement the regular academic program of participating students; and

(3) offer families of students served by community learning centers opportunities for literacy and related educational development.

STRATEGY
Vender provide training on the use of the software and other materials obtained to provide effective instruction for the students.

Activities to Be Carried Out to Accomplish Strategy	Positions Responsible	Timeline	Effectiveness Indicators
Training on the Science, Social Studies, PLATO, HOSTS, Kurzweil, Reading Plus, Lexia, Failure Free, and Visagraph programs	Venders	Starting in November using the vender's recommended training times on all programs	The staff will be able to use the software and instructional materials to assist the students in being successful academically.
The staff will develop integrated lesson that use these non-traditional instructional methods and materials	Principals	October	The staff will have lesson plans that show the integration of these items into the at-risk students' instruction

GRANT FUNDS WILL BE USED TO PAY ONLY FOR ACTIVITIES OCCURRING BETWEEN THE BEGINNING AND ENDING DATES OF THE GRANT AS SPECIFIED ON THE NOTICE OF GRANT AWARD.

TEXAS EDUCATION AGENCY

Standard Application System (SAS)
Texas 21ˢᵗ Century Community Learning Centers, Cycle 3
Spring, Summer, and Fall of
2005, 2006, and 2007
SCHEDULE #4B--Program Description - Part 3
Program Activities/Budget Year 1: October 1, 2004 - December 31,
2005

(Enter Component Area if applicable)

For TEA Use Only

Adjustments and/or annotations made on this have been confirmed with

by telephone/FAX on _____

by _____ of TEA.

Use as Many Pages as Necessary, front only, font size not less than 9 point.

LOCAL PROGRAM OBJECTIVE

Increase by 5% each year the number of participating students who pass all sections of TAKS.

STRATEGY

Provide supplemental learning activities for participating students.

The goals of the program are:
The purpose of 21st Century Community Learning Centers, Cycle 3, is to provide opportunities for communities to establish or expand activities in community learning centers that—
(1) provide opportunities for academic enrichment, including providing tutorial services to help children, particularly students who attend low performing schools, to meet State and local Student academic achievement standards in core academic subjects, such as reading and mathematics
(2) offer students a broad array of additional services, programs and activities, such as youth development activities, drug and violence prevention programs, counseling programs, art, music, and physical education and fitness programs, and technology education programs that are designed to reinforce and complement the regular academic program of participating students; and
(3) offer families of students served by community learning centers opportunities for literacy and related educational development.

Activities to Be Carried Out to Accomplish Strategy	Positions Responsible	Timeline	Effectiveness Indicators
1. Implement HOSTS Math and Language Arts programs in the Integrated Education Archive Center After-school Program: a) Conduct initial two-day training on all facets of HOSTS implementation—diagnostic assessment, learning plans, mentoring. b) Conduct HOSTS Math and Language Arts instructional sessions. c) Provide mentors for individualized instruction. d) Provide smaller class sizes through HOSTS Math and Language Arts.	HOSTS Education Consultant Teachers TTU mentors Community mentors	October -May	Afterschool teachers are trained in content and strategies; 5% increase in the number of participating students passing TAKS Reading and Math.
2. Provide "TAKS Night" to prepare for TAKS exams.	Teachers TTU mentors Community mentors	October -May	5% increase in the number of participating students passing TAKS Reading and Math.
3. Provide homework assistance.	Teachers TTU mentors Community mentors	October -May	5% increase in the number of participating students passing TAKS Reading and Math.

GRANT FUNDS WILL BE USED TO PAY ONLY FOR ACTIVITIES OCCURRING BETWEEN THE BEGINNING AND ENDING DATES OF THE GRANT AS SPECIFIED ON THE NOTICE OF GRANT AWARD.

For TEA Use Only

Adjustments and/or annotations made on this have been confirmed with

by telephone/FAX on _____

by _____ of TEA.

TEXAS EDUCATION AGENCY

Standard Application System (SAS)
Texas 21st Century Community Learning Centers, Cycle 3
Spring, Summer, and Fall of
2005, 2006, and 2007
SCHEDULE #4B--Program Description - Part 3
Program Activities/Budget Year 1: October 1, 2004 - December 31,
2005
(Enter Component Area if applicable)

Use as Many Pages as Necessary, front only, font size not less than 9 point.

LOCAL PROGRAM OBJECTIVE

Decrease by 5% each year the number of students who are retained in grade.

The goals of the program are:
The purpose of 21st Century Community Learning Centers, Cycle 3, is to provide opportunities for communities to establish or expand activities in community learning centers that—
(1) provide opportunities for academic enrichment, including providing tutorial services to help children, particularly students who attend low performing schools, to meet State and local Student academic achievement standards in core academic subjects, such as reading and mathematics
(2) offer students a broad array of additional services, programs and activities, such as youth development activities, drug and violence prevention programs, counseling programs, art, music, and physical education and fitness programs, and technology education programs that are designed to reinforce and complement the regular academic program of participating students; and
(3) offer families of students served by community learning centers opportunities for literacy and related educational development.

STRATEGY

Offer homework assistance.

Activities to Be Carried Out to Accomplish Strategy	Positions Responsible	Timeline	Effectiveness Indicators
1. Identify students needing homework assistance.	Classroom teachers	Each grading period.	All eligible students have a place in the Learning Center.
2. Canvas classroom teachers to determine homework assignments to be addressed in the assistance sessions.	Teachers TTU/Community Mentors	Weekly, October -May	Current homework assignments are secured for each student; the number of students earning passing grades in the core curriculum increases by 5%.
3. Conduct homework assistance sessions.	Teachers TTU/Community Mentors	Weekly, October -May	The number of students earning passing grades in the core curriculum increases by 5%.
4. Review student performance in class to determine effectiveness of the homework assistance sessions.	Teachers TTU/Community Mentors	Weekly, October-May	The number of students earning passing grades in the core curriculum increases by 5%.

GRANT FUNDS WILL BE USED TO PAY ONLY FOR ACTIVITIES OCCURRING BETWEEN THE BEGINNING AND ENDING DATES OF THE GRANT AS SPECIFIED ON THE NOTICE OF GRANT AWARD.

For TEA Use Only

Adjustments and/or annotations made on this have been confirmed with

_____

by telephone/FAX on _____

by _____ of TEA.

TEXAS EDUCATION AGENCY

Standard Application System (SAS)

Texas 21st Century Community Learning Centers, Cycle 3

2005, 2006, and 2007
Spring, Summer, and Fall of

SCHEDULE #4B--Program Description - Part 3
Program Activities/Budget Year 1: October 1, 2004 - December 31, 2005

(Enter Component Area if applicable)

Use as Many Pages as Necessary, front only, font size not less than 9 point.'

LOCAL PROGRAM OBJECTIVE

Increase by 5% each year the number of participating students who increase proficiency in reading and math as determined by pre- and post-testing.

STRATEGY

Diagnostic assessment of learning needs.

The goals of the program are:
The purpose of 21st Century Community Learning Centers, Cycle 3, is to provide opportunities for communities to establish or expand activities in community learning centers that—

(1) provide opportunities for academic enrichment, including providing tutorial services to help children, particularly students who attend low performing schools, to meet State and local Student academic achievement standards in core academic subjects, such as reading and mathematics

(2) offer students a broad array of additional services, programs and activities, such as youth development activities, drug and violence prevention programs, counseling programs, art, music, and physical education and fitness programs, and technology education programs that are designed to reinforce and complement the regular academic program of participating students; and

(3) offer families of students served by community learning centers opportunities for literacy and related educational development.

Activities to Be Carried Out to Accomplish Strategy	Positions Responsible	Timeline	Effectiveness Indicators
1. Conduct training on the administration and use of HOSTS assessments.	HOSTS Education Consultant	May	Program evaluation shows that teachers administer assessments and use data to develop learning plans.
2. Continually assess students' individual learning needs using HOSTS Reading Diagnostic Assessments, HOST Math Placement Inventory, and TEKS/TAKS data. Reassessment takes place weekly, bi-weekly, monthly as required each year.	Teachers TTU/Community Mentors	October - May	Program evaluation shows the use of assessment data to develop learning plans; learning plans are updated following re-assessment; pre- and post-tests show that 80% of participating students master benchmark objectives.

GRANT FUNDS WILL BE USED TO PAY ONLY FOR ACTIVITIES OCCURRING BETWEEN THE BEGINNING AND ENDING DATES OF THE GRANT AS SPECIFIED ON THE NOTICE OF GRANT AWARD.

152-906
County District No.

Lubbock-Cooper ISD
Applicant Agency

Amendment No. _____

TEXAS EDUCATION AGENCY

Standard Application System (SAS)
Texas 21st Century Community Learning Centers, Cycle 3
Spring, Summer, and Fall of
2005, 2006, and 2007
SCHEDULE #4B--Program Description - Part 3
Program Activities/Budget Year 1: October 1, 2004 - December 31, 2005

Use as Many Pages as Necessary, front only, font size not less than 9 point.   *(Enter Component Area if applicable)*

LOCAL PROGRAM OBJECTIVE

Increase by 5% each year the number of participating students who increase proficiency in reading and math as determined by pre- and post-testing.

STRATEGY

Regular monitoring of student progress toward learning goals.

The goals of the program are:
The purpose of 21st Century Community Learning Centers, Cycle 3, is to provide opportunities for communities to establish or expand activities in community learning centers that—
(1) provide opportunities for academic enrichment, including providing tutorial services to help children, particularly students who attend low performing schools, to meet State and local Student academic achievement standards in core academic subjects, such as reading and mathematics
(2) offer students a broad array of additional services, programs and activities, such as youth development activities, drug and violence prevention programs, counseling programs, art, music, and physical education and fitness programs, and technology education programs that are designed to reinforce and complement the regular academic program of participating students; and
(3) offer families of students served by community learning centers opportunities for literacy and related educational development.

Activities to Be Carried Out to Accomplish Strategy	Positions Responsible	Timeline	Effectiveness Indicators
1. Conduct training on HOSTS continuous progress strategies.	HOSTS Education Consultant	October	Program evaluation shows that teachers are monitoring progress using pre- and post-testing.
2. Gather pre-data.	Teachers TTU/Community Mentors	November	Data is available for benchmarks.
3. Continually assess students' individual learning needs using HOSTS Reading Diagnostic Assessments, HOST Math Placement Inventory, and TEKS/TAKS data. Reassessment takes place weekly, bi-weekly, monthly as required each year.	Teachers TTU/Community Mentors	May	Learning plans are updated following re-assessment.
4. Gather post-data.	Teachers TTU/Community Mentors	May	Pre- and post-tests show that 80% of participating students master benchmark objectives.

GRANT FUNDS WILL BE USED TO PAY ONLY FOR ACTIVITIES OCCURRING BETWEEN THE BEGINNING AND ENDING DATES OF THE GRANT AS SPECIFIED ON THE NOTICE OF GRANT AWARD.

<table>
<tr><td colspan="2">

For TEA Use Only

Adjustments and/or annotations made
on this have been confirmed with

_____

by telephone/FAX on_____
by _____ of TEA.

</td><td>

TEXAS EDUCATION AGENCY
Standard Application System (SAS)
Texas 21st Century Community Learning Centers, Cycle 3
Spring, Summer, and Fall of
2005, 2006, and 2007

SCHEDULE #4C--Program Evaluation Design

</td><td>

152-006
County District No.
Lubbock-Cooper ISD
Applicant Agency

</td></tr>
</table>

Font size not less than 9 point. (Arial or Times New Roman)

THE APPLICANT AGREES TO COMPLY WITH ANY REPORTING AND EVALUATION REQUIREMENTS THAT MAY BE ESTABLISHED BY THE TEXAS EDUCATION AGENCY AND TO SUBMIT THE REPORTS IN THE FORMAT AND TIME REQUESTED BY THE AGENCY.

Part 1: Component Description	Limited to the Space Provided

Ongoing Monitoring / Continuous Improvement

The West Texas Community Learning Centers evaluation committee will meet regularly to oversee program evaluation and to ensure that ongoing feedback is provided to program decision makers (21st WTCLC Advisory Committee) on program progress and financial activities. WTCLC will contract with an experienced firm with grant management, program development and program evaluation experience to provide continuous program evaluation and refinement. The external evaluation team will include a cadre of experienced evaluators, on-site assessment staff, and technical assistance experts. External Evaluator will utilize formal and informal observations to assess program effectiveness, including pre/post-test surveys containing both open and closed questions; Likert-type scales directed at students, parents, teachers, and project staff; and records, including course grades, internal behavioral and disciplinary actions, and attendance. Using a "tiered-approach," quantitative and qualitative outcome components will be used along with baseline assessments, benchmarks, and other markers for continuous program assessment and refinement. The evaluation team will meet monthly with program staff to provide ongoing feedback so necessary program adjustments can be made as needed to enhance program outcomes. The day-to-day evaluations will be facilitated by the program director and will work with the staff to improve the program in a continuous manner. In addition to the program director, the program coordinator will provide data analysis and program linkage of the out-of-school-time programs to the regular curriculum of each of the school districts to assure that students are obtaining Adequate Yearly Progress in meeting state standards and are obtaining graduation and promotion credits in a timely manner. He will also coordinate the activities of the preK Learning Center model with the overall campus improvement planning (CIP) process. At a district level he will coordinate the activities designed to link this analysis to the district improvement planning (DIP) process. The goals will be to create an after school program that increases student learning, fitness, and belonging while involving more community stakeholders with the grant activities through the HOSTS mentoring program and other opportunities that will be developed to involve all of the stakeholders. During the yearly School Report Card the public will be given an overview of all aspects of this program.

Qualitative and Quantitative Data Collection Methods

In collaboration with the external evaluator and the Evaluation Committee, the 21st CCLC Site Coordinator will be responsible for supervision of data collection. The district currently collects a wide array of student statistics, including enrollment, attendance, discipline, grades, course history, testing scores, and demographic information, such as school-wide and disaggregated by population categories. Our five Center campus principals agree and understand that we must provide baseline data for three years preceding and following receipt of the 21st CCLC grant. **Quantitative** data will include statistics and information regarding student achievement, academic rigor, student retention, and school climate. Through monthly visits, the external evaluator will use various **qualitative** data collection methodologies, such as observation by different evaluators, focus groups, parent-teacher-student surveys, and Likert-type surveys to assess program progress. Written feedback will be provided regularly to 21st CCLC Coordinator. Quarterly reports will be provided to the Texas Education Agency and to the Advisory Council throughout program implementation and operation. Annual Reports required by the Texas Education Agency and more in-depth annual analyses will be prepared by the external evaluator for review by our Advisory Council.

Data Collection Methods and Schedule: Data will be collected by four primary methods as summarized below according to the schedule listed:

Collection Method	Description of Data Collection	Collection Schedule
Interviews. Focus Groups	Interview with project personnel, students, family, and community members. Purpose is to assess: a) Needs of individuals b) How project met needs; c) Project strengths and weaknesses; d) Project benefits; e) Changes needed to better meet identified needs.	Beginning, middle, and end of project activities
Observation	Evaluators observe site activities using standard observation protocols	8 times for the duration of project
Surveys	Survey will follow up on issues from interviews and focus groups	Quarterly -four times/year
Extant & Project Data	School and project attendance records, school grades, State test scores, discipline records, Safe School data, and other data as needed and available	Beginning, middle, and end of project

These qualitative data will be combined with quantitative measures that will be obtained from various vender day-to-day assessments, teacher generated tests, TAKS practice tests, AEIS analysis and testing, and other standardized measures. When taken collectively all of these data points will allow the hard data to drive changes in the program. This will provide a base in real data that is both quantitative and qualitative in nature and will employ all of the system at each of the school districts for data collection. This will be done to maximize the information obtained from all sources so that the best decision regarding teaching can be made. This system will employ several of the systems that the school districts had developed while working with other service providers.

For TEA Use Only	TEXAS EDUCATION AGENCY	__152-906_
Adjustments and/or annotations made on this have been confirmed with	**Standard Application System (SAS)** **Texas 21st Century Community Learning Centers, Cycle 3** **Spring, Summer, and Fall of 2005, 2006, and 2007**	County District No. **Lubbock-Cooper ISD_** Applicant Agency
by telephone/FAX on_____ by _____ of TEA.	**SCHEDULE #4C Program Evaluation Design**	

Formative Evaluation	**(Limited to Space Provided)**

a. Formative Evaluation: Formative evaluation will begin during project development and continues throughout the life of the project. Its intent is to assess ongoing project activities and provide information to monitor and improve the project. It will be conducted at several points in the developmental life of a project and its activities.

b. Process Evaluation. The process evaluation will examine the conduct of the project, including a determination of the effectiveness of the planning, design, implementation, and evaluation of the project. The purpose of process or implementation evaluation will be to assess whether the project is being conducted as planned. This process will occur several times during the life of the program. The underlying principle is that before you can evaluate the outcomes or impact of a program, you must make sure the program and its components are really operating and, if they are operating according to the proposed plan or description. A series of implementation questions will guide our process or implementation evaluation to determine the following:

- the quality, type, and degree of planning, implementation, and evaluation of project activities;
- the quality, type, and degree of collaboration with project partners;
- the quality and level of communication with project management on the progress of the project and any problems encountered;
- the quality, type, and degree of involvement practiced by the principal(s), teacher(s), parent(s), and when appropriate, student(s);
- the quality, type, and level of professional development activities;
- the quality, type, and level of services actually provided to the targeted population;
- the quality of any products/documents developed as part of the project;
- the strengths and weaknesses of the project design, implementation, and evaluation; and
- the extent to which recommendations for enhancing the project as a result of ongoing evaluation activities were implemented.

c. Product Evaluation. The purpose of progress or product evaluation will be to assess progress in meeting the goals of the program and the project. It will involve collecting information to learn whether or not the benchmarks of participant progress were met and to point out unexpected developments. Progress evaluation will collect information to determine what the impact of the activities and strategies is on participants, curriculum at various stages of the intervention. By measuring progress, program staff will be able to eliminate the risk of waiting until participants have experienced the entire program to assess likely outcomes. If the data collected as part of the progress evaluation fail to show expected changes, the information will be used to fine tune, revise or modify the project. Data collected, as part of a product evaluation, will form the basis for, a summative evaluation conducted at final stages of the project. We plan to collect data and provide information with regard to the required performance measures to determine the extent to which the project achieved the desired results and to measure the impact of the program on the participants related to the following overall performance objectives:

- increase in number of families of participating students from eligible campuses that show gains in literacy and educational development as well as involvement in school-related education activities relevant to their children's school(s)
- improvement in citizenship/character education as demonstrated by student participants and their families as measured by attendance reports for both in school and WTCLC program days, decrease in office referrals, assignment to alternative education centers and juvenile justice alternative education programs, and non-criminal and criminal incidents and an increase in activities that demonstrate student responsibility and obligation to the school and community through projects such as community service and service learning opportunities.
- perceived impact as evidenced by an increase in the academic success of all students in the schools implementing Texas 21st Century Community Learning Centers such as increased numbers of students passing all TAKS tests, being promoted to the next succeeding grade level, graduating from high school, entering college, etc.

Summative (Final) Evaluation
Summative evaluation will assess the project's success in reaching its stated goals at its final stage. Summative evaluation will addresses many of the same questions as a progress evaluation, but it will take place after the project has been established and the timeframe posited for change has occurred. A summative evaluation will address these basic questions:

- The extent to which the activities of the project were implemented as planned.
- The effectiveness of the activities in achieving the goals and objectives of the project.
- The impact of the project activities on the participants.

Summative evaluation will attempt to collect information about outcomes and related processes, strategies, and activities that have led to them.

Term Activity Progress Reports
Progress/activity reports will be submitted thirty days after the completion of each term, specifically fall term as of December 31, spring term as of May 31, of each year, and summer session as of August 31, of each year. The reports will focus on data and information gathered through the effectiveness indicators included in program activities. The data collected will also reference the educational and literacy opportunities offered for participating students' family members, both adults and young siblings. Documentation will serve as proof of achievement and will be used to establish a foundation for sustainability after the grant funds are no longer available. Logs and records of activities for families, adults and younger siblings, will also be records that demonstrate the impact the program has immediately and over time.

Final Evaluation Report: WTCLC will provide a final evaluation report in requested TEA format within 30 days after the end of the project.

Continuous Improvement Reports: The Program Director will work with the staff of the school districts on a weekly basis to improve the program. The Program Director will inform the evaluation committee of the changes that have occurred to improve the program.

Continued Funding of the Program: The linkage of the program successes to specific grant funded programs will allow these items to be built into the ongoing plans of the campus and the district. This will proved a method to integrate these successful programs into the normal budget.

14

Conclusions

In this book, I have provided a host of strategies, techniques, and resources that will assist you in your pursuit of large and small grants and gifts for your classroom, school, or school district. Data was presented showing that fundraising is a billion-dollar business in America, and that grants and gifts from individual donors are, by far, the largest source of outside funding at the college, university, and private school levels. The implications of all this, combined with the enormous transfer of wealth that is going to take place in America over the next 50 years, has many positive implications for the public schools and should provide some direction for planning and implementation purposes well into the future.

Research data was presented showing that education ranks second only to religion in total contributions received from corporations and foundations. The research also disclosed that more than 80 percent of all contributions made, including bequests, come from individual donors, and that individual donors provide, by far, the most contributions to worthy causes. Solicitation of grants and gifts from individuals should become a major part of a school district's total big-time fundraising effort.

I have emphasized in this book that millions of people all over the United States are graduates and strong supporters of the public schools. They view the public schools as being truly representative of our democratic ideals and values as a nation. Many of our best and brightest are graduates of the public schools, live or work in our communities, and have children or grandchildren attending our schools. At this time of tight education budgets and budget shortfalls, many of these graduates and the organizations they represent are interested in helping the schools. They want to experience the joy and fulfillment of giving gifts to the schools, and many want to become personally involved in your cause. Learning how to ask for big grants and gifts from individual donors is a major part of this book.

Public school foundations and public education funds were examined and reported on in relationship to the good they are doing around the country. Assistance was provided on how to form a foundation for those schools and school districts that do not have foundations at this time. I highlighted some of the most successful school foundations and public education funds around the country, and I suggested that more coordination and cooperation should take place among foundations in schools and school districts.

A number of issues of concern were discussed, mainly centering on the need to adequately fund public education in the United States and to explore ways to equalize outside funding among schools of poverty and schools of wealth. Wealthy schools and school districts are able to raise significantly more outside dollars than poorer schools and school districts, thus making for an unequal playing field. I mentioned that states, the federal government, and local school districts need to adequately fund public education in this country. Schools and school districts should not have to look for outside dollars to fund basic programs, buy materials and equipment, and provide for teacher salaries. These school funding issues are real and must be dealt with by boards of education around the country as well as by legislators and taxpayers who are responsible for adequately funding public education.

As one of the major goals of a big-time fundraising effort, I recommended establishing a development office at the district level with full-time staff. It was mentioned that the development office should become a profit center in two to three years or less. This is a good investment! The need to delineate fundraising roles and responsibilities in a big-time fundraising effort was also presented, and the roles of the superintendent of schools, the school board, teachers, principals, parents, volunteers, and other staff were discussed.

Concrete strategies and examples of how to obtain big grants and gifts from corporations, foundations, and the government were provided. It was mentioned that there are millions of dollars in corporate, foundation, and government grant opportunities out there waiting to be tapped. Knowing how to pursue these grants and gifts is very important in a big-time fundraising effort.

Grantwriting techniques for both minigrants and major grants were presented in much detail, including needs assessment documentation, goals, objectives, activities, evaluation specifications, and the budget. Actual examples of two winning minigrants and one major government grant were provided for review. I emphasized that it has been my experience and the experience of others that first learning how to write a successful minigrant will facilitate the writing of a successful major grant.

Many ideas and strategies were offered on how to ask for big grants and gifts from people of wealth and others. In a big-time fundraising effort, learning how to "friendraise" will be just as important as learning how to fundraise. Obtaining big gifts of cash and noncash assets from individual donors will help to build your endowment just as professional development staff do at colleges, universities, and private schools. This, I believe, is going to be key to the success of your fundraising efforts now and into the future. It's big grants and gifts that will help you build creative and performing arts centers, new gymnasiums, state-of-the-art computer learning stations, and other high-end facilities and programs.

To save you time and energy, I have provided a comprehensive bibliography of some of the finest books and materials on fundraising available as well as many Web addresses that I have gathered along the way. Additionally, I have included a comprehensive sampling of available corporate and foundation grants, including funding information and Web addresses, job descriptions for key fundraising staff, a sample letter that would accompany a corporate or foundation grant application, and a glossary of terms to help you decipher some of the fundraising lingo.

Schools, school districts, and school foundations are at the threshold of something very big and very beautiful. Many individual donors, corporations, and foundations want to see the public schools succeed as never before, and they want to give gifts to the schools. You must seize the opportunity by hiring competent, experienced staff and consultants, training those in need, identifying potential donors, and going after big grants and gifts with gusto! You must become big-time fundraisers. The kids deserve nothing less! Good luck along the way.

Resource A

Some Examples of Grant Opportunities for K–12 Schools

The following examples of grant opportunities for K–12 are reprinted with permission from *eSchool News*. The entries are extensive and provide you with a starting point for pursuing grants and gifts from the many funding sources that are out there for K–12.

Grant Title: "I Will LEARN Today!" Grant Program

Organization: LearningStation Inc.

Eligibility: K-12 schools or districts interested in using technology to enhance teaching and learning

Value: $500,000 total

LearningStation Inc., a provider of customized web-based desktops for teaching and learning, has initiated a grant program entitled "I Will LEARN Today!" Through this program, LearningStation will provide grants for schools to receive access to the company's Education Desktop. The Education Desktop gives students and teachers access to a comprehensive suite of instructional programs, software content, and professional development programs of their school's choice; schools can choose from more than 12,000 programs from 75 content publishers. This desktop portal also gives administrators tools to track and report on program use, features password-protected access to all content titles, and includes features for file storage, eMail, and many other functions. LearningStation will provide $500,000 worth of subscriptions to this web service to K-12 schools or districts chosen to receive the grant. The number of LearningStation subscriptions grant recipients will get varies according to their circumstances.

Contact: http://www.learningstation.com/grantapp

Grant Title: Acellus Matching Grant Program

Organization: The International Academy of Science

Eligibility: Schools or districts that teach grades 6–12, junior college, or university

Value: 50 percent match

The International Academy of Science developed the Acellus Matching Program to help qualified schools purchase Acellus Learning Systems so they can raise students' math scores. The Acellus Learning System is a video-based interactive education tool that is helping students master Mathematics. Approved schools will be required to cover the remaining cost of the software. The eligible software programs and their full prices are listed on the grant application.

Contact: Julianna Habing or Martha Asay, (816) 229–3800, julianna@science.edu

http://www.science.edu/AcellusGrants

Grant Title: Adobe Software Donation

Organization: Adobe Systems Inc.

Eligibility: Schools and nonprofits

Value: Software

Adobe Systems Inc. supports K-12 schools and nonprofits by donating up to four packages of its latest software. Eligible organizations have a core mission that focus on at least one of the following: improving K-12 student performance; developing curriculum for K-12 classrooms; developing and providing K-12 teacher training and development; and working to prevent hunger and homelessness. The program is managed by Gifts In Kind International. Requests are reviewed every other month based on the primary services the organization provides. Organizations may only apply once in a 12-month period.

Contact: http://www.adobe.com/aboutadobe/philanthropy/software.html

Grant Title: Adopt-A-Classroom Grants

Organization: Adopt-a-Classroom

Eligibility: Teachers

Value: $500 credit

Teachers who register at the Adopt-a-Classroom web site can be adopted by an individual, a business, or a foundation. Once adopted, teachers will receive $500 worth of credit to purchase items that enrich the learning environment, including classroom technology. Teachers help solicit their own sponsors by downloading and distributing fliers within their community or by sending out a personalized, pre-written eMail from the Adopt-a-Classroom web site. Every donor receives information about the classroom it has adopted, including an itemized list of what teachers bought so donors can see the impact of their donation.

Contact: http://www.adoptaclassroom.com

Grant Title: Advancing Student Achievement Grants

Organization: The Actuarial Foundation

Eligibility: Schools and nonprofit organizations in the U.S. and Canada

Value: Up to $25,000 total

Through its Advancing Student Achievement program, the Actuarial Foundation awards monetary grants to schools and nonprofit groups throughout the United States and Canada. The basic requirement for schools or groups seeking funding is that they develop a viable mentoring program involving actuaries in the teaching of mathematics to children in private or public schools. The program brings together actuaries and educators in local classroom environments with the belief that interaction with real-world mentors will boost students' interest and achievement in math. The Actuarial Foundation provides a local network of actuaries ready to participate, as well as suggestions on how to integrate math concepts from the workplace into the classroom. Groups applying for grants will be given wide latitude in designing programs that enhance learning and create a "love of math" in each student.

Contact: asa@actfnd.org

http://www.actuarialfoundation.org/grant/index.html

Grant Title: Allstate Foundation Grants

Organization: The Allstate Foundation

Eligibility: Schools

Value: Up to $10,000

The Allstate Foundation makes grants to nonprofit organizations, including public K-12 schools, for projects that are related to automobile and highway safety, homes and neighborhoods, and personal safety and security. Under the personal safety and security initiative, programs that raise awareness of poverty, child abuse, drugs, and violence prevention are eligible for consideration. Applicants should offer safeguards against gangs, guns, sexual harassment, and domestic violence. Grants typically range from $5,000 to $10,000. There are no deadlines.

Contact: allfound@allstate.com

http://www.allstate.com/foundation

Grant Title: AMD Corporate Contributions

Organization: Advanced Micro Devices Inc.

Eligibility: K-12 schools and districts

Value: Varies

AMD's K-12 initiatives target programs that increase student interest and/or proficiency in literacy, math, science, and computer technology. Because great teachers are the key to successful learning, AMD also funds programs aimed at developing and supporting effective classroom instruction. Applications are due twice a year: May 1 and Dec. 1. Funding decisions are communicated no later than six months following the application deadline.

Contact: http://www.amd.com/usen/Corporate/AboutAMD/0,,51_52_7697_7702,00.html

Grant Title: American Express Philanthropic Program

Organization: The American Express Foundation

Eligibility: Nonprofits located near American Express six service centers: Phoenix, Ariz.; South Florida; Minneapolis, Minn.; Greensboro, N.C.; New York, N.Y.; and Salt Lake City, Utah

Value: Varies

The American Express Foundation makes grants under three program themes that reflect its funding priorities: Community Service, Cultural Heritage, and Economic Independence. The third category, Economic Independence, supports initiatives that encourage, develop, and sustain economic self-reliance through programs that: serve youth, emphasize school-to-work efforts, and work experiences; build awareness about career and employment options for individuals facing significant barriers to employment; and provide education, training and workplace experiences so they may actively pursue these options. The American Express Foundation also targets its grants in cities where American Express has significant business and/or employee presence.

Contact: http://home3.americanexpress.com/corp/philanthropy/

Grant Title: American Honda Foundation Grants

Organization: American Honda Foundation

Eligibility: Schools and youth-focused nonprofit organizations

Value: Between $10,000 and $100,000 per award

The American Honda Foundation makes grants of $10,000 to $100,000 to K-12 schools, colleges, universities, trade schools, and other youth-focused nonprofit organizations for programs that benefit youth and scientific education. The foundation is seeking programs that meet the following characteristics: imaginative, scientific, creative, humanistic, youthful, innovative, and forward-thinking. Grant applications are accepted four times per year: Nov. 1, Feb. 1, May 1, and Aug. 1.

Contact: http://www.hondacorporate.com/community

Grant Title: AOL Time Warner Foundation Grants

Organization: The AOL Time Warner Foundation

Eligibility: Schools and districts

Value: Funding & partnerships

The AOL Time Warner Foundation supports technology-related projects in four major areas of priority: Equipping Kids for the 21st Century, Extending Internet Benefits to All, Engaging Communities in the Arts, and Empowering Citizens and Civic Participation. Rather than simply providing grant monies, the foundation prefers to enter into sustainable, strategic partnerships with organizations that have demonstrated a commitment to pioneering innovative ways of meeting these priorities. As a general rule, the foundation does not fund unsolicited proposals except in very special circumstances. Proposals are reviewed throughout the year, and the foundation responds to requests within 8 to 12 weeks.

Contact: (800) 818–1066, AOLTWFoundation@aol.com

http://aoltimewarnerfoundation.org/grants/grants.html

Grant Title: Assisting At-Risk Youth

Organization: The Home Depot Foundation

Eligibility: Schools and districts

Value: Up to $25,000

The Home Depot Foundation gives cash and materials to help provide young people with safe places to play and learn, leadership programs that teach skills through community engagement, and job readiness training. The Home Depot Foundation focuses its support on programs that serve at-risk youth ages 12 to 18. Grants typically range from $5,000 to $25,000. The foundation gives first priority to organizations that have been invited to apply for a grant. However, the foundation also will consider unsolicited requests that match its eligibility requirements. The foundation will consider only one proposal from the same organization in a 12-month period. Applications are reviewed four times per year and are to be submitted online.

Contact: http://www.homedepotfoundation.org

Grant Title: AT&T Foundation Grants

Organization: The AT&T Foundation

Eligibility: K-12 and higher ed

Value: Varies

The AT&T Foundation awards grants to education projects that focus on improving the quality of teaching and learning through the effective use of technology; developing workforce skills for the information technology industry; and advancing diversity in education and the workplace, especially in the fields of science, math, engineering, and technology. Accredited public and private elementary and secondary schools, accredited public and private two- and four-year institutions of higher education, and educational nonprofit organizations are eligible for consideration. AT&T funds are typically distributed through invitational programs or through projects that it proactively develops with nonprofit organizations. Unsolicited applications are reviewed, but rarely are supported. Those who wish to submit an unsolicited proposal should send a brief letter of introduction and description of their organization and project to: Secretary, AT&T Foundation, 32 Avenue of the Americas, 6th Floor, New York, N.Y. 10013.

Contact: http://www.att.com/foundation

Grant Title: Boeing Co. Charitable Contributions Program

Organization: Boeing Co.

Eligibility: K-12 schools near Boeing's facilities and institutions of higher education nationwide

Value: Grants and volunteer support

Education is one of the Boeing Co.'s four areas of support. The largest single block of company contributions goes to education, including K-12 and college and university programs across the nation and in the countries where Boeing has operations. Boeing is a major supporter of systemic reform in public education. The company works in partnership with public school districts located near major Boeing facilities and encourages employees to become active volunteers engaged in sharing their knowledge and skills with K-12 students.

Contact: http://www.boeing.com/educationrelations

Grant Title: Books for Children

Organization: The Libri Foundation

Eligibility: Rural libraries in the United States

Value: Up to $700 per award

The Libri Foundation is a nationwide nonprofit organization that donates new, high-quality, hardcover children's books to small, rural public libraries in the United States through its Books for Children program. The books donated through the Books for Children program are used for storytelling; toddler, preschool, and after-school programs; summer reading programs; "book buddy" programs, in which older children read to younger children; holiday programs; teacher check-out and curriculum support; early childhood development programs; school projects; and to just provide children with a "good read." Applicants' Friends of Library programs or other local initiatives are expected to contribute up to $350 toward the project, which the Libri Foundation will match on a 2-to-1 ratio. The foundation awards grants three times a year. The application deadlines are March 15, July 15, and Dec. 15.

Contact: librifdn@teleport.com

http://www.librifoundation.org

Grant Title: Box Tops for Education

Organization: General Mills Inc.

Eligibility: K-8 schools in the United States

Value: Up to $60,000 per year

The Box Tops for Education program offers three ways for schools to earn cash through everyday activities such as buying groceries, shopping online, and making purchases with a credit card. When parents and community members clip box tops from General Mills products, schools can get 10 cents per box top. Schools also can earn up to 10 percent of each qualifying purchase made online at the Box Tops Marketplace. Box Tops also offers a Visa card that returns 1 percent of each purchase back to your school. Each program can generate up to $20,000 per year per school, for a maximum of $60,000 per year. Each participating school must designate a school coordinator to be enrolled in the program. Check the Box Tops for Education web site for more details.

Contact: http://www.boxtops4education.com

Grant Title: Breaking Down Barriers to Assistive Technology

Organization: Premier Assistive Technology Inc.

Eligibility: Schools and nonprofit organizations

Value: Software

Since 2002, Premier Assistive Technology Inc. has been offering its full suite of Accessibility software products to educational and nonprofit organizations through its Breaking Down Barriers to Assistive Technology grant program, which has benefited more than 1,300 school districts nationwide. To help meet the accessibility needs of students with learning and/or visual disabilities, the program offers a range of software that reads printed text out loud. The software suite includes titles such as Scan and Read Pro, Talking Calculator, Talking Word Processor, Text to Audio, Ultimate Talking Dictionary, and more. Applicants have no obligation to buy, but after the grant period has expired, applicants will have the option to pay a nominal fee to continue the product maintenance, technical support, and upgrades. Grant applications take two to three weeks to process.

Contact: (815) 722–5961 or (517) 668–8188, info@readingmadeeasy.com

http://www.premier-programming.com/grant/grantform.htm

Grant Title: Broad Foundation Grants

Organization: The Broad Foundation

Eligibility: K-12 school districts in eligible urban areas

Value: Varies

The Broad Foundation's mission is to improve K-12 urban public education through better governance, management, and labor relations. The foundation seeks applications that aim to enlist talent, redefine roles and authorities, develop high-performing leaders and systems, provide incentives for results, and honor and showcase success. Organizations seeking funding should carefully review the foundation's web site to ensure that their proposals are consistent with its mission and that the focus of the work is located in one of the eligible districts. The foundation considers concept papers at the end of the month in which they are received. All concept papers will receive a response within 60 days, and applicants whose concept papers are of interest to the foundation may be asked to submit a full proposal. Note that the foundation funds less than five percent of unsolicited inquiries.

Contact: Wendy Jones, Wendy Jones, grants@broadfoundation.org

http://www.broadfoundation.org

Grant Title: Cartridges 4 Kids Fundraising Program and Contest

Organization: Cartridges 4 Kids

Eligibility: North American nonprofit organizations

Value: $50 giveaways, plus cash for recycled components

Cartridges 4 Kids, an environmentally smart fundraising program, is giving away $50 every two months to one lucky winner. To enter, participants must return an Easy Return Collection Box of qualifying printer cartridges and/or cell phones during the contest period. Every qualifying box returned will increase an applicant's chances of winning. For its fundraising program, Cartridges 4 Kids pays up to $10 for empty printer cartridges and up to $25 for cell phones. The company estimates that organizations can earn up to $1,500 per year by recycling.

Contact: http://www.cartridges4kids.ca/contest/contest.htm

Grant Title: Citigroup Smarter Schools & Smarter Classrooms Grants

Organization: The Citigroup Foundation

Eligibility: Schools and districts

Value: Varies

The Citigroup Foundation, the philanthropic arm of Citibank Corp., dedicates approximately 75 percent of its charitable contributions to community development and education programs. The foundation's K-12 giving focuses on strengthening education in low-income neighborhoods. Its grants emphasize the creation of "smarter schools" and "smarter classrooms." The "smarter schools" initiative supports improvements in the governance of public schools and higher standards for student performance. It also funds alternative schools that offer more individual attention to students, as well as mentoring and tutoring programs. The "smarter classrooms" initiative supports innovative classroom technologies and successful school-to-work programs. The Citigroup Foundation prefers to solicit proposals from grantees with demonstrated successes. Unsolicited proposals will be accepted, but a favorable decision is less likely. For guidelines, see the foundation's web site.

Contact: Charles V. Raymond, citigroupfoundation@citigroup.com

http://www.citigroup.com/citigroup/corporate/foundation

Grant Title: Classified Ad Pages for Your School

Organization: Classroom Classifieds

Eligibility: Schools

Value: Varies

Classroom Classifieds, a new web-based business, gives school districts classified advertising web pages on which community members can sell unwanted goods in exchange for donating part of their proceeds to the school system. Classroom Classifieds works on the honor system. Those posting ads agree to donate anything from 1 percent (or less) to 100 percent of the sale to the education foundation. Participating schools are charged fees for creating the web pages and the amount of ads that run, but the company says schools can offset the costs with their donations. A basic site, with 100 classified ads a month, costs $20 per month.

Contact: Carolyn Gillis, (207) 797–2168, classroomclassifieds@yahoo.com

http://www.classroomclassifieds.com

Grant Title: Coca-Cola Foundation Grants

Organization: The Coca-Cola Foundation

Eligibility: Schools, higher ed

Value: Varies

The Coca-Cola Foundation supports high-quality education and encourages new solutions to the problems that impede educational systems today. It also supports programs that have been proven to work. The foundation makes grants to public and private colleges and universities, elementary and secondary schools, teacher training programs, educational programs for minority students, and global educational programs. The Coca-Cola Foundation Board of Directors reviews funding proposals in quarterly meetings. All requests receive a written response when the review process is complete.

Contact: http://www2.coca-cola.com/citizenship/foundation.html

Grant Title: Common Good Grants

Organization: Newman's Own

Eligibility: Nonprofits

Value: Varies

Actor Paul Newman donates to charity all of his after-tax profits from the sale of his Newman's Own line of products, which include steak sauce, salad dressing, and lemonade. Since founding the company, he has donated more than $150 million to thousands of projects in the areas of education, children's issues, disaster relief, arts, affordable housing, elderly groups, environmental causes, and hunger relief. You can contact Newman's Own in writing at: Newman's Own, 246 Post Road East, Westport, CT 06880.

Contact: http://www.newmansown.com/5_good.html

Grant Title: Computers for Learning

Organization: The federal government

Eligibility: Schools

Value: Surplus computers

Through its Computers for Learning program, the federal government has placed hundreds of thousands of surplus computers in schools across the country on a needs-first basis. Schools register and request equipment on the Computers for Learning web site, and federal agencies match their surplus equipment to schools with those needs. Most, but not all, of the available computers are Windows-based PCs rather than computers made by Apple. Most of the donated machines are older models, but as the government continues to upgrade its computer systems, the number of surplus Pentium computers will sharply increase. Computers and equipment are not refurbished by the government before being shipped to schools, nor are they covered by warranty.

Contact: (202) 501–3846, computers.learning@gsa.gov

http://www.computers.fed.gov

Grant Title: Corning Foundation Grants

Organization: The Corning Inc. Foundation

Eligibility: Schools and districts

Value: Up to $2.25 million

The Corning Inc. Foundation, established in 1952, develops and administers projects in support of educational, cultural, and community organizations. Over the years, the foundation has contributed more than $83 million through its grant programs. Each year, the foundation fulfills approximately 225 grants totaling some $2.25 million. Corning's areas of involvement have included community service programs for students, curriculum enrichment, student scholarships, facility improvement, and instructional technology projects for the classroom. The foundation also supports youth centers, YMCAs, and local chapters of Girl Scouts and Boy Scouts of America. All requests for support must be made in writing.

Contact: http://www.corning.com/inside_corning/foundation.asp

Grant Title: CVS Innovations Grants Program

Organization: CVS Charitable Trust

Eligibility: K-12 schools near CVS locations

Value: $75,000 per award

CVS pharmacy has been promoting innovative thinking in public schools for more than a decade. The CVS Innovations Grants program provides three-year grants totaling $75,000 along with annual conferences, access to nationally known educators, and on-site assistance to help "innovators" implement their ideas. Access to this program begins with a request for proposal to schools within a geography selected by CVS.

Contact: (401) 770–7240

http://www.cvs.com/corpInfo/community/innovation_grants.html

Grant Title: DIRECTV Goes to School

Organization: DIRECTV

Eligibility: K-12 schools

Value: Equipment, content

The DIRECTV Goes to School program offers educators a free, nonviolent educational programming package and satellite equipment to reach students through auditory, kinesthetic, and visual means. The programming package, called SCHOOL CHOICE, is available to state-accredited public and private schools serving students in grades K-12. A free DIRECTV Multi-Satellite System also will be provided, although there is a limited quantity available. Installation costs are not included.

Contact: http://www.directv.com/school

Grant Title: Dow K-12 Education Grants

Organization: The Dow Chemical Co.

Eligibility: School districts

Value: Grants

Each year the Dow Chemical Co. supports many school districts/school boards and efforts in and around communities in which Dow is located with cash or product donations, research grants, in-kind services, or volunteered time. Dow prioritizes its areas for K-12 education funding to: math and science; teacher training; and parental involvement. Dow further categorizes the qualified K-12 programs to: national, state and local programs that benefit Dow communities; programs that promote systemic education reform in math and science; and school districts and school boards, rather than individual schools.

Contact: http://www.dow.com/about/corp/social/ei.htm

Grant Title: Earthwatch Education Awards

Organization: Earthwatch Institute

Eligibility: Teachers

Value: Fellowship

Earthwatch Institute, an international nonprofit organization founded in 1972, offers fellowships for K-12 educators to join two-week field expeditions in the summer. Projects range from archeological digs in Peru, to habitat studies in Oregon, to running transects through reefs in the Bahamas. The institute aims to promote multidisciplinary science and social studies curriculum in schools nationwide, as well as enrich teachers and enhance the academic experience of students. While in the field, fellows work side by side with researchers on one of more than 60 ongoing research projects worldwide. In most cases, no special skills are necessary. The institute is looking for adventuresome, curious, and innovative people who are committed to lifelong learning. Applications are accepted on a rolling basis, but most decisions are made during the spring.

Contact: Matt Marino, (800) 776–0188 ext. 118, EducationAwards@earthwatch.org

http://www.earthwatch.org/education/educator/fellowships.html

Grant Title: EcoPhones Fundraiser

Organization: EcoPhones

Eligibility: Schools and universities

Value: Varies

The EcoPhones Drive is a cellular phone fund-raising and recycling program that pays organizations up to $100 for each used digital cell phone they turn in. No buying or selling is required to participate, just recycling. EcoPhones provides a free marketing kit to help launch community phone drives. Once you have collected a full box of cell phones, EcoPhones will pick them up for free. Within 60 days you'll receive a check.

Contact: http://www.ecophones.com

Grant Title: Education & Literacy Grants

Organization: The Entergy Charitable Foundation

Eligibility: Schools and non-profit organizations

Value: Varies

The Entergy Charitable Foundation is dedicated to creating and sustaining thriving communities where Entergy employees live and work. To do this, Entergy funds programs that aim to eliminate illiteracy by providing reading and writing skills. The Foundation staff reviews and evaluates funding requests before they are presented to the Board of Directors. Generally, the Board evaluates applications three times per year. Applications must be postmarked by the following deadlines: Feb. 1, May 1, and Aug. 1.

Contact: (877) 285–2006

http://www.entergy.com/content/corp/community/foundation_app.pdf

Grant Title: Education PC Program

Organization: Intel Corp.

Eligibility: Schools and districts

Value: Discounts

Intel Corp.'s Education PC Program provides the opportunity for teachers, staff, students, and parents to purchase high-quality educational computers at discounted prices. The program's web page provides links to computer and equipment manufacturers that support schools through the Intel Model School Program by delivering reliable PC systems to schools. By clicking on any of the links on the page, you can view products and services that are discounted through this program from companies such as Acer, Dell, Gateway, and HP. Schools purchase directly from the manufacturer at prices discounted for education.

Contact: http://www.intel.com/modelschool/educationpc.htm

Grant Title: Education Scholarship/Grant Rebate Program

Organization: Troxell Communications and Hitachi America Ltd.

Eligibility: K-12 and higher-education institutions

Value: Varies

Troxell Communications, a supplier of audiovisual equipment to the scholastic market, and Hitachi America Ltd., a global electronics company, have partnered to offer cash rebates to schools that purchase audiovisual equipment from a comprehensive list of products made eligible for the program. With the intention of supplementing strained district budgets, the rebates return actual money to schools' general funds at the direction of district administrators. Educators can use the funds for school programs, books, supplies and equipment, fuel, and transportation costs, or any purpose deemed appropriate by the district. The program starts July 1, 2004.

Contact: (602) 437–7240 ext. 1705, leigh.carter@trox.com

http://www.trox.com

Grant Title: Education Spotlight Program

Organization: PLUS Vision Corp.

Eligibility: Schools

Value: Presentation equipment

PLUS Vision Corp., a maker of ultra-portable projectors, has announced a new program called Education Spotlight. Through the program, PLUS Vision will donate one projector and an electronic copy board to a selected school each quarter, reflecting a commitment to increase the effective use of multimedia in K-12 education. Applicants are asked to give a unique example of how the projector will be used when applying for the award. Recipients are chosen based on the creativity of their response, and PLUS Vision will share innovative applications with other educators on its web site.

Contact: http://www.lightware.com/site/spotlight.html

Grant Title: Educational Foundation of America Grants

Organization: The Educational Foundation of America

Eligibility: Non-profits

Value: Grants

The Educational Foundation of America (EFA) makes grants to qualifying non-profit organizations for specific projects related to the environment, the crisis of human overpopulation and reproductive freedom, Native Americans, arts, education, medicine, and human services. The Educational Foundation of America was established in 1959 to preserve the lifelong altruistic commitment of its founders, Richard Prentice Ettinger and his wife, Elsie P. Ettinger. Applicants are required to send a Letter of Inquiry as the first step. Check the foundation's website for more details.

Contact: Diane M. Allison, (203) 226–6498, efa@efaw.org

http://www.efaw.org

Grant Title: FedExKinko's Educator Savings Program

Organization: FedEx Kinko's Inc.

Eligibility: Educators

Value: Discounts

The Kinko's Educator Savings Program aims to provide relief for teachers who often dig deep into their own pockets to purchase supplies for their classrooms. Through this program, educators can save 20 percent on most Kinko's products and services. Teachers and administrators from kindergarten through college can now enjoy discount pricing on such offerings as black and white and color copying and finishing, oversized copies, posters, signs and banners, paper, and desk supplies.

Educators may obtain their 20 percent discount card through a program brochure available at participating Kinko's locations nationwide. Free discount cards are also available online.

Contact: http://www.kinkos.com/educatorsavings

Grant Title: Ford Motor Co. Fund Grants

Organization: Ford Motor Co. Fund

Eligibility: Nonprofit organizations

Value: Varies

The Ford Motor Co. Fund makes awards in six categories: education, environment, public policy, health and social programs, civic affairs and community development, and arts and humanities. Across these areas, Ford Fund grants to nonprofit organizations totaled $83.8 million in 2002 and $77.4 million in 2003.

Contact: http://www.ford.com/en/goodWorks/fundingAndGrants

Grant Title: FundingFactory Recycling Fundraiser

Organization: Epson America Inc. and FundingFactory

Eligibility: U.S. schools

Value: Varies

Epson America, in partnership with FundingFactory, allows schools and nonprofits nationwide to return ink cartridges for rewards that can boost fundraising efforts and help the environment. Educational and nonprofit organizations can earn points by collecting genuine Epson ink cartridges and sending them to FundingFactory for recycling. The cartridges will be converted to energy through an environmentally sound incineration process at a licensed waste-to-energy recycling facility. Participation in FundingFactory is completely free to all schools and nonprofit organizations. Once an organization registers at FundingFactory's web site, materials are sent to help them launch the program and start earning points in an easy-to-use online account. Their account is credited with points for every eligible Epson cartridge sent in; those points can be redeemed by the organization for cash and/or equipment.

Contact: http://www.FundingFactory.com

Grant Title: GAERF Mini-Grants

Organization: Graphic Arts Education and Research Foundation

Eligibility: U.S. schools and colleges

Value: $2,500 per award

The Graphic Arts Education and Research Foundation (GAERF) has provided more than $4.5 million to fund more than 125 projects at more than 45 institutions since it was founded in 1983. GAERF awards two types of grants: full grants and mini-grants. Mini-grants are awarded for projects such as one-day workshops, specialized conferences, and the production of career and educational materials. Funding is limited to $2,500 per project and may be submitted at any time. Four mini-grants are awarded per year. Requests for mini-grant funding should be submitted in the same manner as other foundation proposals.

Contact: http://www.gaerf.org

Grant Title: GeoMedia Education Grants

Organization: Intergraph Mapping and GIS Solutions

Eligibility: Schools and higher ed

Value: Software, worth $6 million

Intergraph Mapping and GIS Solutions will award GeoMedia Education Grants valued at more than $6 million. The grants will recognize innovative teaching that advances the use of geographic information sciences by educators and students in the classroom. Grants will be awarded on two levels: (1) community colleges, technical schools, and universities; and (2) K-12 primary and secondary schools. By taking advantage of these grants, students and teachers can use GeoMedia's leading-edge technology to explore new possibilities and impact the future of geographic information systems (GIS). They can learn GIS principles and methodology, spatial analysis techniques, GIS data construction, and a variety of other application capabilities. Products that will be part of the grant program are GeoMedia Professional, GeoMedia WebMap Professional, IntelliWhere OnDemand, and IntelliWhere LocationServer with Intergraph's powerful location-based services technology.

Contact: Shanthi Lindsey, (713) 954–8010, education@intergraph.com

http://www.intergraph.com/gis/education/edgrant.asp

Grant Title: Google Grants Program

Organization: Google Inc.

Eligibility: Nonprofit organizations

Value: Free advertising space

The Google Grants program supports nonprofit organizations focused in areas such as science and technology, education, global public health, the environment, youth advocacy, and the arts. Google Grants harnesses the power of its flagship advertising product, Google AdWords, to nonprofits seeking to inform and engage their constituents online. Google Grant recipients use their award of three months of free AdWords advertising on Google.com to raise awareness and increase traffic. Google Grants has awarded AdWords advertising to hundreds of nonprofit groups whose missions range from animal welfare and literacy to supporting homeless children and promoting HIV education.

Contact: http://www.google.com/grants

Grant Title: HOBO Lab Contest

Organization: iScienceProject.com

Eligibility: Teachers

Value: Equipment

Teachers, whose ideas are selected by iScienceProject.com, will be loaned a classroom set of HOBO data logger equipment for up to two months to run their experiments. A HOBO data logger is a matchbox sized, battery-operated device that can measure air temperature (Fahrenheit and Celsius), water temperature, matter (solid, liquid, and gas) temperature, relative humidity, dew point, light, vibration, contact closure (open/closed), motor (on/off), AC sensors, and more. Once teachers return the sets and their experiment results, teachers are eligible to win HOBO gift certificates ranging from $40 to $300.

Contact: http://iscienceproject.com/contest/5598_aboutcontests.html

Grant Title: ImpactSchools.org

Organization: Lawson Software

Eligibility: Schools

Value: Varies

On March 9, Lawson Software launched www.ImpactSchools.org, an online giving tool that allows donors to provide direct funding to the elementary or secondary school of their choice within a participating district. This tool allows school advocates to choose to donate to a specific program within each school, such as music, computers, sports, or field trips. In total, 97 percent of every tax-deductible donation goes directly to the school and program of choice. St. Paul Public Schools is the first district, with 68 participating schools, to benefit from this program. In the coming year, St. Paul-based Lawson plans to roll out ImpactSchools.org to districts across the nation. To get more information or to sign up, send an eMail to the address listed below.

Contact: impactschools@lawson.com

http://www.ImpactSchools.org

Grant Title: Innovation Grants and Learning & Leadership Grants

Organization: The NEA's National Foundation for the Improvement of Education

Eligibility: Schools, higher ed

Value: Up to $5,000

The National Education Association's Foundation for the Improvement of Education (NFIE) now offers more than 300 small grants of $2,000 to $5,000 each on an ongoing, year-round basis. These grants fund classroom innovations or professional development for improved practice in public K-12 schools and higher-education institutions. NFIE will award up to 250 Innovation grants worth $5,000 per year and 75 Leadership & Learning grants ranging between $2,000 and $5,000. Grants will fund activities for 12 months from the date of the award.

Contact: (202) 822–7840

http://www.nfie.org/programs/howtoapply.htm

Grant Title: Intel Foundation Grants

Organization: Intel Corp.

Eligibility: Schools and districts

Value: Grants

Intel Corp. offers a wide range of support for many technology- and science-related initiatives. On a national level, Intel funds programs that advance math, science, or technology education, promote science careers among women and under-represented minorities, or increase public understanding of technology and its impact. National grants are made either to national projects or to local projects that serve as pilots for national programs. Community grants are viewed with the same priorities and are subject to the same rules as national grants, but they are limited to communities where Intel has a major facility: Chandler, Ariz.; Folsom and Santa Clara, Calif.; Rio Rancho, N.M.; Hillsboro, Ore.; Fort Worth, Texas; and DuPont, Wash. Finally, Intel's Teach to the Future program aims to train two million teachers worldwide. Combined with software and equipment discounts from companies such as Microsoft, Hewlett-Packard, IBM, Premio, and Toshiba, Teach to the Future represents approximately a half-billion dollars invested by leading U.S. computer firms in bringing technology to the classroom. Applications for all these programs can be found on Intel's web site.

Contact: http://www.intel.com/community

Grant Title: Internet Technology Grants

Organization: eProfessional Association

Eligibility: K-12 schools and districts

Value: $500 to $100,000 per award

Professional Association, the nonprofit arm of Minnesota-based Distributed Weesite Corp., is providing $10 million in grants for web-based applications to help K-12 schools and districts add new features to their existing school web sites. For the grant process, eProfessional Association will conduct a needs assessment with the requesting organization's technology or administrative staff. Only schools that are found to benefit from reduced operational costs as a result of the technology will be provided with grants. Grants range from $500 to $100,000 depending upon the applicant's need. Applicants are required to contribute a portion of the cost, which will be determined based on the school's financial capability.

Contact: Mark Kevitt, (507) 453–5153, Mark@eProfessionalAssoc.org

http://www.eProfessionalAssoc.org

Grant Title: K-12 Public Schools Foundation Grants

Organization: State Farm Companies Foundation

Eligibility: K-12 schools

Value: Varies

The State Farm Companies Foundation awards grants to K-12 public schools in the United States and Canada to support the following education initiatives: education reform or curriculum changes that improve student achievement; after-school programs; improving teacher quality; and school-to-work programs. Proposals are accepted year-round and are reviewed in a timely manner. However, approval time depends on the requested amount and completeness of the proposal. Requests exceeding $100,000 are considered quarterly. The foundation accepts one proposal per organization per year. See the foundation's web site for more details.

Contact: http://www.statefarm.com/foundati/foundati.htm

Grant Title: K-12 School Teacher Enhancement

Organization: Waksman Foundation for Microbiology

Eligibility: K-12 science teachers

Value: Up to $20,000 per award

The Waksman Foundation supports projects that enhance teachers' use of microorganisms to teach science in the K-12 classroom. Eligible projects are designed to enhance K-12 education through teacher training, course or curriculum development, construction of laboratory exercises, or innovative use of electronic media. There are no fixed application deadlines, but proposals submitted by the end of September or January can be assured of action within a month or two. Applicants are encouraged to contact the foundation by telephone or eMail before submitting a proposal.

Contact: Nan Waksman Schanbacher, (610) 668–8644, nanws@juno.com

http://www.waksmanfoundation.org

Grant Title: Lowe's Foundation Grants

Organization: Lowe's Charitable and Educational Foundation

Eligibility: Nonprofit organizations located near Lowe's stores

Value: Varies

The Lowe's Charitable and Educational Foundation, founded in 1957, funds large-scale education and community improvement projects that address issues of importance to local communities and are supported by the management of local Lowe's stores. The foundation has a long and proud history of contributing to grassroots community projects. Requests are processed within three to four weeks, and a written response will be sent via U.S. mail within eight to 10 weeks. Owing to the large volume of requests, the foundation is unable to fulfill every request. Unsolicited requests and proposals not aligned with Lowe's focus areas will not be funded.

Contact: http://www.lowes.com/lkn?action=pg&p=AboutLowes/Community#charitable

Grant Title: MainBrain School Grants

Organization: MainBrain Inc.

Eligibility: North Carolina schools

Value: Software discounts

MainBrain Inc., which makes web-based software to improve parent-teacher communication, is giving grants of more than $10,000 to select schools in North Carolina so they can acquire the company's software at cost. The company's flagship product, MainBrain School, provides parents with access to information about the school, classes, and grades. The software reportedly can send alerts about school closings, grades, absences, or upcoming special events directly to a parent's eMail account or cell phone; allow parents to fill out and return permission slips online; easily update and manage the school's home page with current events and information; and enable users to create Web pages for classes, sports, clubs, and other activities simply by pointing and clicking, putting everything from cafeteria schedules to homework assignments online.

Contact: http://www.mainbrainschool.com

Grant Title: Mathematica Academic Grant Program

Organization: Wolfram Research Inc.

Eligibility: Schools

Value: Software

Wolfram Research Inc., the maker of a technical computing software system called Mathematica, is donating Mathematica Classroom Pack licenses to applicants who show outstanding creative promise in using Mathematica to enhance their education and research activities. Recipients also should demonstrate a commitment to expanding the use of Mathematica within their school and should be able to act as a reference for other schools.

Contact: (217) 398–0700, ext. 703, Mathematicagrants@wolfram.com

http://www.wolfram.com/company/programs/academic

Grant Title: Merrill Lynch Foundation Grants

Organization: The Merrill Lynch Foundation

Eligibility: New York City, national organizations, school districts

Value: Grants

In 2000, Merrill Lynch adopted children and youth as its global cause for 2000 to 2005. The foundation supports programs that meet the educational needs and interests of underserved children and youth, and it gives priority to specific programs and projects that are innovative, sustainable, easily expanded from a local to a global perspective, and have a measurable impact. Technology skills in particular were cited by the foundation as one of several elements a project can address. The Merrill Lynch Foundation gives priority to grant requests from New York City and national organizations that reflect its focus, but the foundation does consider a small number of unsolicited requests from nonprofit organizations, including school districts. All requests outside of New York City should be submitted to the branch managers of local offices. When making a grant decision, the foundation considers other types of support an organization already might be receiving (e.g., matching gifts, United Way funds, etc.).

Contact: http://www.ml.com/philanthropy/grants/index.htm

Grant Title: Microsoft's Unlimited Potential Initiative

Organization: Microsoft Corp.

Eligibility: Non-profit organizations

Value: More than $1 billion

Microsoft Corp. plans to commit more than $1 billion over the next five years to Unlimited Potential (UP), a global initiative focused on providing technology skills to disadvantaged individuals through community-based technology and learning centers. In the first round of UP grants, Microsoft awarded $8.1 million in cash and software to 82 nonprofit organizations. Initially, UP will provide funding to help community-based technology and learning centers hire and train technology instructors. Subsequent phases of the initiative will offer an online global support network delivering technology curriculum, research, tools, and help-desk services. UP also will sponsor a global and regional awards program, which will invest in technology solutions that deliver a social benefit. The awards are designed to encourage innovation and provide the funding necessary to help the best technology solutions scale for broader use.

Contact: http://www.microsoft.com/mscorp/citizenship/giving/apply

Grant Title: MissionFish Fundraising

Organization: MissionFish and eBay

Eligibility: Nonprofit organizations

Value: Varies

Since 2000, MissionFish has helped nonprofits raise hundreds of thousands of dollars through eBay's online auctions. Schools and districts can register for free to appear in MissionFish's database of benefiting organizations. When eBay sellers list their item for sale through MissionFish, they can then pick your school and indicate a percentage of the proceeds to donate, ranging from 10 to 100 percent.

Contact: http://www.missionfish.org

Grant Title: Model School Program

Organization: Intel Corp.

Eligibility: Schools

Value: Grants

Intel Corp.'s Model School Program gives every school in the United States the chance to apply for potential seeding of equipment. To apply, schools must submit an innovative proposal for using technology to enhance instruction, and if Intel likes what it sees, it will match grant recipients with companies that can provide the equipment necessary to meet their needs. Whitney High School in Cerritos, Calif., and Miami Carol City Senior High School in Miami are the program's first two recipients.

Contact: http://www.intel.com/modelschool

Grant Title: Music Education Program Grants

Organization: The Mockingbird Foundation Inc.

Eligibility: Schools

Value: Grants

The Mockingbird Foundation Inc., which generates charitable proceeds from fans of the rock band Phish, funds music education programs for children. The foundation looks for projects that encourage creative expression in all musical forms (including composition, instrumentation, vocalization, and improvisation), but also support more basic needs within conventional instruction. The foundation is particularly, though not exclusively, interested in funding programs that benefit disenfranchised groups. Interested parties should review the funding guidelines available at the Mockingbird Foundation web site. In its first three rounds of funding, the foundation contributed more than $250,000 to music education.

Contact: Kristen Godard, grants@mockingbirdfoundation.org

http://www.phish.net/mockingbird/funding

Grant Title: NASA Educator Astronaut Program

Organization: NASA

Eligibility: U.S. teachers

Value: Employment

NASA is recruiting individuals with specific experience and expertise in K-12 education to become Educator Astronauts who will help the Agency develop new ways to connect space exploration with the classroom. Selected Educator Astronaut applicants will be designated astronaut candidates and assigned to the Astronaut Office at the Johnson Space Center in Houston. Educator Astronaut candidates must successfully complete a one-to-two year training and evaluation program prior to receiving a space flight assignment. Educator Astronaut candidates who successfully complete their training will be eligible for multiple flights aboard the Space Shuttle and, possibly, the International Space Station.

Contact: http://edspace.nasa.gov

Grant Title: Partners in Education

Organization: Symbol Technologies Inc.

Eligibility: K-12 schools and higher-education institutions

Value: Varies

Through Partners in Education, Symbol Technologies supports a number of educational institutions locally and nationally, but is particularly eager to assist students pursuing technical careers. Symbol prides itself upon its scientific and entrepreneurial innovations; therefore, the company is dedicated to supporting a number of initiatives that propel the continuation of research and innovation within universities and colleges, as well as other venues.

Contact: http://www.symbol.com/about/overview/overview_community_affairs.html

Grant Title: Pay It Forward Mini Grants

Organization: Pay It Forward Foundation

Eligibility: Teachers and principals

Value: Between $50 and $500 per award

Each month during the school year, the Pay It Forward Foundation awards $500 grants to K-12, service-oriented projects that benefit the school, neighborhood, or greater community. When completing an application, teachers should explain the project thoroughly, include specific details about its educational value, and attach a clear and concise budget. Funds may be used for supplies, materials, equipment, or transportation to a service site.

Contact: http://payitforwardfoundation.org/educators/grant.html

Grant Title: PLUS Vision Copyboard Grant Program

Organization: PLUS Vision Corp. of America

Eligibility: Schools

Value: More than $1,500 in equipment per award

For a limited time, with every purchase of a PLUS Vision U5 series projector, school administrators also will receive a free copy board with their order. The U5 series is PLUS Vision's newest value-based projector line geared for the education market. The PLUS Vision copy boards allow for text and drawings to be copied directly from the board's surface to a memory card, eliminating the need to connect to a PC. PLUS Vision said it paired these two products for education because recent studies indicate that students who are taught with interactive technology, like a copy board and a projector, tend to be more engaged in the classroom.

Contact: (800) 211–9001

http://www.plus-america.com

Grant Title: PNC Grow Up Great

Organization: The PNC Financial Services Group

Eligibility: Nonprofit organizations located near PNC facilities (counties in Delaware, Kentucky, Indiana, Pennsylvania, New Jersey, and Ohio)

Value: $503,000 total

Part of a $100 million investment in early childhood education by the PNC Financial Services Group, the PNC Grow Up Great grant program offers $503,000 to better prepare children, from birth to age five, for school. Grants will be awarded to 12 early-education organizations, including Head Start centers. Nearly $50 million of PNC's overall investment will be devoted to grants to nonprofit early-education organizations over the next 10 years.

Contact: Mia Hallett Bernard, (412) 762–7076, Marianna.hallet@pnc.com

http://www.pncgrowupgreat.com

Grant Title: Polycom Special Offer

Organization: Polycom Inc. and the United States Distance Learning Association

Eligibility: Recipient must purchase $500 in Polycom educational equipment

Value: $125 per membership

Polycom Inc., a provider of collaborative communications solutions, will give a complimentary individual membership in the United States Distance Learning Association (USDLA) to Polycom customers when they purchase at least $500 worth of educational equipment. The USDLA monitors new technologies and supports systems that are fully integrated, teacher-friendly, and network-supported. Membership includes USDLA news alerts via eMail; discounts for all USDLA-sponsored events, including conferences, national policy forums, and distance learning meetings; benefits of national legislative representation from USDLA; and member discounts for USDLA products and services, including offerings from USDLA premium sponsors. The membership is available for primary and secondary school educators.

Contact: (800) POLYCOM

http://www.polycom.com

Grant Title: Print Art Education Program

Organization: Lexmark International Inc.

Eligibility: K-12 school districts

Value: Free printers, artwork, and lesson plans

Lexmark's Print Art Education Program donates art-inspired lesson plans, CD-ROMs, and printers to schools across the country to help children learn history, language arts, math, and science. Through this program, Lexmark donates either a Lexmark Z53 or a Lexmark Z45 color art-quality inkjet printer to each elementary, middle, and high school in the district. The hardware comes with a warranty and the proper cabling. With this technology, Lexmark also donates a "Print Gallery" CD-ROM—the product of an exclusive collaboration between Lexmark and the largest consortium of art museums in Europe. The disc includes software and approximately 100 high-resolution works of art that allow the students to view, explore, and learn about art masterpieces from the great museums of Europe. Each school also receives a teacher's guide with sample lesson plans. This guide includes academic exercises that put the CD to use in virtually every discipline, from art, to language, to social studies, to math and science. In addition, program participants are eligible to receive one donated inkjet cartridge for every three inkjet cartridges purchased. Every order is shipped free of charge.

Contact: Maria Gambrell, (859) 232–6707, mgambrel@lexmark.com

http://printart.lexmark.com

Grant Title: Process, Power & Marine Educational Grant Program

Organization: Intergraph Corp.

Eligibility: Universities worldwide

Value: Software, support, training, and maintenance

Intergraph Corp.'s Process, Power & Marine educational grant program is an initiative meant to train educators and send fully-equipped students into the process, power, and offshore industries. The program is designed to introduce and stimulate the use of Intergraph's plant lifecycle engineering software at educational institutions with strong plant-oriented engineering programs. Intergraph says its educational grant program puts cutting-edge engineering applications in the classroom. It includes Intergraph's engineering software, program options dependent on institution curriculum and expertise, maintenance for the life of the grant (which is renewable each year), training for instructors, technical assistance in on-site product installation, and one registration to Intergraph's annual user conference.

Contact: Faun Clark Langston, (256) 730–2318, faun.clark@intergraph.com

http://ppm.intergraph.com/education/

Grant Title: Project Enhance Program

Organization: Computers for Youth

Eligibility: New York City public school districts

Value: Free computers

Through its Project Enhance Program, Computers for Youth (CFY) distributes working Pentium-level computers to New York City public schools for use within the school building. School administrators interested in being considered for Project Enhance should eMail the program. CFY fills requests for donations on a first-come, first-served basis, while also balancing requests to ensure equity among boroughs and districts. CFY is best known for its project, Take IT Home NY, that helps improve the educational, social, and economic prospects for low-income students and their families by providing them with home computers and the skills to use them. To distribute the computers through this program, CFY partners with local area schools.

Contact: (718) 349–5682, enhance@cfy.org

http://www.cfy.org

Grant Title: Reading Pen Grant for K-12 and Higher Education

Organization: The Reading Pen Group

Eligibility: K-12 and higher-education institutions in the U.S

Value: 10 free Readingpen devices worth $1,000 total

The Reading Pen Group is offering two types of grants: the Readingpen K-12 Grant and the Readingpen Higher Education Grant. The K-12 Grant provides assistance to pioneering educators who want to use Readingpen in effective and creative ways to improve students' reading skills. The Higher Education Grant is designed to support innovative and valuable uses of Readingpen at the college and university level for teacher professional development or research. Proposed projects for both the K-12 and higher-education grants must focus on using Readingpen devices in daily instruction with K-12 students, whether in the classroom or during homework.

Grant recipients get 10 Readingpen devices; teacher support materials that include a Teacher's Guide, student activities, and white papers; and guidance from a mentor or senior reading specialist with experience in integrating technology into the K-12 environment. The approximate value of each grant package is $1,000.

Contact: http://www.readingpen.com/learn/educators.htm

Grant Title: Ready to Learn

Organization: The Prudential Foundation

Eligibility: Academic institutions of higher learning, not-for-profit organizations, K-12 education institutions

Value: Up to $200,000 (larger amounts require board approval).

The Prudential Foundation's Ready to Learn grant program provides support to innovative direct-service education programs that address the needs of communities the company serves. Ready to Learn funds initiatives that strengthen public education at the elementary school level. The program supports education reform efforts that strengthen public education at the elementary school level. Within this framework, the Foundation will emphasize systemic school reform meant to improve the quality of teachers, principals, and other school leaders, and arts education. The program funds early childhood care and education initiatives, focusing on programs that support professional development for pre-kindergarten through third-grade teachers or create model classrooms. Funds are also provided for strategies to improve literacy that address professional development for teachers, family literacy programs, or literacy in the early years. The Prudential Foundation serves the Newark and surrounding New Jersey urban centers. It also funds programs in cities where Prudential has a significant presence. These cities include Atlanta, Chicago, Hartford, Houston, Jacksonville, Los Angeles, Minneapolis, Philadelphia and Phoenix. The Foundation may also fund national programs that further their objectives and can be implemented or replicated in cities where Prudential has a substantial presence. The Foundation receives and reviews proposals throughout the year. Grants that exceed $200,000 must be approved by its board of trustees, which meets three times a year.

Contact: http://www.prudential.com/productsAndServices/0,1474,intPageID%253D1444%2526b

Grant Title: RGK Foundation Grants

Organization: The RGK Foundation

Eligibility: Schools and districts

Value: Varies

The RGK Foundation awards grants in the broad areas of education, community, and medicine or health. The foundation's primary interests within education include programs that focus on formal K-12 education (particularly mathematics, science, and reading or literacy), after-school tutoring and enrichment, integrating technology into the curriculum, teacher development, and higher education. The foundation is particularly interested in programs that attract female and minority students into the fields of mathematics, science, and technology. The foundation does not consider unsolicited grant proposals; instead, applicants are required to submit an electronic Letter of Inquiry on the foundation's web site. Letters of Inquiry are reviewed on an ongoing basis, so there is no deadline for submission. The foundation will respond to letters by eMail within three weeks to let applicants know if they should submit a formal proposal.

Contact: Jami Hampton, (512) 474–9298, jhampton@rgkfdn.org

http://www.rgkfoundation.org/guidelines.php

Grant Title: SafeDesk Solutions' Quick Start program

Organization: SafeDesk Solutions

Eligibility: K-12 and higher-education institutions, as well as other nonprofit organizations

Value: $4,000 per 30-user license

The Quick Start program from SafeDesk Solutions allows organizations to begin exploring how thin-clients can benefit their infrastructure. By providing a 30-user SafeDesk Standard configuration free of charge, the company enables school IT professionals to deploy a Linux-based thin-client network in less than an hour—and be supported along the way. A thin-client network is a networking system that uses underpowered computers as workstations on networks powered through a central server. Chosen applicants will receive a free SafeDesk Basic thin-client server configuration for up to 30 concurrent users; a periodic web-based newsletter show-casing new features and best practices; tiered phone and eMail-based deployment support; 60 days of free upgrades and maintenance service; and discounts on future purchases.

Contact: (866) 465–8636

http://www.safedesksolutions.com/quickstart

Grant Title: School Donation Program

Organization: Ohana Educational Supplies

Eligibility: Educators

Value: $100 per school

Each year, Ohana Educational Supplies donates $100 worth of much-needed school supplies to 1,000 different classrooms across the country. Chosen schools will be asked to pay only the standard shipping rate. There are no obligations with this donation, except to use it where it's needed most.

Contact: http://www.ohanaed.com/donation.html

Grant Title: School Homepage Offer

Organization: webEdition Software Ltd.

Eligibility: Schools in North America

Value: Free software valued at $249 U.S.

webEdition Software Ltd. is offering its web site content management system (CMS) software for free to schools throughout North America to help schools build current and informative web sites for teachers, administrators, students, and parents alike. North American primary and secondary schools who apply will receive full access to webEdition's Standard Version of their software at no cost. All other webEdition products and modules can be purchased for research and teaching purposes at a discount of 25 percent off of the regular purchase price.

Contact: http://www.webedition-cms.com/education/home_page_offer

Grant Title: Share the Technology Computer Recycling Project

Organization: Share the Technology

Eligibility: Schools, nonprofit organizations, and individuals

Value: Donated computers

Share the Technology is a web site that provides a way for donors and potential recipients to connect no matter where they are in the country. Schools, nonprofit organizations, and individuals can search message boards and databases on the site to find computers and equipment available for free in their region. The web site warns schools and other donation seekers that while some of the equipment is in excellent condition, not all equipment is in good working condition. Therefore, recipients should carefully evaluate the donated items before accepting them.

Contact: http://www.sharetechnology.org

Grant Title: Sprint Foundation Grants

Organization: The Sprint Foundation

Eligibility: Schools

Value: $500,000

The Sprint Foundation supports educational projects that foster school reform through the use of new technologies and through fresh approaches to the enhancement of teachers' skills. Although Sprint does not have an application form, the foundation recommends that applicants identify how their projects support Sprint's objectives: innovation and the use of technology in the classroom; enhanced education for minorities and/or the disadvantaged; and increased employee and public support of education. Because these grants are supported by employee contributions matched by foundation funds, grants are available primarily for projects in areas with a significant employee presence, such as Kansas City, Atlanta, Dallas, and Sacramento.

Schools and other education-related nonprofit agencies can apply for grants totaling about $500,000 per year. The Sprint Foundation reviews unsolicited proposals on a continuous basis. Applicants typically will receive a response within four to six weeks.

Contact: (913) 624–3343

http://www.sprint.com/proposals

Grant Title: Staples Recycle for Education

Organization: Staples Inc.

Eligibility: U.S. public schools

Value: Varies

Staples Inc. will donate $1 to public schools for every eligible ink cartridge they collect. Staples created the "Staples Recycle for Education" program in July 2003 to encourage cartridge recycling at its 1,100 U.S. stores but has now expanded the program nationwide. Staples now provides prepaid postage for shipping the cartridges and an account number so schools can monitor the status of reimbursement checks and total collection counts. Parents or teachers can log on to the web site below to register their school and receive a welcome kit that includes flyers to announce the program.

Contact: http://www.staplesrecyclefored.com

Grant Title: SUSE LINUX Education Program

Organization: SUSE LINUX

Eligibility: Schools and nonprofit education organizations

Value: Discounts on software

Students, schools, universities, and nonprofit organizations participating in the SUSE LINUX Education Program will receive 40-percent discounts on open-source Linux software through SUSE's partners CCV Software and RICIS Inc. This new program helps schools provide flexible, cost-efficient software solutions at a fraction of the cost of proprietary software. Applications available range from server software to text processing, spreadsheets, eMail clients, internet browsers, and more.

Contact: http://www.suse.com/edu

Grant Title: Teaching Tolerance Grant Program

Organization: Southern Poverty Law Center

Eligibility: K-12 teachers

Value: $2,000 per award

The Teaching Tolerance project of the Southern Poverty Law Center offers grants of up to $2,000 to K-12 classroom teachers for implementing tolerance and youth activism projects in their schools and communities. Proposals from other educators, such as community organizations and churches, will be considered on the basis of direct student impact. Projects must be sustainable rather than one-time-only events or activities. Salaries, stipends, presenter fees, overhead costs, travel expenses, food items, and computer hardware are not normally funded.

Contact: http://www.tolerance.org/teach/expand/gra/guide.jsp

Grant Title: Teaching Tools Guides & Videos

Organization: ConocoPhillips Co.

Eligibility: Teachers

Value: Free educational videos

For the past 25 years, ConocoPhillips Co. has been producing high-quality educational videos and teachers' guides for math, science, and environmental topics. These materials have been offered to qualified teachers for free and have been seen by millions of junior high and high school students. These free teaching guides and videos cover topics ranging from math and science to problem solving and protecting wildlife. To order one of ConocoPhillips' educational films, visit the Teaching Tools web site or fax your request to (570) 822–8226.

Contact: http://www.teachingtools.com

Grant Title: Teammates for Kids Foundation Grants

Organization: Garth Brooks' Teammates for Kids Foundation

Eligibility: Nonprofit organizations

Value: Varies

The Teammates for Kids Foundation accepts proposals for grants from nonprofit organizations that specialize in working with children. Grants support the ongoing work of operating organizations that help needy children in the areas of health, education, and inner-city services. The foundation's priorities focus on educational achievement in areas of documented weakness; advanced learning opportunities to gifted children who would otherwise lack the resources necessary to pursue dreams and talents; and exposing children to learning opportunities they would otherwise not experience because of insufficient financial resources. The foundation will accept applications twice in 2007: Feb. 1 and July 31.

Contact: http://www.teammates4kids.com

Grant Title: Tech Corps: Mobilizing Technology Volunteers into K-12 Schools Nationwide

Organization: Tech Corps

Eligibility: School districts

Value: Volunteers, mentoring

Since 1995, privately-funded Tech Corps has provided no-cost assistance in maintaining their technology systems to schools connected to the internet. The Tech4schools Online Mentoring Program provides online, volunteer technical assistance to educators and school technology coordinators. Typically, a team of as many as 10 volunteers (each with a specialty, such as software or networking) will support a single technology coordinator, who may represent an individual school or an entire district. Tech Corps volunteers are available in 43 states.

Contact: (978) 897–8282, info@techcorps.org

http://www.techcorps.org

Grant Title: Tellabs Grant Program

Organization: The Tellabs Foundation

Eligibility: Non-profit organizations

Value: $10,000 or more

The Tellabs Foundation, created by telecommunications provider Tellabs Inc., supports local and national education programs with a particular focus on curricula for engineering, science, mathematics, and technology. The Foundation focuses its support on programs in areas in which Tellabs employees live and work. Unless invited by the Foundation Board to submit a full grant proposal, all new applicants or programs first must submit a letter of inquiry. The deadline for letters of inquiry or invited proposals is four weeks prior to every Tellabs Foundation Board meeting, which are held quarterly, usually in January, April, July and October. Proposals received after the deadline will be considered at the next meeting. It is recommended that letters of inquiry be submitted at least four months before funding is needed.

Contact: Meredith Hilt, (630) 798–2506, meredith.hilt@tellabs.com

http://www.tellabs.com/about/foundation.shtml

Grant Title: Texas Instruments Foundation Grants

Organization: The Texas Instruments Foundation

Eligibility: Schools and districts

Value: $5,000 to $10,000 per award

The Texas Instruments Foundation requires no special application form. Grants usually range from $5,000 to $10,000, but the foundation has awarded some schools up to $100,000. Approximately 65 awards are granted each year. Applicants are encouraged to submit one- or two-page proposals that briefly outline the following: purpose of the organization, population served, amount requested, how the requested funds will be used, how the proposal matches funding interests of the foundation, and a copy of 501(c)(3) designation. Proposals are considered from civic, research, educational, health, welfare, charitable, and cultural organizations that have been ruled to be tax-exempt under section 501(c)(3) of the Internal Revenue Code and that are not private foundations as defined by the code.

Contact: (214) 480–3221

http://www.ti.com/corp/docs/company/citizen/education

Grant Title: The Design & Technology in Schools Program

Organization: Parametric Technology Corp.

Eligibility: High schools

Value: Free software, classroom materials

Parametric Technology Corp. is proud to offer technology teacher-led training workshops, free unlimited licenses of Pro/DESKTOP 3D design software, classroom materials, and projects. We also encourage teachers to allow students to install Pro/DESKTOP at home. The Design & Technology in Schools Program introduces students to 3D design technology as early as middle school, so they can become better problem solvers, critical thinkers, and collaborators. The program is about more than just free software—it teaches technological literacy, problem solving, and critical thinking skills.

Contact: http://www.ptc.com/for/education/schools

Grant Title: The GLOBE Program

Organization: The National Science Foundation

Eligibility: U.S. school teachers

Value: Professional development

The GLOBE program, which stands for Global Learning and Observations to Benefit the Environment, is a hands-on, school-based science and education program. It was formed through a partnership between several organizations including the National Science Foundation, the National Oceanic and Atmospheric Administration, the National Aeronautics and Space Administration, and the Environmental Protection Agency. The program teaches students how to research environmental topics while encouraging them to share their findings via the web. Specifically, the program provides resources for students to monitor the environment through the use of soil samples, atmospheric readings, land cover, and phenology. Teachers also benefit from this program through free training at GLOBE workshops, complementary educational videos, and continuous access to a teacher's help desk.

Contact: http://www.globe.gov

Grant Title: The Melody Program

Organization: Mr. Holland's Opus Foundation

Eligibility: K-12 music programs

Value: Musical instruments and instrument repairs

The Melody program is designed to provide musical instruments and instrument repairs to existing K-12 school music programs that have no other source of financing to purchase additional musical instruments or materials. Applicants whose music programs lack institutional financial support and whose students qualify for financial assistance will receive greater consideration. The applicant school must have an ongoing music program that is at least three years old.

Contact: http://www.mhopus.org/apply.htm

Grant Title: Think Ink Contest

Organization: Virtual Ink Corp.

Eligibility: Teacher

Value: Presentation equipment

Each month, Virtual Ink Corp. will award a free mimio electronic whiteboard system to an educator who submits the most original, innovative, or creative entry incorporating the use of mimio at his or her school. Mimio, which works with PC and Mac platforms, attaches to any whiteboard and electronically captures everything that is written or drawn in color and in real time. Rooted in the classroom, mimio originated at the Massachusetts Institute of Technology as a practical solution to a frustrating teaching dilemma: Students were so focused on accurately duplicating the drawings on the classroom's dry-erase whiteboard that they often missed important lecture details and failed to actively participate in class discussions. The contest is open to educators from around the world. Educators interested in entering the Think Ink contest can do so by visiting the company's web site and completing an entry form. Entrants should describe the creative ways in which they would incorporate mimio to foster greater student-teacher collaboration and productivity within the classroom.

Contact: http://www.mimio.com/education/winmimio.php

Grant Title: TI Volume Purchase Program

Organization: Texas Instruments

Eligibility: Schools

Value: Free TI handhelds

By taking advantage of Texas Instruments' Volume Purchase Program, educators can get free technology and classroom activities when they purchase qualifying TI educational handhelds. Under the program, K-12 educators collect proofs of purchase and earn points toward free TI handheld technology, and they can earn double points when they purchase the TI-83 Plus Silver Edition. For additional details, check the company's web site. Contact: (866) 848–7722 or ti-educators@ti.com

Contact: Volume Purchase Program, (866) 848–7722, ti-educators@ti.com

http://education.ti.com/us/resources/vpp/instructional.html

Grant Title: Tiger Woods Foundation Grants

Organization: Tiger Woods Foundation

Eligibility: U.S. urban cities

Value: Varies

The Tiger Woods Foundation provides grants that focus on providing opportunities to underserved children and families in the four program areas: education, youth development, parenting, and family health and welfare. In the education area, the foundation funds school programs and projects that enhance the learning process for children and transitional school programs for young adults to become productive adults. The foundation considers and awards grants four times each year: Feb. 1, May 1, Aug. 1, and Nov. 1. Applications submitted after one cycle has closed will be considered during the next cycle. Organizations may apply for a grant only one time during a calendar year.

Contact: (714) 816–1806, grants@twfound.org

http://www.twfound.org/grants/funding.sps?section=grants&sid=941&lid=1&gra=0

Grant Title: Toshiba America Foundation Grants

Organization: The Toshiba America Foundation

Eligibility: Schools

Value: $550,000

The Toshiba America Foundation awards grants for programs and activities that improve the classroom teaching of science, mathematics, and technology for middle and high school students. Public and private schools, local educational agencies, and youth organizations across the United States may apply. Projects should provide direct benefits to students and should include teacher-led, classroom-based experiences. The Small Grants Program awards grants of up to $5,000 monthly throughout the year. The Large Grants Program awards grants of more than $5,000 in March and September, with deadlines of Feb. 1 and Aug. 1, respectively. The foundation's total annual grants budget is approximately $550,000.

Contact: Toshiba America Foundation, (212) 588–0820, foundation@tai.toshiba.com

http://www.toshiba.com/about/taf.html

Grant Title: Tuition-Free Computer and IT Training for Teachers

Organization: The National Education Foundation

Eligibility: School districts

Value: $30,000 to $10 million in matching grants

CyberLearning, a project of the National Education Foundation, aims to help bridge the digital divide by giving K-12 schools, colleges, universities, government agencies, and nonprofit organizations the opportunity to receive matching grants to access more than 1,000 online courses in information technology (IT), management, and SAT preparation. Applicants must write a one-page proposal that describes their target population and how they would use the courses to improve the IT, management, or SAT skills of their target population, including students, teachers, and staff. One-year matching grants ranging from $30,000 to $10 million are awarded to applicants based on the poverty level of the target populations or communities. Recent awards include $50,000 to Seattle Shoreline Community College, $250,000 to the New Haven School District in Connecticut, and $4,000,000 to the New Jersey State Department of Education to train 75,000 disadvantaged high school students and teachers.

Contact: (703) 823–9999

http://www.cyberlearning.org/links/schools.asp

Grant Title: Tyco Electronics Foundation Grants

Organization: The Tyco Electronics Foundation

Eligibility: Pennsylvania and North Carolina communities

Value: Grants

The Tyco Electronics Foundation, the charitable arm of Tyco Electronics Corp., provides extensive funding for projects that enhance learning opportunities for students. In addition to a matching-gifts program for employee contributions to accredited high schools, the foundation makes direct grants for programs that address a business or community concern of Tyco Electronics. Organizations (public or private) that support pre-college math and science education receive special attention. As with many companies, Tyco focuses its support on communities—especially Pennsylvania and North Carolina—where it operates. Past projects have included wiring schools with fiber-optic cables to allow rapid internet connections. Although the foundation makes funding decisions on a quarterly basis (Dec. 15, March 15, June 15, or Sept. 15), it gives the majority of its grants in the first quarter of the year. Therefore, the best time to send in requests is ahead of the Dec. 15 quarterly deadline.

Contact: Mary Rakoczy, (717) 592–4869, mjrakocz@tycoelectronics.com

http://www.tycoelectronics.com/about/foundation/application.stm

Grant Title: Uno School Partner Programs

Organization: Uno Chicago Grill

Eligibility: Schools near Uno restaurants

Value: Varies

Uno Chicago Grill offers a variety of programs that support school curriculum and help schools raise money. For the Uno fundraiser, schools distribute Uno Fundraising Tickets throughout their community and, for every person who dines at Uno's and presents a ticket during the agreed time period, Uno will donate 20 percent of their check plus tax and tip to your organization. Through Uno School Awards, the restaurant offers certificates and free meal coupons that teachers can use as incentives to motivate students. Uno's also throws Uno Pizza Maker Parties for elementary school classes. Students visit the restaurant, tour the kitchen, learn about cooking safely, and then make their own pizzas.

Contact: (800) 411–2544

http://www.unos.com/uno_fund.html

Grant Title: WaMoola for Schools

Organization: Washington Mutual Inc.

Eligibility: Schools

Value: Varies

With the help of its customers, Washington Mutual expects to drive millions of dollars in donations to K-12 schools through a new check-card program that will provide unrestricted funding to local schools for school supplies, computers, musical instruments, playground equipment, or whatever a school needs. The program, called WaMoola for Schools, ties support for local schools to check-card usage. Customers simply enroll by designating a local school to benefit and use their Washington Mutual check card. For each purchase, the school receives a point, which is worth approximately 5 cents. At the end of the year, points are converted to cash and schools are sent checks.

Contact: http://www.wamoolaforschools.com

Grant Title: Westinghouse Charitable Giving

Organization: Westinghouse Electric Co.

Eligibility: Nonprofit organizations

Value: Varies

Westinghouse actively contributes to programs that benefit nonprofit organizations. Areas of emphasis include health and welfare, education, and civic and social pursuits. Within each area, Westinghouse encourages programs that help to meet the needs of populations such as the disadvantaged, the young, the elderly, minorities, and people with disabilities. In the area of education, emphasis is given to elementary, secondary, and high school educational programs that emphasize math and science, although consideration will be given to other relevant, non-fine arts programs.

Contact: http://www.westinghousenuclear.com/E2.asp

Grant Title: William and Flora Hewlett Foundation Education Grants

Organization: The William and Flora Hewlett Foundation

Eligibility: Schools and districts

Value: Grants

The William and Flora Hewlett Foundation seeks to achieve greater quality and equality of educational opportunity in the United States and throughout the world through grants that support increased student achievement, improved access to exemplary educational content, and other goals as outlined on its web site. The foundation will not consider requests to fund student aid, individual scholarships, construction, equipment and computer purchases, health research, or health education programs. Applicants should submit a brief letter of intent for initial review, after which proposals may or may not be requested. Full proposals will not be accepted unless they are requested. Check the foundation's web site for details before sending a letter of intent.

Contact: Grants Administration Department, loi@hewlett.org

http://www.hewlett.org

Grant Title: XPRESS Loan Program

Organization: Genieve Systems

Eligibility: Nonprofit organizations

Value: Equipment

Nonprofit organizations, such as teachers' associations and school foundations, are eligible to apply for this free, four-week loan of the XPRESS Audience Response System from Genieve Systems. XPRESS enhances audience involvement by allowing instructors to take votes and receive instant feedback from up to 300 people. The system is capable of administering quizzes, tests, buzz-ins, games, and training, according to the company.

Contact: http://www.genieve.com/XPRESS_Loan_Homepage.htm

Resource B

Sample Ads for Key Positions

DIRECTOR OF DEVELOPMENT

- Advises the superintendent, the school board, and other key staff on overall development strategy and on major gift cultivation and stewardship
- Is responsible for supervision and evaluation of development office staff
- Researches and assists in the writing of grant applications for corporate, foundation, and government grants
- Assists in training of staff people, volunteers, teachers, school administrators, and others
- Participates, as a member of the management team, in strategic planning across school departments, and represents the school district to key constituencies, internal and external, in partnership with other staff

Education, Training, and Experience

- At least a bachelor's degree
- Minimum of five years experience in grant and major donor development and management
- Experience in K–12 education and school administration a strong plus

NOTE: Development office is expected to be a profit center within two years of the starting date of employment.

Application Details

- Applicants are encouraged to submit materials by _____
- Salary and relocation package—negotiable

DIRECTOR OF INDIVIDUAL GIVING

- Reports to the director of development
- Is responsible for researching, identifying, and cultivating individual donors, including major gift prospects

- Plans and implements a comprehensive individual giving program, including annual campaigns, capital campaigns, solicitation of major gifts, and high-profile fundraising events
- Prepares for and implements plans, budgets, and timelines related to the district's overall individual giving program
- Meets personally with prospects and solicits gifts individually and with other volunteers and staff

Education, Training, and Experience

- At least a bachelor's degree
- Three to five years of nonprofit fundraising experience, preferably in a school setting
- Strong commitment to the public schools
- Strong verbal, written, planning, and time management skills
- Desire and ability to work in a diverse, dynamic, cooperative, school district environment
- Thorough knowledge of fundraising management software preferred

NOTE: Position is expected to be a profit center within two years of the starting date of employment.

Application Details

- Please send cover letter, salary requirement, and resume to _____

COORDINATOR OF CORPORATE, FOUNDATION, AND GOVERNMENT GRANTS

- Is responsible for pursuing corporate, foundation, and government grants that meet the needs of the schools and the school district
- Reports to the director of development
- Does prospect research to match the needs of the school district and the interests of funding agencies
- Responds to requests for proposals that have relevance for the district
- Assists in nurturing corporate and foundation funding agencies, including setting up school site visitations from corporate and foundation staff as well as visitations to corporate and foundation offices
- Coordinates district's grantwriting effort on all government grant applications, including state and federal grants as well as corporate and foundation grants.
- Notifies school site principals and their staff about funding opportunities open to them

Education, Training, and Experience

- Thorough knowledge of corporate, foundation, and government grant opportunities
- Experience in grantwriting in a school or district setting desired
- At least a bachelor's degree
- Three to five years of experience in a nonprofit setting, preferably in a school setting
- Strong commitment to the public schools

NOTE: Position is expected to be a profit center within two years of the starting date of employment.

Application Details

- Please send a cover letter, salary requirement, and resume to _____

GRANTWRITER

- Is primarily responsible for researching and writing all major (over $25,000) corporate, foundation, and government grants in cooperation with teachers, administrators, parents, and others
- Reports to the coordinator of corporate, foundation, and government grants
- Provides school sites with information related to available grant opportunities
- Trains teachers, principals, and others in researching and writing grant applications, including applications for minigrants (under $5,000)
- Develops a district grantwriting library of relevant books and periodicals
- Develops a relevant grantwriting link to the district's Web site that assists teachers, administrators, and others
- Has other duties as assigned

Education, Training, and Experience

- At least a bachelor's degree
- Successful, relevant, grantwriting experience in a school setting
- Ability to relate well to the total school community

NOTE: Position is expected to be a profit center within two years of the starting date of employment.

Application Details

- Please send a cover letter, salary requirement, and resume to _____

Resource C

Sample Cover Letter to
Accompany a Grant Application

Letterhead Stationery

Date

Mr. Maury Moneybags, President

ABC Foundation

7474 Main Street

Anytown, USA 85111

Dear Mr. Moneybags:

As superintendent of the XYZ School District, I am pleased and excited about the enclosed grant application for the expansion of the ALLBRIGHT ACADEMICS PROGRAM at XYZ High School. This unique program allows students to have contact with the same teachers for three hours each day, thus enabling them to develop close student-teacher relationships that are meaningful and significant. In addition, the program plans to incorporate cutting-edge technology into the curriculum by providing all students in the ALLBRIGHT ACADEMICS PROGRAM with laptop computers. This will enable them to integrate technology into their lives as a working tool for productivity and organization and to involve their parents in the education process.

XYZ High School, an acclaimed Blue Ribbon Distinguished School, is the ideal target site for this highly innovative project. The staff is very competent and dedicated, the principal is a respected leader in the school community, the parents are very supportive, and the students are highly motivated. Unfortunately, at this time our budget will not allow for the full implementation of this worthy project. We are respectfully requesting that ABC Foundation assist us by providing a grant in the amount of $144,856.

We feel that this project has positive implications for other schools and districts in this county and elsewhere. If funded, we would be pleased to publicize the grant to the community and welcome ABC Foundation as an educational partner with the XYZ School District. If you have any questions or concerns, please don't hesitate to contact the principal of XYZ High School, Dr. Al Ready, or me.

Thank you very much for your interest, and I look forward to hearing from you at your earliest convenience.

Sincerely,
Nancy Needsmoremoney, PhD
Superintendent
Encl: Grant Application

Resource D

The Foundation Center's Glossary of Funding Terms

Annual report

A voluntary report issued by a foundation or corporation that provides financial data and descriptions of its grantmaking activities. Annual reports vary in format from simple typewritten documents listing the year's grants to detailed publications that provide substantial information about the grantmaker's grantmaking programs. Approximately 1,100 foundations issue them.

Assets

The amount of capital or principal—money, stocks, bonds, real estate, or other resources—controlled by a foundation or corporate giving program. Generally, assets are invested and the resulting income is used to make grants.

Associates program

A fee-based membership program of the Foundation Center providing toll-free e-mail and telephone reference, photocopy and fax service, computer searches of Foundation Center databases, attendance at an annual conference, and access to a special Associates-only Web site.

Beneficiary

In philanthropic terms, the donee or grantee receiving funds from a foundation or corporate giving program is the beneficiary, although society may benefit as well.

Capital support

Funds provided for endowment purposes, buildings, construction, or equipment.

CD-ROM

Acronym for Compact Disk-Read Only Memory. CD-ROMs are high-capacity computer disks that allow publishers and other information providers to distribute large amounts of information in a searchable format.

Challenge grant

A grant that is paid only if the donee organization is able to raise additional funds from other sources. Challenge grants are often used to stimulate giving from other donors. *See also* matching grant.

Community foundation

A 501(c)(3) organization that makes grants for charitable purposes in a specific community or region. The funds available to a community foundation are usually derived from many donors and held in an endowment that is independently administered; income earned by the endowment is then used to make grants. Although a community foundation may be classified by the Internal Revenue Service (IRS) as a private foundation, most are public charities and are thus eligible for maximum tax-deductible contributions from the general public. *See also* 501(c)(3); public charity.

Community fund

An organized community program which makes annual appeals to the general public for funds that are usually not retained in an endowment but are instead used for the ongoing operational support of local agencies. *See also* federated giving program.

Company-sponsored foundation (also referred to as a corporate foundation)

A private foundation whose assets are derived primarily from the contributions of a for-profit business. While a company-sponsored foundation may maintain close ties with its parent company, it is an independent organization with its own endowment and as such is subject to the same rules and regulations as other private foundations. *See also* private foundation.

Cooperating Collection

A member of the Foundation Center's network of libraries, community foundations, and other nonprofit agencies that provides a core collection of Center publications in addition to a variety of supplementary materials and services in areas useful to grantseekers.

Cooperative venture

A joint effort between or among two or more grantmakers. Cooperative venture partners may share in funding responsibilities or contribute information and technical resources.

Corporate foundation

See company-sponsored foundation.

Corporate giving program

A grantmaking program established and administered within a for-profit corporation. Because corporate giving programs do not have separate endowments, their annual grant totals generally are directly related to company profits. Corporate giving programs are not subject to the same reporting requirements as corporate foundations.

DIALOG

An online database information service made available by the Thomson Corporation. The Foundation Center offers two large files on foundations and grants through DIALOG.

Distribution committee

The committee responsible for making grant decisions. For community foundations, the distribution committee is intended to be broadly representative of the community served by the foundation.

Donee

The recipient of a grant. (Also known as the grantee or the beneficiary.)

Donor

An individual or organization that makes a grant or contribution to a donee. (Also known as the grantor.)

Employee matching gift

A contribution to a charitable organization by an employee that is matched by a similar contribution from his or her employer. Many corporations have employee matching-gift programs in higher education that encourage their employees to give to the college or university of their choice.

Endowment

Funds intended to be invested in perpetuity to provide income for continued support of a not-for-profit organization.

Expenditure responsibility

In general, when a private foundation makes a grant to an organization that is not classified by the IRS as a "public charity," the foundation is required by law to provide some assurance that the funds will be used for the intended charitable purposes. Special reports on such grants must be filed with the IRS. Most grantee organizations are public charities and many foundations do not make "expenditure responsibility" grants.

Family foundation

An independent private foundation whose funds are derived from members of a single family. Family members often serve as officers or board members of family foundations and have a significant role in their grantmaking decisions.

Federated giving program

A joint fundraising effort usually administered by a nonprofit "umbrella" organization that in turn distributes the contributed funds to several nonprofit agencies. United Way and community chests or funds, the United Jewish Appeal and other religious appeals, the United Negro College Fund, and joint arts councils are examples of federated giving programs. *See also* community fund.

Field offices

The Washington, DC, Atlanta, Cleveland, and San Francisco reference collections operated by the Foundation Center, all of which offer a wide variety of services and comprehensive collections of information on foundations and grants.

Fiscal sponsorship

Affiliation with an existing nonprofit organization for the purpose of receiving grants. Grantseekers may either apply for federal tax-exempt status or affiliate with a nonprofit sponsor.

501(c)(3)

The section of the tax code that defines nonprofit, charitable, tax-exempt organizations; 501(c)(3) organizations are further defined as public charities, private operating foundations, and private non-operating foundations. *See also* operating foundation; private foundation; public charity.

Form 990-PF

The public record information return that all private foundations are required by law to submit annually to the IRS.

Form 990

The information return that public charities file with the IRS.

General/operating support

A grant made to further the general purpose or work of an organization, rather than for a specific purpose or project; also called an unrestricted grant or basic support.

General purpose foundation

An independent private foundation that awards grants in many different fields of interest. *See also* special purpose foundation.

Grantee financial report

A report detailing how grant funds were used by an organization. Many corporate grantmakers require this kind of report from grantees. A financial report generally includes a listing of all expenditures from grant funds as well as an overall organizational financial report covering revenue and expenses, assets and liabilities. Some funders may require an audited financial report.

Grassroots fundraising

Efforts to raise money from individuals or groups from the local community on a broad basis. Usually an organization's own constituents—people who live in the neighborhood served or clients of the agency's services—are the sources of these funds. Grassroots fundraising activities include membership drives, raffles, auctions, benefits, and a range of other activities.

Guidelines

Procedures set forth by a funder that grantseekers should follow when approaching a grantmaker.

Independent foundation

A grantmaking organization usually classified by the IRS as a private foundation. Independent foundations may also be known as family foundations, general purpose foundations, special purpose foundations, or private non-operating foundations. *See also* private foundation.

In-kind contribution

A contribution of equipment, supplies, or other tangible resource, as distinguished from a monetary grant. Some corporate contributors may also donate the use of space or staff time as an in-kind contribution.

Letter of inquiry / Letter of intent

A brief letter outlining an organization's activities and its request for funding that is sent to a prospective donor in order to determine whether it would be appropriate to submit a full grant proposal. Many grantmakers prefer to be contacted in this way before receiving a full proposal.

Matching grant

A grant that is made to match funds provided by another donor. *See also* challenge grant; employee matching grant.

Operating foundation

A 501(c)(3) organization classified by the IRS as a private foundation whose primary purpose is to conduct research, social welfare, or other programs determined by its governing body or establishment charter. An operating foundation may make grants, but the amount of grants awarded generally is small relative to the funds used for the foundation's own programs. *See also* 501(c)(3).

Operating support grant

A grant to cover the regular personnel, administrative, and miscellaneous expenses of an existing program or project. *See also* general/operating support.

Payout requirement

The minimum amount that private foundations are required to expend for charitable purposes (including grants and, within certain limits, the administrative cost of making grants). In general, a private foundation must meet or exceed an annual payout requirement of five percent of the average market value of its total assets.

Private foundation

A nongovernmental, nonprofit organization with funds (usually from a single source, such as an individual, family, or corporation) and program managed by its own trustees or directors. Private foundations are established to maintain or aid social, educational, religious, or other charitable activities serving the common welfare, primarily through the making of grants. *See also* 501(c)(3); public charity.

Program amount

Funds that are expended to support a particular program administered internally by a foundation or corporate giving program.

Program officer

A staff member of a foundation who reviews grant proposals and processes applications for the board of trustees. Only a small percentage of foundations have program officers.

Program-related investment (PRI)

A loan or other investment (as distinguished from a grant) made by a foundation to another organization for a project related to the foundation's philanthropic purposes and interests.

Proposal

A written application, often accompanied by supporting documents, submitted to a foundation or corporate giving program in requesting a grant. Most foundations and corporations do not use printed application forms but instead require written proposals; others prefer preliminary letters of inquiry prior to a formal proposal. Consult published guidelines.

Public charity

A nonprofit organization that qualifies for tax-exempt status under section 501(c)(3) of the IRS code. Public charities are the recipients of most foundation and corporate grants. Some public charities also make grants. *See also* 501(c)(3); private foundation.

Qualifying distributions

Expenditures of a private foundation made to satisfy its annual payout requirement. These can include grants, reasonable administrative expenses, set-asides, loans and program-related investments, and amounts paid to acquire assets used directly in carrying out tax-exempt purposes.

RFP

An acronym for Request for Proposal. When the government issues a new contract or grant program, it sends out RFPs to agencies that might be qualified to participate. The RFP lists project specifications and application procedures. While an increasing number of foundations use RFPs in specific fields, most still prefer to consider proposals that are initiated by applicants. For a current listing of selected RFPs, see our RFP Bulletin.

Seed money

A grant or contribution used to start a new project or organization. Seed grants may cover salaries and other operating expenses of a new project.

Set-asides

Funds set aside by a foundation for a specific purpose or project that are counted as qualifying distributions toward the foundation's annual payout requirement. Amounts for the project must be paid within five years of the first set-aside.

Special purpose foundation

A private foundation that focuses its grantmaking activities in one or a few areas of interest. *See also* general purpose foundation.

Tax-exempt

Refers to organizations that do not have to pay taxes such as federal or state corporate tax or state sales tax. Individuals who make donations to such organizations may be able to deduct these contributions from their income tax.

Technical assistance

Operational or management assistance given to nonprofit organizations. This type of help can include fundraising assistance, budgeting and financial planning, program planning, legal advice, marketing, and other aids to management. Assistance may be offered directly by the staff of a foundation or corporation, or it may be provided in the form of a grant to pay for the services of an outside consultant. *See also* in-kind contributions.

Trustee

A foundation board member or officer who helps make decisions about how grant monies are spent. Depending on whether the foundation has paid staff, trustees may take a more or less active role in running its affairs.

Bibliography

The following bibliography, while comprehensive, is not exhaustive by any means. It is a starting point for you to explore and study. There are additional books, articles, periodicals, software programs, and Web sites that you will discover.

BOOKS AND ARTICLES

Axelrod, T. (2004). *Raising more money: A step-by-step guide to building lifelong donors*. Seattle, WA: Raising More Money Publications. Helps fundraisers raise more money through building relationships with lifelong donors.

Barrett, R. D., & Ware, M. E. (2002). *Planned giving essentials: A step-by-step guide to success* (2nd ed.). Gaithersburg, MD: Aspen. Provides an introduction to the essentials of planned giving and explains how to set up a planned giving program.

Burnett, K. (2002). *Relationship fundraising*. San Francisco: Jossey-Bass. A practical guide to building creative approaches to relationship fundraising written by a respected fundraising executive.

Ciconte, B. K., & Jacob, J. G. (2001). *Fundraising basics: A complete guide* (2nd ed.). Gaithersburg, MD: Aspen. Discusses annual giving, direct-mail fundraising, major gifts, special events, capital campaigns, prospect research, technology, and other issues.

Frye, G. L. (2006). The $1.3 million question: Why does your district need its own development office? *American School Board Journal, 192*(12), 22–24. The author, who is a respected practitioner in the field, provides insight into the advantages of establishing a development office in a public school district.

Joachim, J. C. (2003). *Beyond the bake sale*. New York: Saint Martin's Griffin. Down-to-earth, how-to book written by member of an award-winning fundraising team at P.S. 87 on the upper west side of Manhattan, where they have raised more than $200,000 a year for more than 10 years.

Levenson, S. (2002). *How to get grants and gifts for the public schools*. Boston: Allyn & Bacon. Discusses how to get corporate, foundation, and government grants as well as grants and gifts from individual donors. Also includes comprehensive, practical information on writing successful grant applications.

Levenson, S. (2003). A bigger piece of the pie. *Principal Leadership, 3*(5), 14–18. Provides principals, teachers, and others with the practical help they need to go beyond nickel-and-dime fundraising and into the big time.

Levenson, S. (2003). Beyond the bake sale. *American School Board Journal, 190*(5), 37–39. Helps school board members and superintendents understand what big-time fundraising is and how to implement a big-time fundraising effort in their school districts.

Levenson, S. (2006). The big gift: A new fundraising strategy for public schools. *American School Board Journal, 193*(2), 28–31. Helps school board members and superintendents understand the impact of individual giving and how important it is in a big-time fundraising effort. Provides practical ideas for implementation.

McCormick, D. H., Bauer, D. G., & Ferguson, D. E. (2001). *Creating foundations for American schools.* Gaithersburg, MD: Aspen. Provides the know-how necessary to set up your foundation and keep it running smoothly. Includes sample documents, tax forms, a guide to laws, and more.

Panas, J. (1999). *Finders keepers.* Chicago: Bonus Books. A behind-the-scenes look at the strategies and skills that lead to successful fundraising written in a lively and irreverent style.

Panas, J. (2004). *Asking.* Medfield, MA: Emerson & Church. Very practical ideas on how to ask for and secure gifts by one of the most respected people in modern philanthropy.

Panas, J. (2005). *Mega gifts.* Medfield, MA: Emerson & Church. A very easy-to-read book on the psychology of giving. Includes motives, emotions, and impulses that propel big givers.

Warwick, M. (2001). *How to write successful fundraising letters.* San Francisco: Jossey-Bass. A very practical book that helps you raise serious dollars through letter-writing campaigns written by one of the most respected authorities in the field. Includes sample letters, style tips, useful hints, and real world examples.

Warwick, M. (2005). *The mercifully brief, real world guide to raising $1,000 gifts by mail.* Medfield: MA: Emerson and Church. Tried and true marketing techniques focused on high dollar fundraising written in a brief, clear, and concise format.

Wholey, J., Hatry, H. P., & Newcomer, K. E. (Eds.). (2004). *Handbook of practical program evaluation* (2nd ed.). San Francisco: Jossey-Bass. Presents efficient and economic methods for assessing program results and identifying ways to improve program performance.

GRANTWRITING RESOURCES

Brewer, E. W., Achilles, C. M., Fuhriman, J. R., & Bronson, C. H. (2001). *Finding funding.* Thousand Oaks, CA: Corwin Press.

Browning, B. (2001). *Grant writing for dummies.* New York: Hungry Minds.

Burke, M. A. (2002). *Simplified grantwriting.* Thousand Oaks, CA: Corwin Press.

Carlson, M., & Alliance for Nonprofit Management. (2002). *Winning grants step by step* (2nd ed.). San Francisco: Jossey-Bass.

Karsh, E., & Fox, A. S. (2003). *The only grant-writing book you'll ever need.* New York: Carroll & Graf.

Levenson, S. (2002). *How to get grants and gifts for the public schools.* Boston: Allyn & Bacon.

Miner, L. E., Miner, J. T., & Griffith, J. (2003). *Proposal planning and writing* (3rd ed.). Phoenix, AZ: Oryx Press.

Smith, N. B., & Tremore, J. (2003). *The everything grant writing book.* Avon, MA: Adams Media Corporation.

PERIODICALS

The *Chronicle of Philanthropy.* P.O. Box 1989, Marion, OH 43305–1989. (614) 382–3322. http://www.philanthropy.com. Newspaper of the nonprofit world published 24 times a year. Provides news and information for grantseekers, including lists of grants, fundraising ideas and techniques, statistics, updates on regulations, forthcoming conferences, and other relevant information. Also publishes *The Nonprofit Handbook* on a yearly basis with listings of books, periodicals, software, Internet sites, and other essential resources for nonprofit leaders.

Foundation and Corporate Grants Alert. Capitol Publications, 1101 King Street, Alexandria, VA 22314. (800) 655–5597. Published monthly. Lists grant opportunities, profiles foundations and corporate-giving programs with their grant priorities, and provides helpful suggestions.

Foundation News and Commentary. Council on Foundations, 1828 L Street NW, 3rd Floor, Washington, DC 20036. (800) 771–8187. http://www.cof.org. Provides articles, case studies, questions and answers, and essays on critical issues confronting philanthropy today. News and information on emerging technologies, ethics, regulations, legislation, research, book reviews, and grantmaking videos.

Grants and Funding Alert. Published by *eSchool News,* 7920 Norfolk Ave., Bethesda, MD 20814. (800) 394–0115. http://www.eschoolnews.com. Biweekly e-mail newsletter that provides an extensive listing of grant opportunities available for K–12.

Grants for K–12 Hotline. Quinlan Publishing, 23 Drydock Ave., Boston, MA 02210. (617) 542–0048. http://www.quinlan.com. Subscription includes 24 biweekly issues as well as weekly e-mail updates, access to electronic issues, special grant alerts and resource listings, application aids and grantwriting ideas, and profiles of funding sources.

The NonProfit Times. 120 Littleton Road, Parsippany, N.J. 07054. (800) 535–8207. http://www.nptimes .com. The leading business publication for nonprofit management.

Planned Giving Today. G. Roger Shoenhals, Publisher, 100 Second Avenue South, Suite 180, Edmonds, WA 98020. (800) 525–5748. http://www.pgtoday.com. Professional newsletter that serves the charitable gift-planning community as a practical resource for education, information, inspiration, and professional linkage.

School Technology Alert. Published by *eSchool News,* 7920 Norfolk Ave., Suite 900, Bethesda, MD 20814. (800) 394–0115. http://www.eschoolnews.com. News, tools, and grants listings to help capture some of the $30 billion in school technology funding. Funding success stories, grant analysis, latest listings of new and hidden grant opportunities, techniques, and unwritten rules from some of the nation's successful grantwriting consultants.

SOFTWARE

Crescendo Plus. Crescendo Interactive, Inc. Planned giving software provides customizable brochures, ads and articles for newsletters and promotions, and marketing gift plan ideas such as wills, bequests, gift annuities, unitrusts, and more. http://www.crescendointeractive.com

Donor Perfect Fundraising Software. SofterWare, Inc. Use to review and update data, generate reports, and manage direct mail and other campaigns and events. http://www.donorperfect.com

The Foundation Directory Online. Foundation Center. Provides comprehensive and accurate information, updated weekly, on thousands of U.S. grantmakers and their grants. Several subscription plans available. http://www.fdncenter.org

GiftMakerPRO. Blackbaud, Inc. Manages fundraising data and efforts, including donors, prospects, gifts, events, and volunteers. Also includes top prospect tracking, credit card processing, and online donations. http://www.blackbaud.com/bb/gmp/welcome.aspx

Kintera Sphere. Kintera, Inc. Provides online software tools, including contact relationship management, Web content management, e-marketing and e-mail, payment processing, events management, directed giving, and major gifts and wealth screening. http://www.kintera.com

SIX SPECIAL WEB SITES

Chronicle of Philanthropy Web site. The newspaper of the nonprofit world. Provides comprehensive coverage of grant opportunities, gifts received, ideas and resources, consultant guide, announcements of workshops, seminars, and conferences, and employment opportunities. http://www .philanthropy.com.

EducationNews.Org Web site. Provides education news from around the world on a daily basis. Helps to keep you up-to-date on what's happening in K–12. http://www.educationnews.org.

eSchool News Web site. An excellent news source for K–12 technology, including funding opportunities, publications, announcements, conferences, and related links. Also includes a *Grants and Funding Alert* e-mail newsletter. http://www.eschoolnews.org.

Foundation Center Web site. The most comprehensive website in the United States for corporate and foundation grantseeking. Has links to hundreds of funding sources and other relevant sites. http://www.fdncenter.org. See also *The Foundation Center's User-Friendly Guide to Funding Research and Resources* at http://www.fdncenter.org/learn/ufg_all.html.

The Grantsmanship Center Web site. Offers grantsmanship training and low-cost publications to nonprofit organizations and government agencies. Conducts more than 100 workshops each year and provides technical assistance over the Internet. *The Grantsmanship Center Magazine* is mailed to the staff of 200,000 nonprofit and government agencies in the United States and more than 50 countries overseas. http://www.tgci.com.

Public Education Network Web site. Provides information on how to start a local education foundation, including characteristics, mission, bylaws, committees, meetings, staff, office, and 21 steps to follow when forming a local education foundation. Also includes the excellent, free, *PEN Weekly NewsBlast* that goes to more than 40,000 subscribers. http://www.publiceducation.org.

ADDITIONAL TOP-NOTCH WEB SITES

The following 28 Web sites are provided to assist you in your search for grants and gifts for K–12 schools as well as in professional development. Many of the sites listed have been referred to in this book. Others will broaden your perspective and make you more aware of funding opportunities that are out there for the asking. Some sites offer special assistance in obtaining grants and gifts, while others offer help in grantwriting, individual solicitation, and planned giving. Note that Web addresses change from time to time, and it is possible that some addresses below will also change.

Organizations	Web Address
American Association of Fundraising Counsel	http://www.aafrc.org
Association of Fundraising Professionals	http://www.nsfre.org/
Castle Technology Consultants	http://www.castletechnology.com/
Catalog of Federal Domestic Assistance	http://www.cfda.gov/
Council For Corporate & School Partnerships	http://www.corpschoolpartners.org/
Donors Choose	http://www.donorschoose.org
Federal Register	http://www.ed.gov/legislation/FedRegister/announcements/index.html
Fund$Raiser Cyberzine	http://www.fundsraiser.com
GrantsAlert.Com	http://www.grantsalert.com
GrantSmart	http://www.grantsmart.com
Kintera	http://www.kinterainc.com
Stan Levenson & Associates	http://www.grantsandgiftsforschools.com
National Association of Philanthropic Planners	http://www.napp.net
National Center for Charitable Statistics	http://nccsdataweb.urban.org/FAQ/index.php?category=90
National Committee on Planned Giving	http://www.ncpg.org
National Endowment for the Arts	http://www.nea.gov/grants/
National Endowment for the Humanities	http://www.neh.gov/grants/
National Science Foundation (NSF)	http://www.nsf.gov/
Parents-Planet	http://www.parents-planet.com
Planned Giving Today	http://www.pgtoday.com
PTO Today	http://www.ptotoday.com
School Funding Center	http://www.schoolfundingcenter.com
SchoolGrants	http://www.schoolgrants.com
Scholastic Administrator Grants & Funding	http://www.scholastic.com/administrator/funding.htm
Kathy Schrock	http://www.discoveryschool.com/schrockguide/business/grants.html
The Taft Group	http://www.taftgroup.com
Urban Institute	http://www.urban.org
U.S. Department of Education	http://www.ed.gov
U.S. Department of Energy	http://www.energy.gov/
U.S. Department of Health & Human Services	http://www.hhs.gov/

Index